199 Questions

PARENTS ASK

Answered by

Dr. GRACE H. KETTERMAN

BY *Grace H. Ketterman, M.D.*

How to Teach Your Child About Sex
The Complete Book of Baby and Child Care (Revised)
You and Your Child's Problems
You Can Win Over Worry
Before and After the Wedding Night
199 Questions Parents Ask, Answered by Dr. Grace H. Ketterman

199 *Questions*
PARENTS ASK
—— *Answered by* ——
Dr. GRACE H. KETTERMAN

Fleming H. Revell Company
Old Tappan, New Jersey

Library of Congress Cataloging in Publication Data

Ketterman, Grace H.
199 questions parents ask.

1. Child rearing—Miscellanea. 2. Parenting—
Religious aspects—Christianity—Miscellanea.
I. Title. II. Title: One hundred ninety-nine
questions parents ask. III. Title: One hundred
and ninety-nine questions parents ask.
HQ769.K42 1986 649'.1 85-14299
ISBN 0-8007-1447-4

TO my parents,
who answered more of my
questions than they ever knew!

Contents

Introduction

The shrill ringing of the telephone grated on my very spirit as I began to relax at 10:00 P.M. My day had begun with a 7:30 A.M. appointment, and I had missed lunch in order to see a grandmother concerned with her rebellious, adolescent grandchild. Frankly, I was tempted to ignore the raucous sound, but because of the lateness of the hour, I was afraid it might be prompted by an emergency.

This call was not a true crisis, but to the anxious mother who was calling, the problem was distressing. Her preteen daughter had been increasingly moody and anxious. On this evening she had refused to go to the dark basement on an errand, and now was refusing to turn out the light in her bedroom.

Only a few days before, the mother of a two-year-old had called to ask if I knew of any classes she could attend to help her in parenting her difficult child. Most of the time she felt quite confident in her role as mother, but there were days, she confided, when she was so angry with her son's limit testing and rebelliousness that she was actually fearful of abusing him.

Not only do I receive countless telephone calls about family matters but also a great many letters arrive daily in response to my five-minute radio program "You and Your Child." The more opportunities I have to know about people everywhere, the more aware do I become of the multitudinous concerns they share. While many of the issues are similar, each is uniquely painful to those who struggle to survive, to cope, and to resolve the problems.

The purpose of this book, then, is to capture in print the practical, to-the-point answers that seem to have helped many people. Perhaps you, too, may find the one burning concern that confronts you addressed here. I hope it will help you and your child.

MY BASIC PHILOSOPHIES

Let me outline for you some of the basic philosophies that have molded my life. It is from those beliefs that I practiced my own parenting, and they have molded my professional life as well.

I believe (along with many child specialists), *in the necessity of a strong, healthy family if children are to develop into well-adjusted adults.*

The hedonism of our society has created a situation in which personal pleasure takes precedence over family well-being. Having one's own desires often becomes so driving that the needs of others—even children—are ignored. Many parents have no awareness of the meaning of commitment and the personal sacrifices entailed in rearing children.

Selfishness permits some parents to abdicate their responsibilities to the family. Some parents actually abuse their children, while others ignore obvious cruelty to their offspring. If the abusing parent fails to seek help or stop the harmful behavior, then the other parent must take steps to protect the children—even if it means separation or divorce.

Alcoholism, drug addiction, and severe forms of abuse are all taking their toll on family solidarity. Their impact on the formative years of little children is immeasurably destructive.

EFFECT OF DIVORCE

Many churches have held the line against divorce under any circumstances. For many years this seemed to be a spiritually sound stand to take, but spouses and children, often abandoned through no fault of their own, have been painfully judged and ostracized by such hard-line forces. Doubly abandoned, by a parent or spouse *and* the Church, such people desperately try to cope with life against extreme odds.

In many families who choose to stay together "for the sake of the children," the disharmony creates emotional damage that is far-reaching. Such disharmony is exceeded in its harmful effects only by the impenetrable coldness and silence that may become a way of life.

Not only does divorce take its toll on the lives of families but its powerful impact penetrates even healthy families. It has been my experience that all sound relationships have areas of disagreement and arguments. However, many children have confided in me that they worry about such sometimes-heated discussions because of a divorce in the family of a friend of theirs. They have overheard similar arguments in those homes and conclude that a separation is certain to happen to their parents as well.

Out of the many divorced families have emerged an increasing number of "blended" families. The complexities of such families create situations that demand superhuman wisdom and energy. The confusion of divided loyalties and the temptations to manipulate parents to gain one's own advantage adds to the plight of children.

THE PROBLEMS OF "NORMAL" FAMILIES

In the face of such extremely difficult situations, the problems of so-called normal families may seem insignificant. Indeed, they are just as important and need help in order to prevent serious problems in the future families of their own children.

A refuge for many troubled young parents and children are the grandparents. They heroically attempt to support their adult children and rescue the troubled grandchildren. Many youngsters would be irreparably damaged were it not for the strength of these special grandparents.

On the other hand, some parents feel dreadfully trapped by the needs and involvement of their parents that unwittingly set up a triangle with their children. When grandparents take sides with the children against their parents, serious trouble is likely.

And then there are a few tired or selfish grandparents who believe they have completed their responsibilities by raising their own children. They do not enjoy children and refuse to be bothered by having grandchildren around without their parents.

These are just a few of the complexities of modern-day families!

IMPORTANCE OF EARLY CHILDHOOD

Whether we consider the strength of an edifice, the straightness of a tree, or the development of a human being, we must know the vital necessity of correctness in early building.

In early childhood, there is an irretrievable opportunity to lay solid, true foundations that will permit the construction of a truly sound and lovely life! It is through the establishment of balances that such soundness is built.

The following are some of those balances:

1. Enough attention and protection to establish trust, but not enough to stifle growth toward individuality and independence.

2. Enough limits to offer security, but not enough to prompt rebellion or promote the despair of helplessness.

3. Enough work to teach the pride of achievement, but not so much that life becomes a grim drudgery.

4. Enough discipline and training to teach a sense of responsibility, but not so much that it destroys a sense of healthy freedom.

5. Enough laughter and play to keep life joyful, but not so much that pleasure becomes a goal in itself.

6. Enough consistency to make life predictable, but not so much that it makes life unbearably rigid.

7. Enough pride to teach the happiness of being productive, but not so much that it makes a child an egomaniac.

8. Enough love to make each day tender and warm and to motivate the painful efforts to grow—for a lifetime!

The significance of training pets is well understood, and when such training is practiced, the animal is loyal and pleasurable. Yet many parents fail to recognize that the basic principles of pet training apply even more practicably to children! Deciding what they want that pet to do, establishing rewards effectively, and applying firm consequences in a highly consistent manner, are the primary rules for such training. It will work equally well for children.

DISCIPLINE IS ESSENTIAL

But training is not enough, and few people see the significant difference between training and discipline. Training is a basic, neuromuscular response that can be taught simply through rewards or punishments.

Discipline, on the other hand, *is a teaching-learning complex that involves reason and understanding.* It is the process, as I see it, of learning why certain consequences go into effect, what is good or bad about certain behaviors and attitudes, and what makes them good or bad. It is the application to all of life of a few meaningful policies and philosophies. In short, good discipline results in the growth of wisdom.

It is not difficult to love most tiny babies. They are so helpless and vulnerable that even those who cry excessively are given constant attention and loving care by most parents. The first teeth, the first steps, the first words—all call forth excitement and pride from doting parents.

How different, though, is the first "No! I *won't!*" It is in the early search for freedom and the checking out of boundaries that many lifelong battles between parents and child begin. Parents who fail to see this as a healthy component of the child's personality are likely to resent him and establish no-win power struggles. On the other hand, they may lazily give in, permitting a damaging sense of power that is not founded on experience or reason.

Thus it is not only in the balances of life that parents may win or lose the struggle for healthy child raising. It is also in their inner core of strength and their attitudes that more (or less) good building takes place. It is rarely what parents want for their children that is wrong, but the methods they employ to gain obedience that go awry.

From such experiences, conflictual or harmonious, the emotions of children are formed. When there is plenty of unconditional love and pride in the child's growing achievements, those emotions are healthy and the child's self-esteem will develop into strength. But when the compassion and understanding are lacking, and when parents' anger outweighs the communication of their love, a child's developing personality becomes blighted. Later on, serious trouble is predictable.

THE FOUNDATION AND THE ADOLESCENT YEARS

It is in the adolescent years that the cracks in the superstructure of the personality become clearly visible. It was, however, *the faulty foundation of the early years that caused the damage.*

When those essential balances were not reached, and when disapproval too heavily outweighed the pride, the child lacked the proper building materials. Those hidden weaknesses emerge in behavioral disorders that are seen by parents as rebelliousness.

Actually there are three primary reasons for adolescent conduct disorders.

1. *Parents are too rigid or strict.* When parents are dictatorial and maintain too much control over too long a period of time, young people are likely to truly rebel in order to establish a semblance of independence. Since the job of teenagers is to do that very thing if they are to become healthy adults, parents must not only allow but *encourage* them to grow steadily in that direction, in order to avoid serious rebellion.

2. *Parents are too lenient or inconsistent.* Teenagers need to have their boundaries enlarged, *but they still need them.* When parents do not establish such limits or enforce them only erratically, adolescents will test them out regularly. The more erratic the parents are, of course, the more strenuously must the young people test them. To stop dangerous behaviors, parents must begin to set limits and enforce them with great consistency.

3. *Adolescents act out emotional pain.* When teenagers feel very inadequate or carry anxieties and worries that are too heavy, they often act out

such painful emotions in wildly erratic behavior. By getting high on chemicals or carrying out antisocial acts, they can temporarily escape their pain. They may even set themselves up to get caught and punished, because such punishment temporarily relieves their guilt. Such young people need a chance to explore their needs and to verbalize those painful feelings, so they will not need to "act out" to avoid them.

Understanding teenagers is fundamental to staying "in love" with them, enjoying them, and seeing them through those difficult years.

INFLUENCE OF OTHERS ON TEENS

During these important years, the availability of the extended family is a prime benefit to both parents and adolescents. On the other hand, if relatives do not share the values of the family, or if the young person uses them to manipulate and win power struggles, they can create more problems than help. When parents, grandparents, and other relatives do not enjoy a really sound relationship (or are frankly at odds), such manipulations can reach dangerous proportions.

In today's rootless society, frequent moves often prevent the forming of a relationship by grandchildren with grandparents or other relatives. In such situations, parents may benefit the family by looking for surrogate grandparents. Mutual enrichment of the "foster" relatives and the lonely family may be the result of such a search.

Tragically enough, there are many persons and groups in our society who relate with teenagers in a destructive alliance against the parents. Those whose values are highly permissive are an easy target for restless youth who search for permission to rebel against parents they see as old-fashioned and rigid.

Among such groups are a host of cults that build immeasurable wealth by deluding curious or distressed youth. Offering them a false security or some esoteric, mystical experience, they lure many people away from loving families and sound opportunities. They convince them that devotion to their "cause" will bring fulfillment and through intricate processes of brainwashing, they mentally and even physically enslave them.

BUILDING A SOUND SPIRITUAL FOUNDATION

A major defense against the successful influence of such cults is a sound spiritual foundation. Through the practical application of their own religious beliefs and traditions, families can build into the lives of their children the basic truths by which they live. Studies have shown that it is such family practices of a faith that create strength and promote family cohesiveness.

A child who lives with the laughter, training, and protection of a loving father is not easily tempted by even the most charismatic of cult leaders. Rather, as they grow, such children find it easy to trust the Heavenly Father.

A frequent question I receive is related to the best methods for teaching spiritual values to children and how to help adolescents validate those. In today's hedonistic society, there are no pat answers to that extremely important question, but there are some practical ideas that I believe will help.

1. *Parents, establish your own values.* When you know what you believe and demonstrate those beliefs in your daily lives, your children will have difficulty denying them.

2. *Teach your beliefs.* While verbally discussing values without living them is likely to go unheeded, so living them without explaining and teaching them may allow them to be taken for granted.

3. *Keep the practices of your faith joyful.* It is easy to focus on the limiting, negative aspects of the Bible without teaching the protective, loving reasons for them. Simple but honest explanations are important.

4. *Pray family prayers—but keep them simple.* I recommend prayers as a family from the wedding on. Those prayers need to be conversation with God—short sentences of joys shared, sorrows comforted, needs presented, hurts healed, and all of life brought regularly to the Heavenly Father. From the time they can speak a few words, children should be led to pray when their families do.

5. *Avoid using God as a threat or punishment.* Be sure to keep prayers affirming yet honest. Lovingly focusing prayers on needs can only be healing and enlightening.

Few people can resist optimistic, outreaching, unconditional love. Even the prodigal son returned to his father. And sure enough, the father was waiting, looking far down the road to glimpse the first sign of that return. So even if your children stray, don't give up your commitment.

Expect them back, and be ready to meet them when they reappear on the horizon of your hearts!

LET GO!

Every young person must grow through those developmental stages so clearly outlined by child psychologists. The temptation to cling too tenaciously to our children could make them social and emotional cripples. Children are born to mature, to establish their own identity, and to separate from their families, in order to establish their own homes in due time. The parents who recognize this and encourage the independence—gradually but confidently—will rarely need to suffer the heartache of serious rebellion and estrangement. With each child the transition is different, but with each it can be full of joy and love of a new and richer sort.

One of the frightening aspects of this stretch toward independence is tied to the social issues of young lives. When children are little, parents can supervise their play and other activities. If a little friend is judged to be harmful, he or she can be excluded from the home. Not so when teen years arrive! The opportunities to establish relationships in school, on jobs, and in the neighborhood, simply cannot be regulated by parents.

The permissiveness of our Western culture, and its relative affluence, create dangers that are truly frightening. The wise parent walks a fine line of guidance that is designed to teach the emerging young adult basic principles for sound decision making. They enlarge the freedoms in proportion to the sense of responsibility they see in that young person. And they encourage them when they fail or make less than optimal choices. They often must set some protective limits, but as much as possible, they lead their teenagers to learn to manage their own lives.

Keeping open the channels of communication is not always easy in these difficult years! But believing in their own good parenting, their adolescent's goodwill and desire to please them—and most of all, trusting in the transcending love of God—will see the parents through, and their children as well.

199 QUESTIONS

The questions that follow are real ones that have been written to me in response to my radio program "You and Your Child." They are, of course, edited, and identifying information is carefully removed to protect the persons who wrote.

Most of these questions have been written during periods of great frustration, confusion, and pain. For each letter that was sent, there must be countless individuals who also suffer from anxiety over the dangers of child rearing.

We hope the questions are representative of all of the people who endure such worries. And I trust that the answers, though brief, will be clear, practical, hopeful, and useful!

GRACE H. KETTERMAN, M.D.

199 Questions

PARENTS ASK

Answered by

Dr. GRACE H. KETTERMAN

Baby Care

1. POSTPARTUM   *Just what are postpartum blues?*

I was taught in medical school that the postpartum blues were due to a very complicated set of hormone imbalances that might happen after a baby was born. Certainly the mother's body does go through a great many changes after the birth of a child, and a very important part of that change is the reestablishment of the normal rhythm of her hormones. A few years ago, I had a visit from a postpartum father, and he was experiencing the postpartum blues just as typically as any mother I had ever seen. As I talked with him, and subsequently with other fathers, I found that they too went through a time of depression and sadness after the birth of their children.

In researching this and thinking about it deeply with these fathers and mothers, I discovered some reasons that may be very helpful to parents of a new baby or an expected baby.

These days most people who have a baby want that baby very much. They want a child to love and enjoy, and they want to show that baby off to their family and friends. During the pregnancy the mother gains a great deal of attention, and the father is excited about watching the movement of the baby, and feeling it inside the mother's body. Those bodily changes, the developing baby, and the fixing up of the room; the parties and the showers and the anticipation are all very much in high gear for anticipatory parents.

But after that long nine-month wait, suddenly the baby is there. The parties are over, the room is fixed up, but the occupant of that room can become a tyrant, and parents can become very worn-out, very tired. They had never realized ahead of time how much of their freedom they were going to have to give up. The facts that become increasingly clear to the new parents, then, are these: *We have lost our freedom.* (And if it's a subsequent child) *we have lost more freedom than we lost before. We have assumed a heavy responsibility 24 hours a day, 365 days a year, for a lifetime. We risk the loss of our attention from one another. We have financial burdens in supplying the needs that are, frankly, mind boggling.* Furthermore, it's just simply inconvenient to deal with these dirty diapers and getting up at night!

Few parents are truly prepared for giving up this many freedoms and assuming this many responsibilities. It's small wonder that when these realizations accumulate, suddenly, for either father or mother, there would be a time of grieving and sadness. The exciting part of all of this is that grief is a well-known process. Once you get through with the grief, you can recover from it and learn to truly appreciate that little bundle of joy that has come to enrich your lives—as well as to create some responsibilities for you as parents.

2.   NEW BABY SUPPLIES   *What clothes and equipment will our new infant require during those first few days at home? Please limit the list to the basics a new baby would need.*

Those basics really are fairly simple, but I would like to start with one that I think is most important, and that is a *rocking chair*. Rocking chairs may have gone out of vogue in many families, but the ability to hold a child and provide that rhythmic motion that the baby really has been accustomed to within the mother's body is very soothing to both child and parent. Therefore, I strongly recommend a rocking chair.

Obviously your baby will need a *bed* on which to lie, and many parents feel they need a series of beds (a bassinet, a portable crib, a baby bed), but really you only need one bed. The bed, however, is important, and it should have a firm mattress that will provide good support to the baby's body. You must be very careful that the bars on the sides of that crib are such that the baby's head cannot get wedged between those bars and be hurt. I strongly recommend that the bed be equipped with a *bumper pad*. You can make that yourself from a long strip of cardboard with some padding and a bit of bright fabric, or you can purchase one for a bit more money. A bumper pad helps to protect your child's head from bumping, just as the name implies, and certainly will help that child not to get caught in the rails.

You will need some *pads* and *sheets* for the bed. I suggest some small waterproof pads, so that you don't have to do the laundry of the entire linen supply each day, but can simply wash the little pads that will absorb the moisture, as the child wets its diaper from time to time. I do *not* recommend a pillow until the child is old enough to handle the head movements very well, because babies can get their noses tucked into that soft pillow and actually suffocate.

You will certainly need a great many *diapers,* because your baby's bladder will function very well for those first months of life. Fabric ones still are cheaper than the disposable ones, but there is certainly a great deal of time and energy spent in laundering them. You, as parents, need to decide what your time and financial resources are. If you have fabric diapers you will need at least three dozen in order to meet the needs of the baby and your needs to do the laundry.

If you have a relative who wants to give you a gift, I suggest they give you either disposable diapers or a diaper service for the first six weeks of your baby's life. A *plastic cover* for the baby's diaper area will again prevent a soggy bed and a soggy baby, and will help to lower your laundry requirements.

Baby shirts are important, and you will need several of those (perhaps three are enough), baby *gowns,* three or four with cuffs that can encase their fists to avoid thumb sucking and scratching and drawstrings to encase the feet to keep them warm; a couple of light *receiving blankets* and *one larger, warmer blanket* complete the list of bare essentials. Babies really do not need very much equipment. What they *do* need is a great deal of loving attention from you, the parents!

3.   NAMING YOUR CHILD   *What suggestions would you have for parents who are deciding on names for their baby?*

This is certainly one of the more pleasant tasks that expectant parents face, for certainly names are important. I am reminded of biblical facts that show names were given considerable thought. God revealed to the patriarchs many times what they were to name their children, and those names certainly had significant meanings. Family names sometimes are very important, and fathers often would like to have a son named after a grandfather or great-grandfather. Sometimes families would like to name a child after a hero. The name a child has certainly can have great significance. Sometimes parents choose a name that they happen to like. They simply may love the sound of it. A name can convey to a child, as he grows into adulthood, the importance the parents placed on the choice of the name. To the child it means that he as a person is more or less important. There are many "name" books available which give the meaning of the various choices. Always call your child's name with love, whatever name you may choose.

4.   BABY'S LAUNDRY   *What special care does a baby's laundry call for?*

That is a very important question because most babies have very tender skin and some of their diapers and linens are extremely difficult to handle. Every mother wants nice white and bright clothes for her little baby, and the sense of her adequacy as a mother may even depend on the condition of that linen! On the other hand, stains are the norm for babies. Urine and bowel movements stain those diapers and what babies spit up can make their best bibs and clothes look dreadful (as well as the sheets when they spit up in bed!). Orange juice and many baby foods leave very difficult stains.

Certainly harsh bleaches and detergents create white, bright linens but they also irritate baby's tender skin and improper washing can cause more rashes than you can clean up in a month. Here are my suggestions for your solutions in taking care of your child's linens and preventing the irritations on that skin:

Rinsing. First of all, rinse all soiled fabrics *at once* in cool water. Hot water will actually set certain stains, so avoid hot water, but do use plenty of cool water. Then I recommend going to your local drugstore or grocery store for an enzyme solution. These come under many trade names, but they will advertise themselves very clearly as to their effectiveness in taking care of a variety of stains. You will find that soaking your baby's linens and clothing in that enzyme solution will be magic. It simply dissolves away the protein substances that create the stains, and yet it does not hurt the fabric and is perfectly harmless to your child's skin. After rinsing in this special solution, I would urge rinsing through clear water again.

Washing. Run the clothes through your washing machine with a very mild soap. I do not recommend detergents for baby's laundry and, in fact, the one soap that I still find to be the very safest is old-fashioned Ivory Snow. I have never found a child's skin to react badly to that particular product. After washing thoroughly in a mild soap, rinse again well and dry the clothes.

Drying. I still like clothes that are hung outside and bleached by the sunshine and fresh air. If you live in an area where that is not possible, then certainly a dryer is just fine.

Bleaches and Softeners. Avoid bleaches; fabric softeners are sometimes helpful in making clothes and diapers very soft, and usually will not hurt a baby's skin. Occasionally, I have found a baby that may react to the scent that is put in those fabric softeners, but most children will tolerate that very well. Keeping your baby sweet and soft and clean is one of the joys of being a good parent.

5. NEWBORN'S CRYING *What's the most common reason for a baby's cry?*

Frankly most babies cry in pain, but there are certainly many other reasons for their crying. One of the worst fears of new parents is that they won't be able to stop their baby's crying. We instinctively want to soothe and comfort a baby, and when we can't, it makes us feel most inadequate.

I can so vividly recall the birth of our first baby, and how anxious I was about her cries. Having just finished medical school, I was acutely aware of all of the serious medical problems and every time she cried, I was certain that she had some dreadful defect or disease that ordinary parents don't have to worry about. I suppose my concerns were even more than the average parent. I found, fortunately, that her cries were usually very simple, very understandable, and relatively easy to cure.

Pain. The first cry of a newborn baby is that of pain—the pain of being born into a rather cold and sometimes cruel world. The spank of the doctor that elicits that first cry is an example of the result of pain in producing a cry. Now the cry that is in response to pain may sound angry, and it is intense. The baby's fists usually double up and draw in toward the body. The eyes squeeze tightly shut, and the cry is indeed a loud and piercing cry. Being *hungry, cold, wet, having an earache, a painful diaper rash*—these are all conditions that can cause that angry cry in response to the indignations that life heaps upon the child.

Crying Checklist. Still other kinds of crying, however, are those of loneliness, boredom, or even perhaps a fear. We know that even newborn babies startle with loud noises or a jolt, and this can cause a different kind of cry and a different body language. Their hands and feet extend, and the eyes open wide, as if in surprise, when they are startled or frightened. Then they may come out with a very loud cry, but it has a different quality from the angry, painful cry.

Then, of course, the lonely or bored cry is more of a whining, fretful one that can in its own turn be quite irritating to parents. By responding too soon to a baby's cry you can actually teach a child to cry for attention. By responding too late or too little, you may teach the baby to become angry, or even to withdraw in silence. So it is important that you respond appropriately, neither too soon, so you spoil the child, nor too little, so you create the angry or withdrawn child.

You will learn to identify the child's cry and check out the baby's functions. Is the diaper wet? Could he be hungry? Does she need to have a little cuddling or attention? By providing that attention just before the baby begins to cry, you may teach that little one to respond to you lovingly and positively, with less of that irritable cry. One of the greatest joys for a parent is the power to soothe a frightened, hungry, or hurting baby. I wish that joy for each of you.

6. WAKING UP BABY   *Sometimes when I come home late, after a long day at work, I'm disappointed to discover that my three-month-old daughter is sleeping. I'm often tempted to wake her, just to play and be friendly, and I admit sometimes I've done just that. Is it harmful to interrupt her sleep like this? If I don't, I could go days without seeing her when she's awake.*

Frankly, I am delighted to have a question like this. It reflects similar questions that I've had recently from young fathers, and I am hopeful that this is an indication of a trend in our society. By all means, Dad, awaken the baby and enjoy her to your heart's content. She needs the bonding with her father, just as much as she does with mother. Dads have a different approach with children, and they help to balance out the more tender and gentle handling that mothers provide. Enjoy your little girl. I would recommend that you change her diaper and clean her up. Feed her and play with her all you like, and then put her back to bed.

I would suggest that you be aware that this child's mother may be a bit tired after taking care of her all day, and it wouldn't be quite fair for you to have the fun of playing with the child, and then expect Mommy to quiet her down and get her back to sleep! You may give Mother a break, as a matter of fact, by taking care of the child and getting her ready for bed for the night. I would suggest that you and the mother together work out a schedule that will eventually coincide with your working hours. It's wonderful for Dad to come home and give the child a bath.

Dad, I would certainly recommend that you be aware of the need of your child's mother to be enjoyed too. Be friendly and playful together with the child, and then when the child has settled down, find time to keep the romance healthy between the two of you. The best gift you can give your child is a mother and father who truly love one another. Keep that love alive.

7. FIGHTING SLEEP *I'm wondering why it's so hard for children to go to sleep. If they are really tired as my three-month-old daughter seems to be at times, why do they fight sleep? Is there anything we can do to help our daughter drop off to sleep more easily?*

That's an important question because parents certainly need their rest, and I know they are anxious for this three-month-old baby to sleep a little more. One of the reasons that little babies stay awake too much is that there may be noises about that startle them. A barking dog, or a car honking outside, a loud radio, television, and so on can be quite frightening to little children and keep them awake, or awaken them, as they are just drifting off. A child may not only have too much stimulation but also may be extrasensitive. Some children are simply born with a keen sense of hearing, sight, touch, and all kinds of things bother them that would not bother a less sensitive child. And then sometimes new babies, particularly first ones, have overreactive parents. I once was called upon to make a house call by a set of parents whose child was crying himself into a real state of hysteria. When I walked into the house I found two sets of grandparents, and two parents extremely upset. I carefully examined the child and thought he must have a severe earache, but both eardrums were just fine. There was no sore throat, no fever, no rash, simply nothing to account for the child's anxious crying. I asked the parents to leave the room and give me a bottle and a rocking chair, which they very gladly did. As I sat with the child and rocked him gently for a moment, he promptly fell off to sleep. My diagnosis in that case was too many anxious relatives. That's understandable, because parents love a child, and when they can't promptly get him to go to sleep, they are bound to become concerned and tense and their tension can be contagious to the little one.

So parents, learn to relax and practice calmness when you hold your child. THINK CALM might be a nice motto for you to put on the baby's crib. Keep the baby's environment as peaceful as you can. Dim lights, soft colors, soft music in the background—these are the things that can help muffle the outside sounds and keep your child relaxed. Avoid handling the baby too much, especially if you are tired or tense. If the baby is going to fuss anyway, she may as well do so on the bed where she can relax against the firmness of her mattress. Play with her when she is good and happy. Don't run quite so quickly when she cries. Be strong and gentle. As you love the child, she will learn to relax.

8. BORED BABY   *We're new parents, and our question is this: Our daughter is two months old and very active and alert. She loves to coo and smile. She sleeps through the night and is awake most of the day. What bothers me is that sometimes she seems bored. What should we be doing to help her grow and learn? Can we spoil her with too much attention?*

I'm sorry to say this question reflects a concern that a great many young parents have. There is so much emphasis on learning in our society, that a great many parents are more worried than they need to be about teaching even little, tiny babies. I am wondering if a two-month-old looks bored, that perhaps it could simply be drowsiness or complacency, contentment of sorts. And perhaps it's the parents' worry that is concerning them more than the child's actual needs. This baby sounds loved and well attended to. So I'd frankly hate for the parents to develop a habit of entertaining the child all of the time, and trying to keep her excited or happy constantly. Here are some suggestions for taking care of a tiny baby:

After a nap pick the child up and play with her as long as you like. Feed her if she's hungry, and change her diaper, and then place her in a reclining seat, such as an infant seat, or even back in her bed. As soon as she can fit into it without discomfort, I like the little canvas swings that can be placed in the family room, and the child can sit there comfortably watching the normal activities of her mom and dad. This sets the stage for a normal family life, where children observe and learn from observing— and where parents can have some of their own individual activities. When she is able to grasp them, offer to a little baby rattles or toys. Put up a mobile that can move about and attract a child's attention; also consider musical toys or bright objects, tied on to the sides of her crib. These can develop a child's color sense and help her to be entertained on her own, part of the time. Enjoy your child but don't become her slave. Entertain her all you like, but don't feel that you must keep her happy twenty-four hours a day. There is an intuitive, instinctive sense that parents were given to help them recognize a child's need of them and theirs of the child. Follow that intuition and you won't go too far wrong.

9. THE FUSSY, NAPLESS BABY   *My little five-month-old baby has never taken a decent nap. She'll sleep for half an hour to forty-five minutes at the longest, and after this she is awake for three* *hours before she'll take another half-hour nap. In between naps she's usually fussy and seems tired. This goes on every day. It's very tiring and wearing on me, because it doesn't give me a good break to get anything done. Also, when she's tired, she requires more attention from me. How can I get her into a better nap schedule?*

This dear mother has a problem, and it becomes a vicious cycle. The more babies fuss and cry and the more tired mothers become, the more tense the mother feels; the baby then feels Mother's tension and cries all the more. You can easily see, parents, how this happens, so please, above all else, do not blame yourselves or feel guilty because you have a tense, rather sleepless child.

Sleeplessness in infants can be due to discomfort or what we have commonly called *"colic."* It can be due to habits or to tension. These kind of children sometimes do become a bit hyperactive as they grow older. You can see it is important that you solve this problem when they are tiny.

If you suspect that your baby may have colic, I recommend that you ask your pediatrician to help you with this problem. Giving a different formula or a different feeding schedule, giving some medicated drops for the child's gastrointestinal spasms that are at least part of colic, can be a miracle cure for some of these difficult babies. Be sure that there is no skin irritation or rectal pain. Ear infections are another source of chronic pain and discomfort that can disturb a child's sleep. So, first of all, be sure that there are no *physical* causes for the baby's sleeplessness.

Try to keep yourself as calm, relaxed, and happy as you possibly can, even with this irritable little one. Make the environment of the baby's nursery as calm as possible.

Now, parents, I would suggest this: Do not feel that you have to comfort, hold, or cuddle a crying baby! If you can do this within five, ten, or even fifteen minutes, that's fine, but then put him back down and get on with your activities. When you hold the baby for an hour, and he is still fussing, you will become more and more tense yourself. Let him cry in his bed, while you go on about your jobs. Then when the baby sleeps, get some rest yourself, so that you will get out of that vicious cycle of tension. Be comforted, because after a while the baby will quit the crying, and you will be able to enjoy each other, I *assure* you!

10. SMALL NIGHT PERSON   *My daughter and her husband are thrilled with their seven-month-old little boy. They both work,* *but they have a lovely woman to baby-sit, and he has excellent care. The problem is sleeping at night. His naps are short in the daytime, but he's a happy baby and the picture of health. My daughter breast-feeds him, even going at noon to see him and feed him. They bathe him in the evening, and play with him. He can go to bed around nine, then wake at 11:00, 12:30, 3:30, 4:30, and 5:30. Sometimes she feeds him, sometimes not. Her doctor says to just let him cry it out. What can be done for a baby who keeps waking up throughout the night?*

Indeed such nights are hard.

Causes. Before we get to the solutions, let's talk first about the reasons little babies cry during the night. There are several causes, and all of these need to be checked out. *Hunger* is certainly one of them, and little children do digest their food at various rates, so that some children need food more often than others. They may have pain. They may have an *earache,* or a *stomachache,* or a variety of pains, any of which can cause them to waken and be restless at night. Frankly, most often a chronic problem of this sort is simply a habit. This child's physician seems to believe that in his case it *is* a habit. It sounds as if he has checked out all of those other possibilities.

The Fatigue Factor. Sometimes babies are just kept up and played with so hard and so long that they cannot relax. They are overly stimulated. However, the fatigue factor also involves parents. When parents are so tired from getting up that many times at night, their own state of fatigue will sometimes cause a failure of the quality of the time they give the child to be happy and satisfying. I wonder in this case if that might not be a part of the difficulty. Almost certainly this mother is going to feel guilty, maybe because she is upset and so tired that she cannot be as patient as she otherwise would be. Of course, the more irritable and the more tense parents become, the worse the child's problem!

Solution. In the evening follow active play with soothing, quiet times. Delay the bedtime a little bit, until the child has that proper balance in good healthy fatigue, without being exhausted, and some relaxation that will make him ready for sleep. Have his room dark and quiet, except for low, steady music or some other monotonous sound that will cloud the peripheral noises. Follow the doctor's advice. I recommend letting the baby cry. You can expect the first night that he'll cry for half an hour or more. The next night about half that long, and the third night perhaps none at all. Teaching babies to respect their parents' needs must begin early. You'll all be glad you did.

11. BREAST-FEEDING AND SOLIDS   *This is a two-part question. First, when would you advise adding solid food to breast-feeding? Second, how long should I breast-feed after solid food is added regularly?*

Those are very commonly asked questions, because there is great polarity in the advice being given. If you parents happen to have a pediatrician who was trained some time ago, he will probably start the child on some solid foods as early as six or eight weeks. More recently, however, there is concern in medical circles about starting solid foods too soon, because we are seeing a great many children who have food allergies. My frank opinion is that it is wise to wait until three or four, or perhaps even six months of age before you add solid foods to your child's diet. The longer wait would be important if your family happens to be one that you know has a great many allergies.

How to Add Solids. Let's discuss how to add solid foods because that's very important. It is essential that you start with simple, single foods and none of the fancy mixtures that are so appealing to interested mothers. I suggest starting a baby on rice cereal, fixed with water, or perhaps with breast milk you have pumped if you are breast-feeding your baby. After three to five or even six days on a little of the rice cereal, fixed according to the directions on the package, you might choose to start bananas, which are a very simple, easily digested food. Almost all babies tolerate them well and enjoy them very much. I suggest then that you start with a yellow vegetable, such as carrots or squash. Add a single, simple meat, such as chicken, and then go back through the list again, adding another cereal, another fruit, another vegetable, until your child has had a variety of the foods that would be appealing to you (and probably will also appeal to your child).

When to Wean. This is certainly another very important question. Some mothers prefer breast-feeding as long as a year and a half or two years, or as long as the child wants to breast-feed. Others feel that the child should stop by nine months, or whenever the child begins to cut teeth. Again this is pretty much a private and personal matter, and I don't think anyone has the right to dictate exactly when a child should be weaned. However, most children in my experience (and all of my own three) chose to give up their nursing at about seven to nine months of age. Frankly, I was a little disappointed! Though I was not able to breast-feed my children, I did give them the bottle and that was a time for cuddling, holding, and rocking them. I frankly enjoyed that a great deal. But they would have no more of it, and so I had to allow them to give it up. Watch your own child's body. When that child is ready to stop the sucking and the oral satisfaction of nursing or bottle-feeding, allow the child to give it up. Physically the child's own body and system knows when the right time is. If you wait too long, it may be very difficult for the child to give up that sucking reflex and the need for the oral satisfaction may become a habit!

12.   WHO HOLDS THE BABY?   *I am thirty-seven years old, and we feel greatly blessed to have been given a child after waiting so long. My question is should young children be allowed to hold and carry babies? Also could you suggest a diplomatic way for a parent to say no to another parent who suggests letting their child hold your baby?*

That's indeed an important question, and I can feel with that thirty-seven-year-old mother who has waited a long time. However, I find that same question arising with younger mothers as well who have several children. You know, babies really are not toys to be dragged around like rag dolls, and yet they need a great deal of attention and stimulation. So here are some suggestions that I think will help all parents of tiny babies:

First of all let's consider the *intimate family members.* This mother has an only child, so she doesn't have older brothers or sisters but many families do. Older siblings especially need a sense of belonging to the new baby, so they won't have the rivalry or jealousy that so often spoils their relationship. I would recommend that older children be allowed, and even encouraged, to hold and play with a new baby. Now if they are very little (two or three years of age), certainly the parents need to help and be there all of the time to support the baby's head and to guide the older brother or sister in exactly how to handle and play with that little baby. Older children, of course, can learn that quite quickly, and it will be a wonderful lesson for them in child care to be given some responsibility for a new baby.

Children *outside of the family* are another problem, however, and many times they may be coming down with a cold, or perhaps not be as clean as your own children can be taught to be. That's where the sensitive handling comes in. I suggest with other children (or even other adults) that you as a parent not allow them to ask, but first of all, if you see them eyeing your baby and acting like they want to get close, that *you* be the one to give some guidance and direction. If you are not comfortable with them taking your child, hold your baby in your own arms very firmly, and ask them if they would like to touch your baby. If it's a younger child, show how to touch the baby's hands and/or stroke the baby's head or in some way get a feel of the child, without taking over the handling of a baby in a way that could be risky at best.

Older people, of course, can handle a baby physically, but may be unaware that being given that child (and having him passed around among them) can create a nervousness and fatigue on the part of the baby. So I'd suggest that the parents set some limits and say to the other person, "I hope you will enjoy our baby, but we've waited a long time for his birth, and so I'm not very comfortable letting other people hold him right now. When he's a little older, of course, I would like to have you hold him," or some such tactful comment.

13. ROCK TO SLEEP? *Our twin boys are now eight months old and are very good-natured and easy to take care of. They seem to feel quite secure. In the past, I've made it a point to rock them and sing them to sleep, both at naptime and nighttime. Many of my friends tell me that I should just put them down and let them cry themselves to sleep, until they realize that crying won't bring them any attention. I've tried this now for about two weeks, but they've both become very whiny and will cry for long periods. Since they are getting older and heavier, it would be much easier for me to just put them down, but I want to do what's right. I'd appreciate your help. It would make me a more relaxed mother to know I'm doing the best thing.*

I think this mother is doing the best thing when she rocks these little children before she puts them down. Prior to a year or year and a half, little children seem to need the security of that holding and cuddling and rocking before going to sleep for the night. You know, little children at this age can't talk, and all they can do to express their needs is to cry and whine, as they are doing. By this whining they're letting their parents know that their needs have not been met. These children don't sound like they're spoiled at all, and the spoiled child needs a little different kind of handling. For that sort of child who is manipulative and power struggling, I would recommend just putting him to bed and letting him cry it out. By her description, I feel that these children need their mother, and I would strongly urge her, even though it is a bit burdensome, to go ahead with the loving and cuddling process and ritual at bedtime.

14.   THUMB SUCKING   *I have a six-month-old girl who has sucked her thumb since I brought her home from the hospital. She was quite a colicky baby, and the only thing that seemed to comfort her was her thumb. People have told me to put a mitt on her hand, but just what is so terrible about a baby sucking her thumb? I sucked my thumb as a child until I was in sixth grade, and never had any tooth disorder. I have tried a pacifier, but she will have nothing to do with it. I am a nursing mother, and she will not take a bottle at all but does take a cup. I would really appreciate your opinions on this subject.*

This is an age-old problem and every parent who has a thumb-sucking child is worried about that poor child's teeth. The old worries about teeth are not necessarily true, however. In fact, dentists with whom I have consulted tell me not to worry about children who suck their thumbs, at least until the permanent teeth erupt, and then only if the child pushes very hard with the thumb against the erupting teeth. Since parents and grandparents are going to worry about thumb sucking, however, let me make some suggestions:

First of all, *it is easier to prevent thumb sucking than to cure it.* This mother's suggestion of putting a mitt on the hand would have worked had she tried that right from the hospital. Babies' gowns have little sleeves that are made so that they will fold over the child's hands and if a baby never finds the thumb, then certainly it can't miss it later on. However, if the child is colicky and fussy, apparently there is some need on the part of the child to have the comfort and reassurance of that little thumb in its mouth. Frankly, I agree with this mother. I do not think that it is so terrible.

However, if there is a problem (and perhaps your mother or an aunt is telling you to make that child quit sucking her thumb), you may try some of these ideas as well as the preventive ones. First of all, *allow plenty of nursing time* when the baby is feeding so that she may fall asleep without the need to suck her thumb. At this age (six months), you may begin to give her toys to hold, so that she can entertain herself, or perhaps put pieces of the toy in her mouth to chew on. You must be very careful not to give the child something she could choke on or put too far into her mouth. Focus the child's waking attention on objects outside of her own body. A cradle gym, a musical toy, or a mobile that you may make yourself can entertain the child, and she will reach for those objects rather than for her own mouth. Play with your child, and teach her to use her hands for activities other than thumb sucking. As your child's interests focus away from her own self, both you and your child will grow in the joy and intimacy of your parenting. I think you will find the thumb sucking will disappear in due time.

15.   TO BURP OR NOT TO BURP   *It seems that the older our daughter gets—she's three months—the more she is spitting up. Should we be burping her more often to prevent this, or is it natural for her to be spitting up more as she grows older?*

This mother has brought up a very interesting possibility. In not a small number of children there is a problem that we call *achalasia*. This problem really relates to a relaxed valve that opens into a baby's stomach. As the baby becomes more active and starts squirming and kicking, he simply squeezes out the contents of the stomach and then spits them out. It isn't serious, and rarely does the child spit up enough to cause a problem with weight gain; but it is most annoying to parents.

Burping will help only slightly. By removing gas bubbles and helping to relax a fairly full little tummy, it may help to prevent some of the spitting up, but it won't help it totally. When this child grows a little bit older, becomes even more active, and starts flopping over on her tummy, the parents may actually expect the problem to become worse before it gets better. However, as soon as the child starts standing up and walking, the problem will disappear almost overnight. Until that time, however, here are some suggestions if you happen to be a parent who has a spitting-up baby:

First of all, I recommend that you have a great supply of old-fashioned bibs. Keeping a bib around the child's neck will catch most of the spillovers, and those bibs can be changed easily and eliminate the laundry of the baby's entire outfit. Being patient is perhaps the most important thing that I can tell you. Once in a while I have had a baby patient whose spitting up was so severe that to keep him from losing weight we had to prop up the bed, and really that's fairly simple. Some wooden blocks that would fit snugly under the head end of the baby's bed would elevate it, and the flow of gravity would simply keep the baby from spitting up as much. You may want to consult your pediatrician if your child has a more serious degree of this problem. I can tell you, however, I have never seen a kindergartener spit up. You and your child will survive this annoying habit.

16. WALKERS FOR BABIES *This question concerns the value of walkers. It seems more and more mothers consider them to be great for babies who don't know how to crawl. Do you feel they encourage the child to walk rather than crawl?*

That is a very interesting question (and one that I rarely have been asked), but I see its importance. I have had friends whose little babies have walked too quickly in those walkers, and unfortunately, have walked right down basement stairs and other precipitous areas, seriously hurting themselves.

As important as that danger is the significant need for babies *to crawl.* We know that some learning-disabled children have somehow gone through their early developmental stages as infants without crawling. There are those who are wondering if crawling is a very essential stage of a child's motor and neurological development.

So I recommend that whether or not you use a walker, you get down on the floor with your little pretoddler, and crawl with that child. Not only is it fun but it also develops that child's body in a fashion that seems to have a great influence on later learning capacities. So help your child to crawl, and get down and crawl *with* him.

Now, when a child needs to be in a walker or a stroller, that's quite all right. There are times when a baby may have mobility and can be around the parents, while you are busy, and that can create a greater sense of intimacy, warmth, and socialization within the family. It's perfectly all right to use a walker, just so you don't have the child in it too much of the time.

I do worry a little bit that walkers have an influence on parents hurrying their babies. I am currently very concerned about the precocious development of many children, and the push that parents unconsciously have for teaching children to grow up. Early walking is one of those symptoms. So, parents, don't be in a hurry to teach your children to walk. They have many years in which to do that.

17. POTTY TRAINING *Would you please review for me your suggestions for potty training? It's been a while since I've had to go through this and I need some help remembering what to do.*

Whether you have one child or a dozen, it seems like every time you face potty training, it's a new challenge. It is one of the most common problems that I receive, and I'm glad to repeat it for this mother. First of all, I urge her not to feel pushed or anxious. Only seriously neurologically damaged college students fail to master this physical skill, and I find that most problems in potty training come from overanxious parents. So relax. Watch your child for readiness to begin potty training. Don't go by someone else's arbitrary recommendation that because he is eighteen months old, he should begin potty training. It simply doesn't work that way.

Now the signs that will help you to know that your child is ready for potty training are these: the child needs to be *dry for over an hour.* When he awakens dry after a nap or in the morning, the *child may be aware that he is ready to begin using the potty.* Sometimes the child shows that he is aware of the process of urination, and when that is so, begin explaining the process to the child. Begin to sit him on the potty. I do recommend that you use a small potty chair (as compared with the little arrangement that can be fitted onto a toilet). Sitting on the low chair is much safer and more secure for a little child. While the child is sitting on the potty, turn on the water in the bathroom, give the child a drink of water, and even let a little warm water flow over the genital area. Many times that will be enough just to start that flow of urine, and the child will be surprised at his success (and certainly you as mother will be delighted!).

Wait a few minutes if this does not work and let him try again. But don't keep the child on the potty so long that he becomes tired or resistant. Let him up, put him in training pants, or even stay in the bathroom with him while he has no panties on and try again in a little while. In fact, if you have the time and want to do it, you may even spend one day in the bathroom, letting the child run about and play rather normally, and then catching him when he begins to urinate. With the potty so close he will quickly get the idea and many parents have found that this really works quite well with their children. If you don't have a whole day to spend, however, be patient. Keep training pants on the child, rather than the diaper. This feels different, and it reminds the child to take care of his wetting in the bathroom, rather than letting it happen in the diaper.

Above all, *avoid scolding and punishment.* When the child is ready, he will use the potty—unless he is so tense, angry, or frightened that he simply cannot. When he does have successes, praise him sincerely. If he has none in a week or ten days, I would recommend that you wait a while and try it later. I know with patience and love your child will learn to use the potty.

18.   VACATION AND BABY   *We have a seven-month-old daughter who is our delight. We have planned a one-week trip to the mountains at the end of this month, when our daughter will be seven and a half months. Right now, we have tentataive plans on having one set of grandparents take care of her for two days, and the other grandparents for six days. We give her lots of attention, and she is a happy baby. She doesn't cry when we leave her at either of our parents, but we are still having second thoughts about leaving her. We wonder what kind of effect it will have on her not to see us for one week. We don't want her to be upset, and there is no way to know how she'll be. What do you think about leaving her at this age, and how could we best prepare her to be away from us? We do want to feel good about our decision and make it as easy as possible on her.*

I certainly urge young parents to get away now and then. The most precious gift you can give your child is loving one another and keeping your romance alive as husband and wife. I know that time alone is very precious. But at the age of your daughter (just seven and a half months), I would advise against a very long time away. The child may very well enjoy her grandparents for a period of some hours, or even a day or two, but a week is quite a long time for a child of her age.

Studies have been done, in fact, that indicate that children under a year of age may become depressed and feel abandoned, when their parents are away from them for as long as a week. Now after a year (or certainly after eighteen months), apparently the harm is much less likely, and the child can survive perfectly comfortably.

Perhaps for this vital first year, you could settle for a long weekend, rather than an entire week or eight days, knowing that later on there will be longer times available. Unfortunately, it's simply not convenient to be a parent. The times that you must deny yourselves the things that you want very much will later on be made up when the child is older and able to tolerate separations much more easily.

However, if you do decide to go ahead and try this week away, let me recommend the following steps. Have that little girl go and spend a night or two with each of the grandparents before you go. Picking her up and bringing her back to her own home will allow her to know that she has not been abandoned, and that you will be there for her. As the child then spends longer times with those grandparents, she will be able to tolerate it, I hope, without undue anxiety. Babies are very resilient.

19. QUALITY TIME   *How much time should a parent spend with her baby and toddler? I'm speaking of quality time during the day. Would you cover how a mother can tell if she's spending too much or too little time with her child? This is my most worrisome area.*

That concern is a valid one, because I know mothers with a little baby and a toddler certainly must feel trapped at times and need to get away. Sometimes mothers have to go to work, and they worry about the damage that might cause to a little child. Ideally, biologically, a mother is meant to be with her baby at least within eyesight and hearing, until the child is mature enough and trained well enough to be safely alone for periods of time. Practically, however, many mothers have to go to work to earn a living, and many mothers get "cabin fever" when they are confined day after day with little children. These tots sometimes are fussy and cross, and the parent becomes irritable and depressed. The only way I think that a mother can spend too much time with her child is in this latter situation. If mother and child come to be at odds with one another and they are miserable, they are going to be better off if she gets away sometimes and feels a little freedom and relaxation. Then she can come back and truly enjoy those children.

Perhaps some mothers pamper and overprotect children and may give in to them so much that they really create spoiled little monsters. Then, too, I would suggest that the parent might do well to get away sometimes from those children. The signs of problems are that sometimes children become overly dependent, whining, or act spoiled, and just uncomfortable and irritating. When there is too little time, the child may become clinging and act frightened, or perhaps withdrawn and emotionally cold. In an older child, the regression to bed-wetting, thumb sucking, or other childish habits may be other indications that the mother's time or the quality of that time are lacking.

What is quality time? Perhaps that also will help this mother. I think quality time is that which is focused on really relaxing and enjoying the child. Playing together happily, attending to the needs of the child, teaching and guiding, cuddling and cooing, laughing and talking together. Those are things that happy parents and well-adjusted children can enjoy. Quality time is freely given because of proper priorities. A neat house certainly is not going to take a great deal of time, but deep cleaning can wait. Reasonable meals without compulsion for elaborate or gourmet types of menus will spare a lot more time for fun with the child. I hope that the quality and the enjoyment of your time with your child will grow and grow.

Behavior

20. TINY SIBLING RIVALRY   *My question is about disciplining a two-year-old. How can I guide his behavior to be more kind to his one-year-old-sister? They are seventeen months apart. If our son thinks we are not watching, he'll kick her, push her, or hit her with a toy. I'm afraid he might really hurt her sometime.*

As a matter of fact I have known older children to seriously hurt a younger sibling. Parents' temptation is one that I would like to warn them against: that is, to protect the child that is picked upon. Actually, the more aggressive, older child is the one that often needs the attention.

Two-year-olds simply cannot play satisfactorily or constructively with younger siblings. They can't even play successfully with children their own age. They are not really developed enough to do that. They are so busy establishing their own rights and their own identity, that they can't cope with the competition of a younger child. The needs for this older child are those to get more time and more attention, especially of the type that he sees and envies in that younger brother or sister. Don't be afraid, parents, of giving too much attention of this loving sort to your older children. The parents' attitude in this case perhaps needs to become a little more loving and relaxed, and a little less worried and critical, and pretty soon the older child will settle down.

21. IMAGINARY FRIENDS   *Should parents be concerned when a small child starts to make up imaginary playmates?*

Not at all. In fact, I worry a little when children don't have an imagination that creates playmates and all sorts of fantasies for their little lives. It's quite normal for three- to six- or seven-year-old children to have a great many imaginary friends and even pets. That's part of the creativity of their healthy little minds. The imagination of tea parties, and the creation of great banquets from them, is something that I can recall from my childhood—and the making of mud pies into artistic creations of great grandeur and playhouses of string and sticks, which were architectural wonders.

All children have their own various themes of creativity that relate to imaginations. You need to enjoy your children's imaginary friends and pets. Enter into that play with them and your own lives will be enriched by their imagination, and theirs, in turn, will be enhanced by your contributions to that sort of play.

Remain quite certain, however, that both you and your child continue to know that these creatures are imaginary. The only concern that I have is for that vagueness that can happen between the imaginary and the real. When children do not know that difference, and where that line exists, then I might become a little concerned about their being too involved in a fantasy world. By simple words you can help them remember that this is a pretend or an imaginary or a make-believe situation. That simple verbiage can keep both you and your child quite clear about what is real.

22. SHARING AMONG PRESCHOOLERS   *Is it at all possible for two- or three-year-old children to play together and share their toys? Or is that just beyond their capability?*

Let's break that down into the two-year-old and the three-year-old, because there is a remarkable difference even in that close age span. The typical two-year-old is truly incapable of interacting in play with other children. The behavior of two-year-olds really is not very social but quite personal. The two-year-old is testing his own strength and finding out what he can do and cannot do. He is competing with everyone, and the motto of every two-year-old is "May the better man win" because that is certainly how they set out to face their day. They need to find out who is the better and stronger.

There are times when they need that strength, and times when they need to give in. It is important that we not rush our two-year-olds into social situations that are truly beyond their abilities, and we ought not to demand that they do what they cannot do. Two-year-olds cannot share, because they don't even know what to do with toys themselves. They need the time and the space to learn that. Require the two-year-old, however, to stop hurting other children, and do not allow him to grab things away from them. Your gentle but firm interference at the times when your child is around other youngsters will be helpful for that child's protection and guidance for the future. Gradually teach the two-year-old how to share, and that he must take turns, so that he can learn to play with others successfully later on.

One of the things that two-year-olds can do very well (and which can help them to learn a great deal about cooperation) is to sit down on the floor and roll a ball back and forth. As you sit down with legs outspread and the child does too, very close to one another, and yet gradually lengthening that distance, the child will get a very fine concept of playing together, when you throw it to him and allow him to roll it back. That can be a very important concept in that two-year-old's life.

Another method for teaching the two-year-old how to play with others is by putting a number of objects together in a container. You as an adult may play with him in putting things in and out of that container. Then import another child and let him do that with someone else of his own age. These simple mechanisms can help a two-year-old to learn how to play with other little people.

Magically, about the age of three, a child will want to play with other children. By then, they have often learned how to share, how to cooperate in all kinds of activities, and how to play imaginatively and creatively together. Be careful of your two-year-old, and you will enjoy your three-year-old's playing together with other young people.

23.   IN PARENTS' BED   *I'd like to find out what your views are on a preschooler coming into bed with his parents during the night. My four-year-old has been doing this for over two years. We thought he would tire and stop on his own. (He has been a very sick child.) He doesn't require much sleep and slept through the night for the first time at fifteen months. What can I do to keep him in his own bed, and let him feel secure and not rejected?*

That is a very special question and it addresses two different issues. One is a general philosophy about preschoolers sleeping with parents, and the other is a special child who has had some unusual medical problems.

Generally speaking I am very much against little children sleeping much of the time with their parents. I think neither parents nor child get adequate rest; it invades the privacy of the marriage; and I think it is very awkward for everyone involved. However, there are times when children are frightened, or when they have been ill, when there are various concerns, and the child needs the assurance and the security of being with those parents at night. With this special child, or any ill child, I would suggest that you parents check with your physician to be sure that the child is perfectly all right—that it will, in fact, be safe for him to sleep in his own bed and in his own room. You might even try putting his bed temporarily in your bedroom, so he is accustomed to having you nearby. You would feel secure at being able to hear him, and yet you have much more comfort and some privacy in your sleeping arrangements.

When you are ready to break a child of the habit of sleeping with you, there is one most important issue that you as parents need to settle. Be sure that you both are committed to his sleeping in his own bed. You need to be quite convinced that you are ready for this, and that it will not hurt the child because it will be difficult to break that habit. When you are convinced that this is proper and right and you're ready for it, then explain to your child what it is that will be different. Explain to him why it is going to be different, and that it includes your need for privacy, as well as his need to grow up a little bit and become a bit more independent. Then establish a ritual for putting him to bed at night. Play with him, quietly rock him, sing to him, read to him, soothe him in whatever way is comfortable for you and then very firmly and lovingly put him in his bed and assure him that he must stay there. The first night he will test you out. I can promise you he will cry, he will struggle; and he will use all kinds of devices to make you give in. Hold firm. Do not give in.

The second night he will do it a little less, and by the third or fourth night, almost all children will give up the struggle and, frankly, will be relieved to have their own privacy, the spaciousness of their own beds. I know that parents are much more comfortable without that little wiggler between them. Whatever you do, *do not relent.* Simply be consistent and be loving, and you can win the struggle for yourselves and your child.

24. HYPERACTIVE CHILD   *We are relatives (grandmother and aunt) of a child who has not been diagnosed as hyperactive and isn't being treated for it. However, he seems to have many problems of hyperactivity. He has been branded as a troublemaker and rebellious child. What can we do to help without overly interfering?*

First of all, I would like to explain some of the very important causes of hyperactivity for these very concerned relatives. Hyperactive children may have physical problems. There can be neurological difficulties, allergies, or some other kind of chronic, physical problem that makes the child irritable. He may seem to be a hyperative, never-resting sort of child. Very often, however, these hyperactive children have simply gotten off to a bad start from the moment of their birth. They are children who by their temperament simply do not match with their parents. Sometimes a very quiet, peace-loving mother has been blessed with a child who is full of energy and ready to go from the moment his first cry is heard in this world. She is likely to become very tense, fatigued, and frankly irritated herself because of the demands of this kind of child. We know that such children and parents, when they are at crosscurrents for such a long time, often evolve into the problem of hyperactivity, resentment, and difficult relationships.

Relatives often may be the most helpful people because they are not personally, emotionally involved in the struggle and by their observations, their objective opinions can be most helpful. On the other hand, I find that parents can be quite sensitive and the suggestions of well-meaning relatives can cause pain and make them feel as if they are doing a bad job. Let me therefore recommend these specifics to you extended family members who are trying to help:

First of all, try to catch those relatives at a time when they are troubled themselves. Responding to their questions and their difficulties, you will probably find them to be much more open to your ideas and suggestions. Then I recommend that you take those hyperactive children and care for them for periods of time yourselves, giving the parents a rest. Being away from the hyperactive children can give the parents a new lease on life and a great deal more patience. Having those children in your own home, or spending time in their home with them, can give you personal insights into the problems. Perhaps some discoveries will be made by you that can be shared with the parents to help all of them. Above all, avoid criticism of the child or the parents. Love them, support them, and encourage them. Showing your concern and offering them your prayers can be a great gift to tide them over a difficult period of time.

25.   BREAKING THE GUM/SWEETS HABIT   *Unknown to us, our toddler was getting hooked on gum, thanks to indulgent relatives and even church nursery workers. Now at age three, she is looking for gum and candy all the time, from before breakfast until she is tucked in bed at night. I don't want to eliminate sweets, but how can we cut down on her habit of asking?*

Actually, this situation includes two questions. One has to do with gum and sweets, and the other has to do with how to help children accept limits and the simple little word *no*. Now all parents do need to deny some things to their children, and certainly having too much gum and candy is one of them, because we know that the sugar in gum and candy promotes bacterial growth in the mouth. Therefore they can make tooth decay much more likely than it otherwise would be. Obviously there is one answer to that—sugarless gum.

I have no strong objections to a child's chewing gum occasionally if it is sugar-free. Chewing, however, stimulates the flow of saliva from a child's mouth, which obviously must be swallowed, and that tends to stimulate the secretion of gastric juices. I have actually known children to have chronic stomachaches because their poor little tummies did not get enough rest, due to chewing gum too much. So this parent's concern is genuine. You can teach a child to gratify the oral needs just by eating proper food, like vegetable sticks, and swallowing the food that is really nutritious and healthy. Chewing gum can actually cut down on a child's eating because the oral satisfaction that is a part of good appetites can be too much satisfied simply by the endless chewing of gum. Of course, gum tastes good, and it's fun in moderation—use it, perhaps, as a special treat.

Now, if you're going to change this child's habits, parents, do the following things. Explain to the child your concern about chewing gum too much, so that she knows your changing her habit comes out of loving protection for her good. Plan with her when she may and may not chew gum. *Stick with that plan.* Ask others not to treat her to gum unless you okay it first. Be very firm and follow through with your plan, allowing her to chew sugarless gum only, and *only* when you and she agree that she could have it. Supply plenty of love and laughter, play and creativity *and healthy food,* and your daughter will soon give up her addiction to gum.

26. CHEATING   *It was very upsetting and embarrassing when my child's teacher called and said he had been caught cheating. Why is it that some children just give in to the urge to cheat, even though their parents have stressed honesty and playing by the rules?*

The Why. Well, frankly the motivation for most cheating is very understandable and even very positive. Children cheat because they want to do well, and every parent and teacher wants the children to do well, too. The problem is that they have somehow learned how to do well without putting in the honest effort that it takes to learn the material. Interestingly, most cheating begins quite by accident. One child sees another do it and get by with it. The opportunity then presents itself to him, and in a moment of weakness, he gives in and finds that he has done quite well because he did cheat.

The payoff has seemed to teach the child that cheating pays. Grades get better. You can get by (the child reasons) without putting in so much work, and so why not do it? Our society, in fact, teaches us to look for easy ways. I suspect there is a bit of natural laziness in all of us that really prefers to take the easy way toward success.

Be School Supportive. The important thing, parents, once you understand something of why the child cheats, is what to do about it. I am appalled at the number of parents who take exception to the reports of misbehavior from schools. There seems to be a growing adversarial relationship between parents and teachers, and oftentimes I find parents taking the child's side, even when the child is sadly doing something very, very wrong. So your first step needs to be to team up with the school or the person who has become aware of the cheating habit of your child.

Be Aware. Notice your own child. See if he plays games with brothers and sisters and wins by cheating. See if there are other little evidences of dishonesty that begin to grow within his personality. When you begin to see these, do not ask the child if he is doing them, or why he is doing them, because he will promptly deny them. But do reveal to your child what you have seen. Interpret to him that this is dishonest; it is not going to be tolerated; and then set about changing it according to these steps:

Checklist for Correction. First, check your own lives, parents. Your children will be very quick to pick up your example, so if you have not been 100 percent honest, work very hard to shape up your own lives. Second, explain to your child directly that you simply will not tolerate cheating and dishonesty. Set up a consequence for any time the child does break that rule, whether at home, playing games, or at school, and follow through with those consequences. Finally, praise your child for changing that habit. Correct him when he does not, and you will win this very important issue.

27. SHY CHILD   *My little girl is three and a half, and I'm sure she is a bright child. She learns things so quickly, like a song or a poem, in less than a day. She knows some of her books by heart, and can also write part of her name. What worries me so is how she responds to other people. If they talk to her, she will hide her face and not answer. She also won't let anyone kiss or hug her except me, and sometimes her two sisters. She also has six brothers, and even though* *they want to love her, she won't let them. She also won't get close to her daddy. The doctor told me she is a very nervous child, so I try to be patient with her. I was forty-six years old when she was born, and had a hard time with her birth. Maybe that is part of her problem. Can you tell me if I'm doing wrong by trying to get her to show love to her family? Is there anything I should be doing for her?*

This mother certainly does have a grave concern and I can sympathize with the fact that she was a little older than most mothers when this child was born. It is not easy to start raising a child at the age of forty-six. Having raised the family beforehand, and having a little more freedom, certainly has created a burden for this dear mother. This does sound like a precocious child with a great deal of sensitivity and intelligence. Now I would like to reassure this mother that children tend to be loving unless they are overwhelmed by too much stress, too much attention, or perhaps too much criticism. And I would wonder if the number of older brothers and sisters may have provided a little too high an expectation for such a young child. It sounds as if in her learning and ability to memorize, this child is very academically oriented. Sometimes in their pride over such giftedness, families push a child more than they realize. I would suggest that possibly this child should be allowed to have a little more freedom. A little lowering of the expectations might give her a bit more relaxation and comfort.

There may very well be some overprotection of this child. Maybe she was overpampered by her brothers and sisters because it seems that now she gets extra attention by withdrawing. The needs of a shy child are these: Parents need to accept her more unconditionally, and stop trying so hard. Allow the child to choose to approach the other person, rather than pushing her toward them. Give her less attention for learning or per-forming, and allow her freedom just to be a little child. When you catch her smiling or responding (if that ever does happen), quietly and enthusi-astically compliment her. Try to find some similar-age playmates, and en-courage her just to relax. As you yourself relax, I think you will find that this child will grow to be a loving, warm person.

28.   TATTLING   *At what point does tattling become a serious problem?*

There *can* be a fine line between tattling and reporting a dangerous or alarming situation that needs adult attention. The difference that helps me understand which is actually happening is whether or not the reporting is intended to get the other child *in* trouble or to keep the other child *from* trouble. That's a very important concept for parents and teachers alike, to understand.

The problems in tattling are these: The child has no other means of gaining favor from the adult and tattles in order to get adult attention (and also to make himself look much better than those other bad children). That of course is a child who is not very secure and who has to resort to a pathological means of seeking that self-esteem. The tattler is almost always insecure; he has been hurt; he may be angry; and he feels inadequate.

Well, what can you do if you have a tattling child? First of all, I recommend that you explain what is wrong with the habit itself and insist that the child stop it. Set up a reminding system for yourselves, parents, to follow through in stopping that particular habit. Then search for the source of the pain or the insecurity in the life of your child that has caused the anger and the insecurity. Work very hard to correct the problems that have produced that situation. Promoting a sense of maturity and an honest sense of responsibility in your child can replace that bad habit with a very good one, using the child's concern and compassion for others.

29. HAIR PULLING/NAIL BITING *I want to ask you about my son, age two and a half. He has a bad habit of pulling out his hair, especially around bedtime, and when he is sleepy. He also bites his fingernails, which I do, too. He has always pulled at his hair when he was sleepy, ever since he was little. Some of it he eats, but I don't know how much. He just likes to have it in his hand. He also keeps a finger in his mouth at bedtime. I would really appreciate your opinion of this matter. (I'm expecting another child in three months.)*

This sounds like a delightful little boy, despite the problems that trouble this mother. He seems to like the softness of the touch and the feel of his own hair. Many children do. If you run your hand over your own hair, there is a soft, textured feel that is rather enjoyable. It is not uncommon that children like to stroke their own hair, or that of the mother, while they are being rocked to sleep as little babies.

Hair Pulling. Pulling out the hair usually begins in an attempt to keep that hair in his hand without having to raise his little arm up and have it suspended in the air, while he strokes his own head. So I would suggest this for this little boy, and let's see how it works for the mother as well: Provide for this child a soft stuffed toy that he might hold when he is sleepy, and while you rock him. I think at this point in his life he may need a little cuddling and babying, since the new child will soon be taking that away from him. Give him something that is silky and pleasing to hold in his hand, while he falls off to sleep, and perhaps he won't need to pull out his own hair. I would strongly suggest that you avoid his eating his hair, because if very much of the child's own hair is swallowed, it will tend to accumulate in his stomach. It is not easily digested, and it may create a problem that could require medical attention.

Nail Biting. This is another common problem, and one that is not serious, but can be annoying. On a practical basis, nail biting almost always begins because of rough, uneven fingernails that cause discomfort to the person. As the child bites off those rough edges, he may develop a nervous habit, and that, of course, can become a lifelong one that is very hard to break. So the treatment for nail biting in little children is that of keeping the nails smooth with a tiny scissors or clippers or a very fine file. I would rub a tiny bit of cream or lotion around the nail bed and the fingernails to prevent the little hangnails and rough edges that can be so annoying. Occasionally, it will be very helpful to use clear nail polish on a child's fingers. This is obviously not for looks, but in order to keep the nails smooth. By giving a different feel to them, it may break the child's nail-biting habit. Give plenty of physical cuddling and attention; play and draw the child's attention outward from himself to his environment, and I think you will find, as almost all parents do, that those annoying habits eventually will come to a halt.

30. TROUBLE IN SCHOOL *You recently talked about a child's need to feel wanted and liked in school. Our son has a problem in this area. He goes to a lot of trouble to make his classmates notice him. He feels he has to be first in everything, and if another child hits him, he'll turn and do the same. He happens to be the one who gets caught and in trouble, not the one who starts it. Consequently, he is in trouble often. He does have some friends, but his attitude toward school is very poor and getting worse. He also feels he doesn't have to share, but I've tried to teach him to share. We've had to move many times, so his school has changed also. My husband does work a lot, which means he doesn't see our son and daughter often, so I do most of the child rearing. We both love our son very much, but he seems very insecure.*

This does sound like a child who is insecure and certainly needs help. I read in this letter a number of pieces of information that can be helpful, not just to this mother, but to many other parents. First of all, it must be understood that every person needs attention. That's simply universal. Now a child prefers a positive, happy kind of attention, but if he doesn't get enough of that, he will settle for just being noticed, even in negative ways. This child sounds as if he is competing and fighting, even though it may be in getting even with someone else who started it. He sounds self-ish because he always has to be first. All of these, of course, are the signs of a child with poor self-esteem, insecurity—a child who, perhaps, is emotionally hungry. I am aware that this family has moved a great many times and the repeated loss of friends, familiar environment, and the unresolved pain and grief of those moves may be a part of this boy's trouble. The absence of his father seems to me to be a major problem in this young man's life. As boys grow up, they need to have a dad for a role model and to provide for them the strength and protection that dads sym-bolize. Sometimes mothers need their son's love and support so much that they fail to be quite as thorough in their discipline and follow-through as they ought to be. So I hope this boy's father can find a little more time to spend with his son.

Stop feeling sorry for your child if he is not getting along well in school. Refuse to rescue him from the consequences of his misbehaviors, because sooner or later his friends and teachers will help him to learn that he must behave more gently and considerately. Find your son's assets, interests, and talents. Develop and encourage them, and help him to feel proud of himself. Help him to work through the grief regarding the constant moves and his probable feeling of insecurity (or even inferiority). Do this by giving him some idea of the adventure in moving, if you must move again. Dad, do find time and develop quality in your relationship with this son and mother. Fail to spoil him and keep a very strict rein on him, until he learns to behave more considerately and lovingly toward those about him.

31. DANGER SIGNS   *What are some of the signs that would tell parents that their son or daughter had a serious problem?*

There are a great many young people who have committed suicide in the last decade. By no means in all of them, but certainly in a great many cases, the lives could have been saved had their parents known these signs:

Physical Signs. These are the first and easiest to define. A major departure from the child's usual physical patterns may include a change in eating habits. Now this may mean the child who has normally eaten fairly regular meals begins eating excessively, or may eat nothing at all. It can be either extreme and that is important to observe. The same is true of sleeping. A child may sleep excessively or very little. The activity level may become excessive or decreased. *Any major change* is worthy of your notice, parents.

Socially. They may withdraw into their own room and their own little world. They may escape into excessive activities, in order to avoid some emotional pain within them. They may become rude and irritable or extremely polite. Again, it is the variation from that child's own unique norm that is worthy of consideration.

Emotionally. Any marked change from the child's normal status should be noted: a child who becomes irritable, when usually he has been fairly mild mannered; depressed when he has usually been happy; excited when he has usually been quiet, unusually worried, anxious, or moody. All of these are signs to be noted.

Personal Habits. These also need looking at. Giving away special treasures, leaving a will or notes that seem to be accidentally left around the parents, deterioration of work at school, can suddenly cause worry on the part of the parents. These are all signs that can help parents to know a child is sad, angry, or in danger.

I hope that you will be aware of your child and his or her behavior in all of these areas of their lives. Do not hesitate *if there is any concern* to seek the advice of a competent family counselor. Get the help that you and your child may need—before it is too late!

32. UNDISCIPLINED VISITORS *I try to be consistent and fair in disciplining my own children, but sometimes I feel like swatting the kids that visit in my home. Often they are unruly and difficult to handle, and yet their parents seem to ignore their obnoxious behavior. Is there a way I can tactfully protect my furniture and belongings, not to mention avoiding the bad example these kids are setting for my children? I don't want to alienate my friends, but this is a sore point with me.*

When children are in your home, without their parents, the problem is relatively easy to handle. Let me make a few suggestions: When your children have friends visiting in your home, have a short meeting of all of the children. Welcome them, feed them something, and lay out the ground rules. Make those rules few but extremely clear. For example, *there is to be no physical violence to each other or objects in this house.* The areas and items they may play with are made very clear, and *there will be no food in the living room. These are the toys and games and snacks you may have, and these you may not.*

Use humor, and tell them that you are a bear, and that you simply will not tolerate their breaking these rules. Then help them have fun. I do recommend that you stay nearby, and plan on supervising and spot checking in order to be sure that they maintain good behaviors.

Now when their own parents are there, it is much more difficult, because parents sometimes feel threatened or criticized by your setting rules for their children even in your house. If it's an occasional or a rare visitor, I would suggest that you try to collect the children in their own play area. Leaving the parents in the living room to talk with your husband, you, as the mother, might go and briefly lay down these same kinds of rules for those children and yours. Ask your own children to help enforce them and to set the example for the guests. (Of course, let your children know that they may call for help at any time.)

If your friends are regular visitors and really *good* friends, explain to them the values that you are trying to teach your children, and frankly seek their help in teaching their children to cooperate with your rules. You must of course avoid being rigid or rude, but with a kind and positive attitude, I think many parents will not only accept your wishes, but respect them as well. Perhaps they may even learn that they need to be a little bit more strict with their own children!

33.   LYING EIGHT-YEAR-OLD   *We have an eight-year-old who has a problem with being honest. He has also been in trouble at school for lying to his teacher about staying after school and assignments. He and his teacher go around and around. My husband and I have tried many forms of punishment, including spanking, grounding, taking away privileges. We've even given extra privileges for being good. We are at a loss for what to do. We can't believe our boy is only in second grade, and we don't know how to handle something like this.*

These parents needn't feel embarrassed because second-graders can be very bright and persistent in their little bad habits. This type of lying is almost always due to the fringe benefits that such lies gain. When I say "fringe benefits," I mean that out of those lies, the child—at least occasionally—may get out of duties or responsibilities, or even get out of punishment. Certainly this gets the child lots of attention, and we may have a child here who has learned to get negative attention, perhaps because he doesn't get quite enough positive attention.

First of all, mothers and fathers, get together and discuss the reasons why your child is lying. The failure to complete and turn in assignments, as this letter states, indicates that the child has somehow gotten by without doing that. The teacher is dedicated, indeed, who will require such a child to stay after school and complete work; and you parents need to back up that teacher. Once you have gotten together as parents, and then with the teacher (or other adult who must work with your child), work out a plan that will help your child to quit lying. A practiced child, who can get by with lying as much as this one does, needs extremely clear rules as part of your plan. Let your child know that all arguments will stop. It takes two to argue. Your word and the teacher's are the law of the day, not the child's opinion. Simply do not accept the child's lies. Don't ask him if he is lying, but if you feel reasonably sure that he is, tell him that you recognize he is lying, and you simply will not accept that.

In order to help him stop that bad practice, deprive him of a special privilege each time he lies *for that day only.* But beyond that, use firm and loving discipline; tell him that you simply will not tolerate this practice of dishonesty. Be certain to give him plenty of positive attention, lots of love and happiness at all times, and I know that you can win the struggle to stop his lying.

34. FIRST-NAME BASIS *I personally prefer to have my young son call me "Mommy" and his father "Daddy," or something indicating we're his parents. My husband is the director of a camp where all the young people refer to him by his first name. Lately I've noticed that my five-year-old is picking this up, and I'm concerned about it. Should we avoid a first-name basis with our children? Will it eventually make a difference in our relationship?*

Certainly names are important, and so are titles. What does it mean when a child begins to have a first-name basis with his parents? In fact, what does a first-name basis imply in any relationship?

First of all, that we're good friends and that we are equals; or it may imply a lack of respect. Children certainly deserve respect, and they won't learn to show respect unless they are treated with respect. But they are and they need to be under parental authority. So one of the expressions of respect is the title by which a child addresses that authority person. Frankly, through all this lengthy explanation, I hope you realize that I strongly recommend that children do call their parents by actual titles of *Mother* and *Father,* or *Mom* and *Dad.* I cannot, however, deny that the basic respect a child shows for the parent is one that is earned, and it's expressed in attitudes and feelings more than exact titles. So I understand parents who choose to allow their children to call them by their first names. A great many parents do that, and frankly, seem to enjoy it. I have known, on the other hand, some parents who were so rigid and irritable about demanding only a certain title that they actually lost the affection and the respect they sought. If you parents decide you want your child to address you as Mommy and Daddy, simply do this: Explain his special relationship with you; that it's different from the campers or a student or other friends. Because your relationship with him is so important, you want to be called by a special name that only children and parents can share. An occasional first-name address can be teasing and fun and can be tolerated, but if you explain what you really want with your child and insist upon it, it can happen.

35.   BAD LANGUAGE   *I've explained to my six-year-old son that it isn't nice to use swear words; but he tells me that the kids on the school bus swear, and he doesn't understand why it's wrong. How do I keep him from picking up this bad habit? Needless to say, it could be embarrassing at church and elsewhere.*

First of all, I would recommend that this parent explain to her son that he will be encountering children every day of his life who do many things that she does not want him to do. Helping him learn to be his own unique individual is a major task for parents, and it is none too soon to start at the age of six. Coming back to the specific problem of swearing, I recommend that you evaluate your own ideas of what is right and wrong about swearing. (If, indeed, there is anything right!) First of all, certainly taking God's name in vain breaks a commandment, and that is very clear. You can explain that to your child with no qualms. The so-called four-letter words that a great many children use in swearing actually describe physiological processes, and they do so in a very undignified and even derogatory way. They take away from the beauty of the human body, as it has been created by God, and therefore I think those words are very unseemly. Words that relate to the devil or evil are very common in swearing, and by using those words we actually give recognition to evil that we need not give. If anyone needs to swear to prove that he is tough or powerful (and frankly I think that's why most people swear), then one may doubt that person really feels such power inside. The swearing becomes a mask to cover up fear or insecurity. Explaining to your child these and any of your own reasons for the wrongness about swearing, can help him decide to stop that bad habit.

Now, certainly all of us have times when something very profound hits us, and we need words of an exclamatory nature to use. A sudden kind of pain, an injustice in life, can make us feel like saying something very intense. So perhaps you can help your child develop a small vocabulary of harmless and not-so-wrong words that he can use when he does need an exclamatory phrase. This will encourage his individual creativity and will acknowledge the need of a special word for a few special circumstances.

36. PUBLIC TANTRUMS   *What can we do when our three-year-old son throws a loud temper tantrum in public? His favorite trick is to throw himself down and scream over some little thing in a store or restaurant. Needless to say, we find this most embarrassing. He doesn't seem to respond to threats of what will happen when we get home, but we also have hesitated to spank him in front of people, for fear they'll think we're child abusers.*

That certainly is an understandably difficult situation. Children very commonly have temper tantrums. They begin at about eighteen to twenty-four months of age and may extend into the early grade-school years. Most children begin having tantrums out of frustration. They simply reach the end of their resources, and in their angry desperation, they throw themselves down and cry and kick. That gets their anger out, but it usually arouses anger on the part of parents. Unfortunately those early tantrums, understandable as they may be, gain for children certain benefits, and children learn to have fits in order to manipulate to get their way. It sounds as if that's what this child is doing. By kicking and screaming, he knows he can embarrass his mother and get that item that he particularly wants. Knowing that helps you understand how to deal with his tantrums. First of all, make it very clear to your child (and at two or three years of age certainly the child will understand what you say) that he will not have any more temper tantrums in public. Explain that *before* you go anywhere at all. Tell your child that you will not tolerate his fits, and decide carefully what you will do.

Now that's up to you as parents. Some of the suggestions I have are these: If your child throws a fit, leave the store immediately and take him home. That usually is quite a punishment because children like going to stores and enjoy the excitement of being with their parents. You may decide, on the other hand, just to take him to the car and give him some firm and gentle swats, so that he will not be embarrassed, nor will you, by doing that in front of someone else. Leaving him home the next time may be another punishment that will help him decide to change. Whatever you decide, be sure that you follow through. Children are quick to detect if this is an idle threat or if you really mean business.

Often children simply are not mature enough to go out in public and if your child is not ready for such privileges, don't hesitate to get a baby-sitter and leave him at home. Above all, do not allow your child's fits to gain him any advantages *ever*. You will be glad that you were firm, and that you went through the inconveniences, when your child finally gives up his fit throwing.

37. WETTING PROBLEM   *I'm asking about my son who is four and a half years old. He wets the bed at night, if I don't get him up, and then sometimes he still wets. He even wets all through the day, unless I constantly remind him to use the bathroom. Many times he will say he doesn't have to go, and then in the next few minutes, he's wet. It doesn't seem to bother him. He never asks to be changed, and leaves the wet clothes on until I make him change. I've talked to his doctor, and he thinks my son is just being lazy. I haven't taken him to any specialists.*

In this case I certainly would recommend that the mother seek the advice of a specialist, because at four and a half, a child who habitually wets may have some special problem, though that is quite rare. All too often wetting is not a physical but an emotional problem. It may be due to worrisome events in the life of a child. The arrival of a new baby, a family move, illness among relatives—all of these events can cause fear, guilt, and anger, a dangerous triad in the life of a child. That can cause him to regress and begin to wet his pants again, even when he has been well trained.

Very commonly, interpersonal conflict between the child and his parents, with its anxiety and tension, is a cause of both bed-wetting and day-time wetting. Sometimes (and I suspect that in the case of this child), he is simply so busy and involved in his own play and activity that he doesn't have time to stop and go to the bathroom. *He* doesn't mind being wet and why should his mother? There are numerous cures for this annoying habit. For bed-wetting, there is a bell-ringing device that can be ordered from a mail-order catalog. This goes into action at the first drops of moisture, as the child begins to wet, and by awakening the child can condition him to awaken before wetting the bed; then he can go to the bathroom.

Sometimes when children are a little bit older and simply will not stop wetting their pants, the parents may need to put them back in diapers for a little while. Now I certainly recommend that you do this carefully, without shaming a child, and let him know that when he is ready to use the bathroom, then he can stop wearing the diapers. Seriously, I recommend that you stop nagging and fussing. That is perhaps the most important single bit of advice that I can tell you. Explain to your child the needs and the reasons for stopping the wetting. I know that's extra work; it creates an offensive odor. This child will be starting school, and those are all reasons for gaining bladder control. Set up a plan with your child, such as, he can play outside only when he chooses to stay dry. Set a timer for him to remind him to go to the bathroom. If he refuses and it becomes a power struggle, there simply is no playing until he cooperates. Lots of love, encouragement, optimism, and patience will help you and your child through the rigors of toilet training.

38. BLACKMAIL *How should parents answer when their children try emotional blackmail?*

I think before they answer at all, they need to stop and think. In my experience, anytime a child is blackmailing a parent, it is symptomatic of the child's having accumulated too much power within that family. It is the *parents* who should be doing the blackmailing, and if there is any threat to be made, the parents should be doing it. Only it ought not be a threat. It ought to be a *promise*. I think many families today have reversed the old parental role in which my father, for example, would say, "If you don't do this, Grace, then this will happen," and I knew it would. Today I'm hearing children say to their parents, "Mom, if you don't let me do this, then I will run away," or whatever. That's a very frightening situation for the child himself as well as for parents. Parents, I would like you to take back your God-given authority *as parents.*

Let me give you a couple of examples of *what not to do*: First of all, *do not act worried or upset* because that may imply that you are giving the child the power to do the very thing that he is threatening. And he does not need that particular power.

Second, *do not counteract that child's threats with pleading or with childish anger of your own.* Be strong, as an adult, in the way you react, and do not try to get the child's love or happiness back too quickly. That will happen in due time, but dealing with the situation is far more important than keeping your child happy all of the time.

What you must do is this: First, *clarify what the issue is.* Why is the child threatening and upset? What is the problem? When you find this out, talk about it. For a younger child, you may need to put into words the child's feelings, because often a child does not have the vocabulary to express that. "I know you are angry or scared [or whatever], and here's what I think you need. . . ." As a parent, when you verbalize what the child is going through, you will help him to calm down and thus alleviate the stress that's making him do this blackmail job.

With an older child, pose a question and help the child learn to focus his attention on his own feelings and what is causing those. Then help the child, as well as yourself, decide what you can do *together* about the problem. You may send the child to his room, to bed, to a time-out spot—wherever you can put that child to help him think through the situation and arrive at a fine decision will help eliminate emotional blackmail.

39. FIGHTING CHILDREN   *Why do some children constantly get into fights?*

First of all, sometimes family philosophies state that it's smart to be aggressive. Now usually it is not said that explicitly, but if you believe as a parent that you have to fight to get along in this world, then unconsciously you may be teaching your children to become fighters, and to be so aggressive that they can get into some problems in their social lives.

Another reason that children fight is that, unknowingly, they feel put down or inferior in comparison to other children, particularly within their own families. A child who does not get enough positive strokes or loving attention may very well learn to fight and act aggressively, preferring to have even punishment or scolding rather than to get no attention at all.

When such behavior is encouraged because of the family situation, it will carry over to those outside the family as well.

Another reason is the reaction to fear. Many children reach out in an angry, attacking manner, as a reaction to their fear and insecurity. Perhaps the typical school bully is the example that we're all familiar with. The bully is a child who is, underneath it all, very insecure and frightened, and covers it up by pretending to be a blusterer. He very quickly gets into fights with other children.

Finally, there is a certain part of aggression and fighting that is an *instinct*. There is certainly that inborn need to protect or defend one's self, and those who are dear to us. That may be why some children fight.

Look through these reasons, parents, and try to understand why it is that your child is a fighter. If your child is fighting because he is afraid, then you need to encourage him to talk out his fear and stop being afraid. If he is fighting because he doesn't get enough positive, loving attention, then simply supply that for him, and help him to feel more confident and secure. Then he may not need to fight. If, unwittingly, you are teaching your child that you have to be a fighter to get along in this world, then change that belief, and teach him how to love as well as to protect himself.

40. BAD EXAMPLE   *There is an eight-year-old boy in our neighborhood that I would rather my six-year-old son not play with, because this boy lies and uses bad language. He also makes children turn against friends. My child often comes home in tears, yet the more I say, "Don't play with him," the more he wants to. It's like forbidden fruit. When will he learn for himself that playing with this boy just isn't worth the pain?*

It may take this child a little while to learn, but perhaps we can help speed it up with the following ideas. Being an older child, this eight-year-old sounds like a bit of a bully. Such children can seem powerful and desirable as models for younger children, who are weaker and perhaps not quite as swaggering as the bully may seem to be.

Let me recommend something that you may not like, at first, but think about it with me for a moment. Have that boy come to your house to play. Try quietly reflecting to him the facts about his destructive behavior and habits. Ask if he would leave those at the door when he comes to your house, and set forth for him and your child some ground rules that would allow for constructive and positive playing together. Perhaps he will learn and can be influenced to become a better person by that input from you.

Sit over some milk and cookies with your son after this playmate leaves, and in as adult a manner as possible, sort of conversationally process with your son what went on with him and his friend. Ask him if he was aware that the boy did some cheating when they played a game, and what did he think about the lie the friend told. Perhaps you might even ask your son if he really admires the swearing, and let him know that his own dad doesn't use those words. When you can find out in this logical fashion what your son honestly feels about the behaviors of that little boy, you may be pleasantly surprised to find that he doesn't like them any better than you do. You may even use this conversation as an opportunity to compliment your child on his good behavior. Make the contrast very clear, and let this be a time when you and your child sort through some values. Then tell your son that you really do not want him to be hurt by this boy, and for that reason you are counting on his own good judgment to stay away from him. Suggest better friends, and find ways to foster his becoming involved with them, if this friend does not show major improvement. If you must, firmly forbid his contact with such a child. Even if he wants to play with him, simply do not allow it. That is tough love, and it works. If at six, your son learns to develop positive relationships, you'll not have to worry when he is sixteen.

41. WHINING   *Within the past few months my four-year-old has become quite a whiner. She whines and stomps her feet and performs what I would call a whining temper tantrum when asked to do something, like clean up her room. She also is quite argumentative if I say she can't do something. She pleads, whines, and argues with my reasons. I can't seem to find a way, short of spanking or sending her to her room, to stop her whining and arguing.*

Certainly whining is a very annoying habit, and I find a great many parents are extremely irritated by it. When a child is four and has just become a whiner, I am very curious about what may have caused that to begin. Is there a new baby in the family, perhaps, that makes her want to be a little child again? Is there a problem because she may be facing attending school in the near future? Any major event or threat that can cause the child to feel a bit afraid or insecure and make him or her want to be younger than he is, can cause whining.

On the other hand, perhaps this child has observed someone else, such as a friend, getting her way by throwing a fit. Fits and whining and tantrums all have something in common. They get for a child something that he or she wants very much.

Here are some suggestions that can help you to eliminate this annoying behavior for your child: When both you and the child are calm (not when you're upset), explain to the child that she will get into trouble with friends, is certain to get into trouble with you, and with teachers in the future, by such behavior. Explain to her or him that you simply will not tolerate it any longer. Tell the child what will happen if she does do it again (and be quite clear about that). I would suggest that you be prepared to follow through. I frankly like the idea of sending the child to time-out or to her room rather than spanking. In this kind of temperamental child a spanking tends to make her more rebellious, instead of helping. Be certain that the child does what you have asked her to do *no matter what*. I find occasionally parents send a child to the room or spank her, and the child still does not have to do the task or follow through with the request of the parent.

Do not let your child's anger or whining influence you. Do not let that habit make you give in, because it will only create a firmer habit and stronger sense of power in the child.

You might find it successful to work with your child to clean her room. Have her help you with jobs; working together can be fun. Changing beds can be a great deal of fun. Teach your child to express her feelings verbally, but require responsibility in spite of how she feels. Praise her when she succeeds. These are techniques that I have found to be highly successful in breaking bad habits. Someday your daughter's husband will love you for sticking with her through this difficult time and helping her overcome her tantrums.

42. BABY TALK   *My eleven-year-old granddaughter talks baby talk to get attention. Isn't she a bit old to be acting like this? She's the oldest of four children, and the apple of Daddy's eye. She often tattles to get her brothers into trouble with their parents. I don't live near them, and I don't see them often, so I can't come down too hard on her. She resents it when I say anything. I'd appreciate some help in how to handle this situation, and yet keep a good relationship with everyone.*

That certainly is a very sensitive situation, and I would recommend to this grandmother that she work very hard to recognize and comment on the good qualities about this granddaughter, both to the child and to her parents. She needs to make some comments that show how much she loves and enjoys the child before she gets into the problem areas. I would suggest that Grandmother wait until the problem becomes so explicit, so clear, that it can't be explained away or denied. After the episode is over (the tattling, or the manipulating of her father, or whatever that particular episode might be), then that grandmother should wait for a quiet time, perhaps alone with one of the parents with whom she can be most open and comfortable. Then discuss with that parent her concerns about the child, and those particular problem areas. Just the concern alone is not very helpful, so I would suggest that the grandmother give them some constructive suggestions that might be useful to them in curing the problems.

Oldest children, unfortunately, have to grow up too soon, and they usually feel displaced by younger brothers and sisters. They sometimes need babying of sorts, and this child's tendency to talk baby talk, I suspect, reflects her need to be treated as a little child now and then. Staying little or reverting to being little from time to time is something that perhaps all of us crave. The parents should understand that need of the older daughter, and give her a little bit of extra affection and attention, alone and away from those three younger brothers.

She particularly may need some special time with Mom. I find that a girl who is strictly Daddy's girl often craves time with Mother, but somehow doesn't feel like she can get it. This mother may want to spend a little more time alone with this girl, and give her some special mother/daughter attention. Dad and Mother, in this case, may need to reverse their roles a little bit. It sounds like the father has been the nurturer for this child, and at this point, the mother, I think, should take over the role. Let Dad become a little bit more the disciplinarian. Grandmothers unfortunately can only go so far, and I would recommend to this grandmother a practice that I follow myself. That is, that she make suggestions, offer advice, particularly offer her love, and then let go. Trust your child and his or her spouse to do a good job as parents. Simply love their child and trust them to do the same kind of job with their children that you did with them.

43. AFTER-SCHOOL ACTIVITIES   *I suppose that many parents who work away from the home would be interested in your opinion about how much supervision a ten-year-old might need during the time between the end of school and when his parents get home*

from work. Do I need to get a baby-sitter, which my son, by the way, doesn't want? Or should I enroll him in some sort of after-school day-care program?

Before I answer that specifically, I would like to share a story of an actual case that I worked with. One of the schools in which I consult was having a major problem with a fifth-grade child. He was getting into a great deal of difficulty at school, and children were coming to school and reporting problems that he created in the neighborhood. When we called his mother to come in and talk with us, she was indignant, and assured us that it couldn't possibly be true that her son was behaving badly after school. She told me that she always insisted that her son telephone her as soon as he got home, and in talking with him, she was convinced that he was just fine. What she did not realize, of course, was that after the son dutifully made his call, he was indeed going out in the neighborhood and creating a great deal of trouble.

Therefore, parents, do not assume that your child of ten or eleven years of age can get along just fine without you. If there is any way at all, I recommend that one of the parents be home within a few moments of the child's arrival home. Certainly I am practical enough to realize that a great many parents have to work and that being home is simply not possible. And if it is impossible, here are some suggestions that can help you decide what to do in providing the proper supervision and protection for your children.

First of all, *evaluate your neighborhood.* Know who lives next door to you and even around the block. Is yours a reasonably safe community in which children can play together outside with the supervision of neighborhood mothers? Are there children, for example, who could influence your child to get into trouble, or who would be ready partners in some mischief your own child could create? (Don't assume that your child is respectful and obedient, as did the mother in my example.) Are your neighbors friendly? Are they at home much of the time, and would they be available in case there was an emergency or some need? Is your own child truly responsible and honest, or is he, as most children are, capable of being deceptive and doing his own thing when he thinks you don't know about it? What is your job like? Does it allow you and your child to contact each other if you need to in case of a problem? Certainly I would consider your child's sense of the indignity of a sitter at the ripe old age of ten, but if several of the above conditions are such that you feel major concern for his safety, your child's feelings will simply have to be comforted and he will have to bow to your good judgment. Don't overprotect your child, but do protect him enough to keep him safe.

Character Development

44. GOOD JUDGMENT

How can I teach my child to be discerning, without being too picky or expecting perfection? I'm afraid he may become too rigid, a difficult person to please.

That's certainly an interesting question and one that brings up a very important value in my life. I think that discernment is an important word to understand. It means that we develop an ability to evaluate what is harmonious, healthy, loving, and pleasing and the wisdom to choose what is best for the most people involved. *Best* does not mean easiest or most expensive, but certainly the most advantageous and the most considerate of all of those involved in a situation.

In a way, I think discernment is a gift. It depends upon a child's or an adult's intellect and the ability to evaluate and make careful choices. It is, however, a quality that can be taught. Here are some suggestions as to how parents might teach discernment to their children. First of all, of course, I believe parents must start with themselves and their example. Look through your own decision-making methods. How do you decide, for example, such a simple thing as what you will wear? How do you put together colors, designs, styles, and fabrics, so that your appearance is harmonious and pleasing?

In another very practical area of life, how do you decide what is good nutrition for yourself and your family? How do you balance your food intake, the times for your meals, mealtime topics of conversation, the mood, the sense of intimacy that focuses around mealtimes? Discernment can be played out and exemplified in such very practical areas. Your choice of friends, your home atmosphere, your time priorities. All of those topics demand the quality of judgment or discernment.

Now, for a young child, here are some very simple, practical suggestions: Give your child some limited choices within the framework of his ability to choose, such as having a whole glass or a half glass of juice for breakfast; whether he wants to wear a pink sweater or a blue one with some dark slacks. Compliment your child on those choices that do show good taste. Give the child healthy feedback when he makes choices that are not quite so good. Help him to see how to choose more wisely the next time, without being too critical or condemning. Tell someone else in the child's hearing about his growing sense of discernment and good judgment. Discernment developed in these small, daily choices will eventually be translated into good judgment in the more complex, moral areas of life. Good emotional health is evidenced by the decisions we make. Discernment makes such decisions possible, for you and your child.

45. DEVELOPING INDEPENDENCE   *My kids seem to be going through a stage when they are challenging everything their mother and I say. We want to encourage them to be independent, yet we're also concerned about keeping them safe. How can we deal with this power struggle without feeling inadequate or doubting ourselves?*

That is indeed a difficult question. First of all, we need to understand that the characteristics of adolescence mainly are these: They are confused in their ideas and thinking; and they are ambivalent or mixed-up in their feelings. Therefore, these are what they need: They need a trusted, loving, understanding adult who is not threatened by their disagreements; one who can see those for what they are, *simply being mixed-up.* Being able to discuss, argue, and debate without becoming angry or rejecting can help that child to think through those confused ideas and come to really solid values and beliefs. Children also need parents who are willing to hold out for their own time-tested values—and yet brave enough to let those young people try out some ideas for themselves. Now, you do have to have wisdom to know where to draw the lines on that, and you have to be wise and strong enough to hold those lines firmly in order to protect those children.

Children need parents who are loving enough to be tough and yet tender (alternately). Young people need parents who are congenial enough to enjoy them, secure enough to admit their own mistakes (and even to laugh at themselves), but *never* to laugh at the children. Congeniality and a sense of humor can tide almost any family through those rough spots. Young people need parents who are patient enough to outwait this fatiguing and often frightening time in life.

Parents, you need to be confident in yourselves and in the work that you have done, and you need to have faith in the Heavenly Father to know that between you and Him you can make things turn out right. Even when your children don't believe in themselves (and they aren't always sure they believe in you or your God either), your faith can hold things steady. Parents, you need to be able to ask for advice when you're too unsure. Trusting your parenting, realizing that most of this stage is temporary, depending on love, all these will see both you and your child through the troubled times of the teens.

46.   RAISING A GOOD FUTURE SPOUSE   *What can parents teach their children now about being a good husband or wife later?*

I think it's important that we also say perhaps not just a good husband or wife, but a good *person,* because some people may choose not to be married or may not have the opportunity to be married. Most people, however, still do get married, and so we will focus on the role of husband and wife. The characteristics of a good adult, be it husband, wife, or single, start with these qualities:

1. *The ability to give and receive with generosity and gratitude.* Far too often, I find people unable to give, and on the other hand, unable to ask or receive from anyone else. This ability must include giving physical affection as well as material things.

2. *The ability to be open, honest, and trusting.* Real intimacy that is involved in a good relationship within families or within friendships depends upon these qualities. Obviously being open and trusting must be balanced with the development of good judgment. There needs to be some area of privacy, and we don't have to be open to the extent of telling everything we know to everyone.

3. *The ability to handle loss or disappointment, and to grieve with simplicity and sincerity,* is essential to being a good parent or a good spouse.

4. *The ability to respect one's self and the other person,* to be proud of one another, and to be respecting in the sense of building up one another's actions, and to express the pride that we feel *with* one another *to* one another.

5. *The ability to negotiate or compromise,* to give in and to work through disagreements with the maintenance of respect and love for one another.

How do you teach these then to your little child? First and most importantly of all, by modeling. By demonstrating these qualities toward one another as mother and father. Second, I think you teach those to your children by sitting down with them now and then and verbally giving them the guidelines for how they must get along with one another, as well as with you as mother and father. Third, through the methods of discipline and training that you employ, you can teach your little child to begin developing the qualities that will help him grow up to be a wonderful spouse and marvelous parent, in turn.

47. PEER PRESSURE   *I have a four-and-a-half-year-old son who is easily led by other children. Even if he knows he shouldn't do something, he does it anyway, because, he says, "They wanted me to," or "They asked me to." How can I help him to think and act on his own?*

That's such an important question, and the timing is certainly very crucial. We usually think of peer pressure as a problem that only teenagers face. In fact, however, even very young children can feel these same pressures to conform and act as their friends do. I find that parents sometimes are successful in teaching obedience to their child, but in teaching obedience, they have forgotten to think about the need for teaching good judgment, and for developing the child's individuality. In addition, there are some children who are simply very adaptive. They are easygoing and tend to just follow the crowd no matter who that crowd might be.

First of all, with a child of this type, explain your appreciation of his willingness to obey. The child needs to feel good about himself, and this is certainly a very valid reason for such good feeling. After you have explained that good quality about him, interpret the need to take another step in his thinking and development. The child needs to consider whom he is to obey—and what he is doing when he obeys someone else. Even young children, for example, understand the inflicting of damage or pain to another child, so give your child the guidelines that go along with that concept. Help him to know what is okay to do (things that are creative and positive), and what is not okay to do (things that are damaging or painful to himself or to someone else). Is what a friend or playmate is asking him to do likely to hurt someone else? Will what this friend is asking him to do make him feel badly about himself later on? Would he be ashamed or sad for you as the parent, or for God, to find out if he did that thing? If someone else did this to him, would he feel badly? These concepts, if taught even to a young child, can help him develop compassion and empathy for his friends, and help him become a very fine person as an adult.

Now giving the child some weeks to work on these questions is also important. He certainly has to have discipline and supervision if he is to live out the answers that you are trying to teach him. Remember, parents, being a leader is not too important. We need only a few. But being an individual, strong enough to take a stand that is right—and wise enough to know what is right—is the essence of good character. Help your child develop it.

48. SELF-ESTEEM OR HAUGHTINESS? *How can I increase my child's self-confidence without creating the kind of pride the Bible teaches against?*

I'm glad to answer that because in talking about self-esteem, certainly there is a bit of a risk that one could develop in a child the egotistical pride that is very obnoxious to everyone around him. True self-confidence is frankly the very best protection against false or carnal pride. That attitude is the result of very low self-esteem, and is a person's intense effort to prove that he or she is really somebody important, when in actual fact, that person does not feel that at all.

Healthy self-esteem includes these values and is based on a certain philosophy. The philosophy really must be based on the belief that we are children of the Heavenly Father. When we think about being children of the Heavenly Father, children of the King, that is something, indeed, that should indicate the respect and honor that God would like us to know as His children. Furthermore, whatever assets, talents, or abilities I have or that anyone is given, truly are a gift from God. And if you think about it for a bit, gifts are for enjoying and using. Whatever is good in me becomes a responsibility. Pleasurable and rewarding to be sure, but nevertheless, it involves the need to use and develop such talents to the maximum. Pride on the other hand really does not acknowledge God or the benefits that others give us in developing that gift. Pride says, "Look at me. See what I did."

Teach your child that his special gifts come from the Heavenly Father and that they're for appreciating and sharing, and haughtiness will not be a part of his character.

49. DOING IT THEMSELVES *Why is it so important for a little child to begin moving toward independence?*

There are two reasons. One is for the parents' sake and the other, of course, is for the child. Parental habits get set early on, just like a child's habits are, and parents who tend to take the easy way in keeping a child dependent and overprotected, can actually stunt the child's development. True enough, it may be easier, they may enjoy doing it, but it is not good for the child. Children on the other hand are eventually going to become independent. That's what they're born to do, and that is right for them. It is a natural, gradual process, and the earlier on in the child's life the parents understand that, and work with it, the better both will be.

If parents miss the child's instinctive cues that he is ready for the next stage of development, then it becomes much harder to make that happen later on. For example, a child of three or four wants very much to help Daddy mow the grass, or help Mommy clean the house and wash the dishes. But believe me, at thirteen and fourteen, they really do not want to do that. So teaching them to help early, and making that experience a happy and pleasurable one, can establish good habits of cooperation and will create a good sense of responsibility in a child. Most rebelliousness later on in the teenage years can be prevented by knowing how to encourage the gradual establishment of independence early in a child's life.

Here are some rules by which you might help yourself and your child in that development. First, watch the child's interests and capabilities as they develop, and encourage them early. Such a simple thing as the coordination it takes to hold a glass or the child's feeding himself with a spoon, encourages his neurological development. It also helps him to feel proud of his independence. Your reflection of pride in the child's accomplishments can motivate him to want to do more complex things later on. Not only does this process teach and motivate your child, creating healthy independence, but it also builds that wonderful self-esteem he needs. An example: "Susie, how nicely you dressed yourself. What a help that was to me when I was so busy." Not: "Susie, let me do it. You have that shirt on backwards." As painful as it is, and as much extra time and patience as it takes, let them do it themselves.

50. LOW SELF-ESTEEM *My question is about our eight-year-old who has a low self-esteem problem. We would like to know how to help her. She doesn't want to hear our opinion or receive our counsel.*

This child sounds like one of those that I find fairly often who learn early in life how to get attention. For some children, the more intense the attention, the better. And how better than through having a big problem with a capital *P!* Some children simply get their parents really hooked into trying to reassure and convince them about what wonderful little people they are. They really don't care about what kind of persons they are; they *really* care about getting attention.

So stop trying to convince this child, and instead do the very opposite. Sympathize with her, and honestly and sincerely draw out her feelings. What can the child do to make better friends? What can she do to help herself look better? Perhaps a different hairstyle would help, or a new dress. Look for every good thing about your child and tell her about it. Don't argue with her; just give her your opinion. Help her to know what she is doing that needs changing, but do so in a positive and constructive way. Find ways to enjoy your child. No one can laugh and play together and still feel bad at the same time.

51.   GIFT-BEARING GRANDPARENTS   *I guess this is one of those universal problems for grandparents and parents alike. Many times when my children's grandparents have come to visit, they've brought small gifts and favors, and now my children have gotten into the habit of always expecting gifts. I'm embarrassed when they ask the grandparents what they've brought for them. I don't want my children to be greedy, and I also don't want the grandparents to feel obligated to always bring gifts. How can I handle this and keep everybody happy?*

A universal rule should be established. Sometimes I think parents forget their job descriptions. *They* are the ones who are to be in charge of the family, not the children. It's quite all right for them to make a law or a rule that governs this particular situation. The rule is very simple: Children, you do not ask your grandparents or any visiting guests for gifts. Now that isn't hard to understand, and if it's repeated each time those grandparents are going to visit, then the children should be quite clear that this is simply not permitted around here. Now, of course children do forget rules and they may forget and go ahead and ask. If that happens, explain kindly but firmly to both children and grandparents that when they ask, they are not to receive gifts. Gifts are the right of the giver to decide whether or not to give.

Make your own arrangements with the grandparents, too. Ask them to bring gifts only rarely and not to feel compelled to bring things simply because the children request them. I think it's very important that children realize that the time and the loving presence of their grandparents are the best gifts of all. And if they get too many material things, they will fail to realize the value of this special kind of love.

Help your children to turn that gift-giving idea around. Help them to make a special gift for their grandparents. Children can create very clever craft items. A photograph or some special little item that the child has found on a nature hike can be a wonderful gift to give to grandparents. Giving is indeed a two-way street.

Teach your children gratitude. I think a great many grandparents would love to bring gifts to their grandchildren—if they showed a little bit more appreciation. So help your children to really value and appreciate the grandparents or other visitors for themselves, and *then* to appreciate the gifts secondarily, and to express that gratitude very honestly. You, your parents, and your children, can learn to enjoy one another most of the time without material gifts.

52. AN UNGRATEFUL CHILD   *What can parents do to help a child who has already established a pattern of being ungrateful?*

I'd like to remind you of a bit of history in order to help parents understand why it is that they have been perhaps too generous with their children. Over the years, the United States has really lived in a culture of affluence. After the serious deprivation of the depression of the 1930s and the tragedy of the wars of the 1940s, an entire generation of parents wanted their children to have everything they had not been able to enjoy. Furthermore, science continues to produce new and exciting vehicles for pleasure. Motorized toys and bikes, talking dolls, video games—all for children's pleasure. Advertising has made all of these things very obvious to children, and the presentation of exciting new items is a daily occurrence on television. Values became those of pleasure in our world, escalating ever upward from ordinary pleasures to new heights of excitement, materialism, and social status. Parents found themselves ever more involved in trying to provide increasingly stimulating and exciting events and toys for their children, usually with less appreciation and more demands by those children.

Here's a system that's almost certain to cure the problem *if parents have the courage to follow it*: First of all, begin by being aware of the fact that you as parents have undoubtedly given to your children far too much. Find ways of showing emotional warmth, love, and real joy in your family. Telling happy jokes, playing a game together, planning a simple outing, something that would really be fun—not costly and not sophisticated—can help your children to know that simple happenings can satisfy their cravings. Stop giving any gifts at all, except a small, carefully selected one for very special events. When the child asks for more, explain simply your new philosophy of giving less and enjoying more what you do have. If your child wants a special item, require him to work and save for it. Give him extra jobs, perhaps, and help him find a job to earn money for it himself. You will find he will be much more appreciative when he has had to sweat to earn it. Require your child to express gratitude and do that yourself. As you teach and model for your child the spirit of gratitude, I think you will find your own joy in life increasing, as well as your pride in your child.

53.   INFLUENCES   *Who is it that has the greatest influence on a child?*

That answer depends upon the family. When parents are really involved in the lives of their children, then they are that great influence. But when they become too busy or involved with other concerns and neglect to give attention to their child, then we must be concerned about other influences. Many people today are concerned about the impact of a child's friends upon his life as well as the influence of teachers who may not always be very godly people. These concerns I share. Television has a very subtle influence upon all of us, because it is on in most homes so much of the time that we tend to ignore the message of the commercials and the programs. If we are not careful and alert, so that we can counteract those influences, then television can have a powerful influence upon our children.

Let me talk for a moment about how mothers and fathers can be the kind of influence they want to be in the lives of their children. In the preadolescent period of time, *mother is generally the major force*. The father is present, and represents strength and power to back up the mother, but she is the one (let's face it) who carries the major load. Mothers need, therefore, to avoid nagging and being irritating to the child. They need to be firm and never permissive or too lenient, but they must be loving, tender, and playful, if they are to create the atmosphere in which the child will respond and respect them. In this way their influence can be a positive one in that child's life. Mother's very best influence comes in that unique balance which I think a mother is instinctively geared to offer:

that of nurturing and guiding, a positive criticalness to discern the problems and dangers in a child's life; the womanliness that can give her son
some modeling for the kind of wife he wants someday; and certainly she
can give to her daughter the essence of womanliness that she will develop
for herself.

Fathers become more powerful and more influential in the teenage years,
though to some degree they are also very important in the preschool period of life. The father is the recognized authority when he carries out
that role well. He demonstrates the protection, guidance, and teaching
that a male can offer if he is willing to assume that responsibility. His approval and disapproval are very powerful factors in a young person's life.
He, too, offers a role model for his son to become a man, and for his
daughter's choice of a future spouse.

Parents, be involved with your children; know what they are being
taught at school; then *you* will be the influence in your child's life.

54.   SOURCE OF SELF-ESTEEM   *What is the true source of personal worth?*

Philosophically, the true source in the ultimate sense, I'm sure, is simply
the fact that the child is a product of God's creation. He is very special, as
the unique, little child God made him to be. On a practical level, however, there are many other factors that parents need to consider. Historically, children used to be valued by families because of the work they
could do. Unfortunately, in many of today's families, a child's worth is
measured by his beauty or her charm or the kinds of success that they are
able to achieve. Those are rather false values.

These are the considerations that are very important for parents to understand and to put to work in helping their child to develop healthy
self-esteem.

The first and most important practical suggestion is that parents *must
love each child unconditionally.* Acceptance and love simply because he or
she exists is the cornerstone of healthy self-esteem.

There needs, also, to be *pride in the child's achievements,* and early in a
child's life, that's very easy. The first tooth, the first step, the first things
that children do are exciting times, and they merit calls to grandparents to
let them know how the child is growing. But very soon that little child
becomes a two-year-old, and gets into all kinds of independence seeking
and negative behaviors. Then that sense of pride in a child can be lost so
quickly that it's tragic.

Sometimes it's the *intellectual achievement* of a child that merits pride on the part of the parents. Sometimes it's an *artistic talent* or *being good at sports.* As the child grows out of the terrible twos and those creative bents begin to become manifest, then again parents' values and pride in the child will naturally take place. When they are not there naturally, then, parents, *you need to look carefully for any area of your child's life that is worthy of praise and development.* Let the child know that you are proud of that, and what's good about it, because it is out of your pride in your child's accomplishments that he or she will eventually come to feel proud of himself. *Peer approval* is another important part of a child's self-worth and as they reach school age, children need very much to be enjoyed by friends and to be a part of a group of young people. The family and the child (herself or himself) learn to recognize worth, then, because of being God's creatures, a valued member of the family, a productive, creative person, a valued friend in society. As for the traits of love, laughter, and honesty (priceless qualities), enjoy those in yourself and cultivate them in your child.

55. BUILDING SELF-ESTEEM   *How can parents build their child's self-confidence without creating a conceited little monster?*

Love and Accept. That is indeed a task and I have seven steps that I would like to outline. The first step, which I cannot emphasize enough, is to *love* and *accept that child unconditionally.* Children must be loved for who they are and not what they do. That acceptance and love should be communicated with absolute honesty. You cannot pretend to love a child and have him believe it. It must be real.

Discipline. The second step is to discipline that child *firmly, lovingly, consistently,* so that he can learn to be and do the things that are worthy of pride and self-respect.

Express Your Pride. The third step is to *express without reservation the pride that you feel in the child and what he does as well as who he is.* Be careful to avoid the mixture of approval and disapproval. Never say to a child, "That's fine but. . . ." In my experience the *but* always eliminates the *fine* in the mind of a child. Whatever it takes, help the child to stick with a task until it is done to his very best. Then give that unqualified praise and compliments that will help the child develop the honest self-esteem that is so needed in building his life.

Laughter. The fourth step is to *learn to laugh and play together.* When life becomes so heavy and is such a worry and anxiety, children lose a very important ingredient in the building of self-esteem. That is just an attitude or an atmosphere of congeniality, warmth, and laughter, which, as the Bible so beautifully says, "does good like a medicine."

Grow Together. The fifth step is *to explore and grow together as a family.* So many times I find parents sending children off to do their thing, while the parents are doing some other activity. Children need to have at least some time together with their parents to get a sense of their significance and value within the family. This will enable them to feel valued and important outside of the family as well.

Share Yourself. The sixth step is *to share your life's interests and activities as well as your feelings with your children.* As parents you can teach children how to understand and communicate their interests and feelings by doing that yourselves.

Share Their Activities. The seventh step is to *invite them to share their interests and activities with you.* Then enter into these activities with honest concern and be involved in a way that your child can sense and know. If you follow these steps, you will be well on your way to building a confident child.

56. ENEMIES OF SELF-ESTEEM   *What are some of the enemies of self-esteem that parents need to guard against?*

One of the most important enemies is that of the *parents' attitude.* I find a great many parents approach their responsibilities as mother and father by feeling that it's their main job to discover what is wrong with their children and correct that, rather than finding what is right and building upon *that.* So be sure that your attitude as parents is positive, and that you do look for the strengths more than you look for the defects.

Another enemy is the *chronic marital strife* that I find so common in families today. A child can hardly feel secure and confident, when he is almost daily faced with the fear of losing one of the parents. Whether or not you as parents know it, children are afraid, when you argue rather intensely and regularly, that perhaps one of you may leave. They go through this with friends and know that lots of arguments can result in divorce, or with one of the parents leaving. They become afraid of that even within a fine Christian family, so, as parents, you need to be aware of this concern.

Discrediting each other as mother and father, *finding fault,* or *criticizing* each other in front of the child can also make the child feel inadequate, because whether you like it or not, the child will see himself as being like one or the other of you and criticizing each other indirectly condemns the child.

Be careful to avoid blaming or name calling in your family. As certainly as you attach a label to your child, he will tend to feel that that's how he must be. That form of destructive criticism is going to destroy each child's self-esteem.

Be careful as parents that you avoid the *yes, but* kind of responsiveness to your child's behavior and performance. Children need to have discipline and guidance in learning how to act and how to do things, but they need to have that done *separately from the praise.* Be careful to keep the approval and the constructive criticism separated.

Being disapproving of your child's choice of friends is a sure way of hurting his self-esteem, so try very hard to accept those friends and let them enter into your family's life in a positive way. Then your child will know that you approve of his choice and his judgment, as well as his own life. Of course if certain friends are clearly damaging to your child, you will need to help him end those relationships.

I hope, parents, that you will avoid these enemies of self-esteem, and that you will remember, as you develop your own self-confidence as good parents, that you will transmit this to your children.

57. HEROES   *What kind of influence do heroes have?*

When I think about that question, I am reminded of the people who played a hero's role in my own life. I would have to name my father and my mother perhaps first of all, because they were the most intimate heroes of my early days. But when I began to read books, I must confess that Marie Curie was one of the most admirable people about whom I read. My father read to us the book of *The Horse and Buggy Doctor,* a Kansas physician who was the first one to do thyroid surgery for people who had goiters—a very important man in my life. I include Helen Keller, the woman who overcame the double handicap of blindness and deafness to become such a force in our society. These all have had a major impact on my life.

When I think of these people, I think of the values that they teach to all of us and specifically, the values that any hero can teach to your children.

Some of the values that children need to learn are these: Courage was exemplified by the pioneers of our country, and certainly Helen Keller is one who taught courage to me. *Tenacity and patience.* These were things I think my father taught me by the will to win over the vicissitudes of a farmer in the Midwest. The humble beginnings of a great many people who overcame handicaps of all kinds and adversities in order to become significant, contributing people in our world; *determination, creativity, service,* the *faith* of my mother—these are the qualities that many of the heroes and heroines of my life brought to me.

Another effect that heroes have is to model the concept of *significance*, of having it make some difference that we have lived at all. Today's children too often lack that sense of personal importance, which can be conveyed to them by the example and model of a hero. The patterns of the lives of heroes can teach children how they too can live in a fashion that gives them some opportunity to serve and grow, to compensate for adversities that every child knows.

Presently, there is a trend to take heroes away from our children by revealing flaws in one-time models. Certainly no one is perfect, but I think we ought not portray to our children all of the negatives that make them suspicious and doubtful about the quality of being that a real hero can convey to them.

Discipline and Training

58. INCONSISTENCY *How can my husband and I avoid being inconsistent in disciplining our children, when we don't always agree on what our family rules should be? How will inconsistency affect our children?*

Certainly inconsistency is a major problem in rearing children successfully. Predictability is one of the basic emotional needs that all children have. Now obviously you cannot be consistent as parents until you are reasonably united. *That's* where you need to start, moms and dads. Talk and negotiate, until you do come to an agreement. If that demands the outside help of a counselor, don't be afraid to seek that help. At least in your basic policies you must be together. The best results in child rearing involve clear, reasonable, and meaningful guidelines enforced consistently day after day.

Now, obviously all parents are going to disagree. When this disagreement involves minor matters, it's quite all right, because your discussions can actually teach your child to learn how to be honest and to disagree lovingly and discuss constructively, in order to reach a successful compromise. In major matters, however, all too often such disagreements create the climate for manipulation. I know one family in which the daughter has learned repeatedly to go to her father for things that she wants, because she's learned that he will be a much softer, easier touch than her mother. That has created resentment, guilt, and fear among these three members of that family.

Here are some simple guidelines, parents, that I think will help all of you in establishing consistency with your family. First, *set the goals that you want to reach for and with your children. Whom do you want your child to become? What do you want him to achieve in his life?* When you think about those goals, it will draw you together, because there is no question that both moms and dads want the very best for each of their children.

Once you have set those goals, *plan the methods for reaching them.* That demands that you establish some basic policies for your family. Part of those rules, of course, demands that there be consequences and rewards for following through with them. It also implies that there must be teaching and modeling of the qualities and values of life that you are talking about. Decide which parent can best enforce or activate each rule. In some cases, the mother may be far more effective, and in others the father may be the one. So determine that, and each one must take the lead in their best areas, *but back one another up in a consistent, united fashion.* Working for consistency is not an easy task. It will be well worth the struggle, as you find a happy and predictable life-style for you and your child.

59. EARLY DISCIPLINE   *I would greatly appreciate any help you can offer concerning the discipline and training of a child between one and two years of age. My specific question is how do you discipline a child in this age bracket?*

The key to good discipline of a child of any age is a clear understanding about the sort of behavior of which that boy or girl is capable. And it's especially important to keep that in mind when you are dealing with a very young child. The question is a vital one, and concerns a very important age at which to master the art of discipline.

I have a very good friend who is a skilled musician. She had a rack full of very expensive sheet music, and her year-old little girl discovered that music. She loved the bright colors on the covers, and would grab and chew on them. Well, obviously, that was expensive material for chewing, and really not very healthy for the child anyway, so my friend blocked out an afternoon of time and decided to teach her child to leave the music alone. These are the steps that she took, and I think you will find this will work for you, as well:

First of all, explain briefly and firmly to the child that he or she may not have the object; in my friend's case the music was off limits. She used the word *no* fairly frequently and very firmly. When the child began to reach for the music, she firmly moved her away from it, and put the music back in the rack. Clearly and firmly she said, "No, you can't have this." She would pull back the child's hand and not allow her to touch it. She repeated this process with firmness and consistency, until finally, after an hour or two, the child began to understand that she could not have the music. Now my friend tells me that she was crying, and her child was crying, but at the end of the afternoon the music was safe. The child had learned a very important lesson, and that is that when Mother says *no,* she means it and will follow through with enforcing that rule.

Parents sometimes ask if it's necessary to swat or spank a little child. I think that's rarely necessary, though there may be times when a fairly firm swat may be less painful than the consequences of a child's touching a hot iron or a stove that could burn him seriously. Be sure if you are disciplining your child at this age that he stays away from the object, or does not touch whatever it is you are working on, *even when you are out of his sight*. My experience is that when the mom's away, the child will play. You need to step back, so the child cannot see you, and find out if the child's self-control will still maintain obedience. Take one step at a time, and I recommend that you choose it for its protective function—protection of the child or of the environment in which the child lives. After the child learns what is off limits, he can be offered substitutes to enjoy and to play with. Keep most of the time you have with your child full of love, laughter, and play, and as you and your child strengthen the bonds of love, he will become more compliant in order to please the parent whom he loves.

60. TOO-PATIENT PARENTS? *I am a grandmother and just heard your talk regarding the too loving and patient parent, and the fear and anger it can arouse in the child. I'm afraid my daughter has fallen into this. She is so loving and patient, and wants so much for her son to do right because he wants to. I think that's beautiful, but as I see it, she doesn't take into account the fact of our old sin nature and our stubborn wills until our faith makes that wonderful and radical change in us. I've seen my daughter very frustrated with her child because she expects too much of herself.*

This grandmother is absolutely right. In fact, I think she would make a very fine counselor herself. We do, unconsciously, expect of others what we expect of ourselves. If that is true, and I believe it is, this mother is likely to expect that her child will return to her the love, gentleness, and patience that she gives to him. She will expect him to adapt to all of her wishes, and be glad to give up his own will; in short, to be a perfect child, almost a robot. Frankly, I don't think she would even like such a child if she had him, and I'm sure that consciously is not what she wants. She expects herself, unfortunately, to be always calm, kind, gentle, and loving, and in short, to be the perfect parent. It sounds as if this mother is afraid that she may be guilty of not loving enough, and therefore, maybe she will be punished in some terrible way. At any rate, it is important to discuss the cure for this problem.

Parents, I want you to work very hard to understand the basically self-ish nature of children. Now, while that selfish nature can develop into a real problem, it can also be trained into a very positive strength. So if you will learn to accept and love that child unconditionally, and accept this apparent flaw, I think you will begin to see that it can be a good and healthy trait. If you will accept that basic selfishness and train it into good strong leadership skills, and if you will accept the occasional anger and frustration that any child feels and teach him to control them, then I think you will help your child begin to feel good enough about himself or herself and work through the problem parts of those issues.

I recommend these steps: Let me propose a simple dialogue. A mother may say, for example, "Danny, when you poke your sister so hard, I feel angry with you. Now I love you, and I want you to become a thoughtful and fine person. If you do that again, you may be certain that I will send you to your room." This sets a fine example for the child. The mother expresses her feelings, tells him why she feels that way, and what she will do about it. When you express your feelings as honestly and simply as described, and when your child learns to do that with you, you will have set up a climate for honesty within your family. The change will be very healthy, and that will allow you and your child to grow together.

61. HOW TO AVOID SPANKING   *Our son is almost four years old, and we're trying to use spanking less often as a form of punishment when he disobeys or talks back. But we're having a hard time getting away from it, because that seems to be all he'll respond to. When I try having him go to his room for ten minutes alone, he'll keep coming out. I've also tried having him sit on a chair as a punishment, but he seems to think of it as more of a game, so I usually end up spanking him anyway, sometimes just to make the original punishment stick. It's not that he's a terrible boy, but usually, about once a day, he'll break a household rule or refuse to obey, and I don't like to let that pass without responding. Any suggestions you have will be appreciated. Also when I spanked him, it seemed to help him get his anger out. He would cry, and then be very loving, but with other punishments he seems to build up resentments.*

That's a very revealing letter, and one that I'm sure a great many other people may have written with their own variations. Spanking does, of course, allow for the alleviation of guilt through suffering pain over the child's misdeed. Often, however, the best of spankings or the worst do not stop or change the pattern of the child's misbehaviors.

My parents were very strict people. My father was certainly the authority in our family, and obedience was demanded. However, I can recall only two spankings in my entire life. When I hear of a child who is getting spanked every day, I certainly feel a little bit sad, because I know there is a great deal of tension and ill will within that family. I hope we can solve that problem.

In good discipline the parent must be creative. Once upon a time, my father got me up late at night to go outside in the cold and darkness to do a chore I should have done when it was light and warmer. That taught me a very important lesson. He did not lay a hand upon me, but the point got across and the irresponsibility was changed. That's a nice example of how to discipline creatively. Giving a child extra work, making him clean up a mess, or fix what was broken (or at least *try* to fix what was broken), can help that child to learn an important lesson more definitely than simply spanking him. Grounding a child, limiting television, making him go to bed a little early, are among many creative ways to teach children that certain behaviors simply will not be tolerated, and *that there will be consequences attached.* In punishment, sometimes parents give vent to their own anger, and they may be the ones who feel relieved. So to be creative, think constructively and lovingly. What life lesson does my child need to learn from this experience? Thoughtfulness, responsibility, and obedience are qualities children must learn.

62. WHEN GRANDMA BABY-SITS *Because my husband and I both work, we leave our small children with their grandmother during the day. But we're discovering the hard way that Grandmother has different ideas about discipline than we do. And often when we correct our children about something, they'll say, "Well, Grandmother lets us do this." We need Grandmother to babysit but we don't need this problem about discipline. Do you have any suggestions?*

First of all, grandmothers who baby-sit have to play a dual role. They essentially wear two hats. They are *Grandma* and they are *baby-sitter.* So you, as parents, will need to try to be understanding of that fact. The second important fact that I would remind you of is that children are born manipulators. They have discovered a neat way of making you give in to them occasionally by quoting their grandmother. So you may want to look at that with a little bit of doubt.

Here are some ideas for solving these problems. First of all, have a loving but a very clear and straightforward talk with Grandmother. Make your values and the goals that you have set for your children very clear to her. Seek her help and cooperation in achieving these. Help her to understand that while she would like to be grandmother, she right now is playing the role of baby-sitter, and that you need her to help in being consistent and firm in following the rules and exerting the disciplines that your children need. Then, because she is a grandmother, the results may not be all that you desire. So you may have to work at this from the other side of the problem. That is, make it very clear to your little children that grandmas are special people who have the right to spoil them a little bit, *but* here are the rules for the children:

1.   They are not to expect you as parents to spoil them as their grandmother does.

2.   They are not to take advantage of Grandmother and try to get her to give in to them, when that really is not good for them.

I think you need to be very careful that you not develop a spirit of resentment between you and this grandmother. Sometimes, moms, I know that you who have to work (and frankly would somewhat rather be at home with your children) may feel resentful that someone else gets the fun of looking after your children. You may even feel jealous of Grandmother's relationship with the children, and fear that they will love her more than you as the mom. Be very careful that you do not give in to such jealous feelings. Do not mistake for respect the manipulation that your children may exert upon Grandmother. Know that you will always be the mother of those children. You can earn their respect, you can gain their love, and you can also enjoy (and so they can enjoy) the services of their grandmother as a baby-sitter.

63.   GREEDINESS   *How can I keep my daughter from asking our friends and relatives to give her gifts on her birthday and at other special times? I'm embarrassed by it, and I feel it's improper to ask.*

In general, training and teaching proper behavior requires only a few simple steps. Following through with those steps is, of course, the hard part. I recommend that parents make a very simple, clear, and definite rule. That rule goes something like this: Don't do that. Instead of saying, "I wish you wouldn't ask"; or "You really shouldn't ask Grandmother for that gift," be very clear and say, *finally, emphatically,* "Don't do it." It is quite all right, and the child will understand exactly what you mean when you make it that clear. You might need, as you go along, to explain that there is a reason for such a rule, and certainly you need to expect the child to cooperate with it. Keep the basic relationship between you and the child loving and positive. Such a relationship is the motivator for the child's cooperation with whatever rules you establish.

Have a consequence available if the child does break the rule. Make the child give up the gift, for example, or take it away until he can learn to be grateful and properly appreciative, or to stop the asking and pestering for a special gift.

Specifically, when it comes to asking for gifts, you, as parents, need to cultivate proper values. Develop love and personal respect as the best gift of all. Help your child know that is what really counts. You might try setting up a birthday or two for a child (with the family's agreement, of course) in which there should be no gifts at all—only a card, letter, phone call, or some special act of service for a child. For example, grandparents taking a child to a zoo, and the gift of time that represents can be a wonderful birthday present. Helping the child by this means to learn to value the presence of friends and the love, rather than the gifts, is very important.

64. EXPANDING LIMITS *What advice do you have for parents who are concerned about future teenage rebellion?*

From the time their children are very small, many parents begin to anticipate with dread the day their boy or girl becomes a rebellious teenager. But I'm glad to be able to tell you that you needn't just sit back and watch it come. The advice that I have is related to a story I heard very recently. That was of a twenty-two-year-old man who was working full-time with a very fine job and good income. He still lived at home with his parents, and they required that he be at home by 10:30, no matter where he went. He was not allowed to get his own apartment until he was married, and he was not prepared for marriage just yet. Here was a man who had a very seriously overprotective family which did not allow him the normal sort of freedom that a man of twenty-two (and a godly young man at that!) should be able to handle very well.

In the patterning of life there are many lessons that parents can learn. As we think about the growth of a little baby physically, I think we can see how a child also needs to grow socially and intellectually and in every area of life, gradually pushing back the boundaries of life. The little baby is born from the confinement of the mother's womb and is placed in a crib. He's gently cradled and nurtured in that larger space. From the crib, the baby usually is promoted to a playpen, and then to a whole room, to the floor of the house, the whole house. Very quickly it seems that child graduates to the yard and the neighborhood, the community, the city, and eventually the world. Now interplanetary space travel means that our children may someday travel infinitely! Just as children must expand their physical limits, so we as parents must be prepared for them to expand the other limits of their lives.

The wise parent observes each child's readiness for a new level of growth and responsibility—and beats the child to the draw, so to speak. As the parent sees that child becoming ready for the new level, he should say to the child, "Son [or Daughter], I have noticed that you are being quite responsible, and you are getting to bed on time, and yet I see that you're really not quite tired enough to need to go to bed. So how about if we put bedtime back a half an hour?" As parents give children that additional freedom, because they've *earned* it by their sense of responsibility, I think you can see that very few children would need to rebel. If the new freedom is too much, both child and parent will be aware and can reconstruct the fences just a bit closer. Your awareness, parents, of your child's readiness to grow and expand his horizons will prevent a great deal of unnecessary teenage rebellion.

65.   POLITENESS   *What's the key to raising children who are sincerely polite?*

The basis of all manners and politeness is a loving concern for the well-being of other people. If parents can somehow convey that to their children, they will have solved the major part of the politeness issue. Children need to learn (and can learn, fortunately) an awareness of their own feelings, and how to keep them positive, loving, and considerate. They need also to learn to be sensitive to the needs and feelings of *other people,* so that they can respond in a considerate and thoughtful way.

How good manners are expressed is something that we need to discuss for a minute. Social interactions very commonly lacking in today's world are the little nuances of simply saying, "Please," or "Thank you," or "Excuse me." Not considering one's own comfort or wishes ahead of those of other people, but putting others first (or certainly at least equal with one's own self) is another one of the essences of good manners.

Teaching manners to children can be done through modeling those as you express "please" and "thank you" to one another as husband and wife, and perhaps even more importantly, directly with your children. You will be teaching your child to use those same good manners back to you, and in turn with other people. Teaching your child verbally to use good manners is another important point.

Sometimes modeling and verbally teaching a child to use good manners are not enough. There are times when children simply do not want to say the right things, and in that case you may need to use discipline. That may be a reality factor. For example, if your child refuses to say "please," he may not get the item he desires. I hope you will make the effort, and that in teaching your child good manners, you will polish your own, because you will find that makes your life more pleasant as well as his.

66. TEACHING SELF-CONTROL   *Sometimes self-control means going against what comes most naturally to a child. I'm wondering if it's even possible to teach a boy or girl that kind of self-discipline.*

It is possible but it certainly is not easy. The question is exactly right because children are born with certain emotions. Those emotions will come out; when they are tiny babies they come out in the angry or frightened crying when they are hurt or startled. We know also that little children, like little animals, tend to want to get even when someone has hurt them.

The steps in teaching self-control are not very difficult. It's the doing of them and the remembering to teach them that are hard for parents. You need, as parents, to have your goal very clear, *and that goal is to teach your child to overcome that instinctive desire to retaliate and to explode with the emotion of the moment.* He must learn to substitute for that an understanding attitude—an understanding of himself as well as the other person. Now that sounds simple, but again it is not easy to put into effect.

Once the goal is established, you need to plan a route in order to get to the goal. You need to guide and talk the child through the process several times, if you expect him to learn how to control his feelings and expresss them appropriately. Let me emphasize that you ought not to teach your child to hide those feelings. He needs to express the anger, rage, or fear, *but* he can learn to do that in a controlled, constructive fashion, rather than a destructive one. The process involves three steps: 1. Verbalize the feeling. 2. Explain why you feel as you do. 3. Determine what you will do about the problem.

Once you have walked and talked your child through that process several times, allow him to try it alone, but observe him for the success with which he will do it. Cheer those successes royally and remind the child in a gentle and positive fashion when he forgets. You need to teach your children the vocabulary with which to express their feelings if they are to do that in a controlled fashion. You need to help them when they succeed to reach out beyond their own controls to help their brothers, sisters, or other family members to reach controls. Parents, you must be a model for this.

It is not so difficult to teach your children to be controlled, but you yourselves may find times when you have reached your limit, and you may want to give up and blow your top. Avoid that temptation, because your model will be the most effective teaching tool of all.

67. STRONG-WILLED CHILD   *I have a six-year-old son who is extremely strong-willed. He can be very loving and giving, but he continually challenges our authority, and is determined to do or not do as he pleases. He has been a very difficult child to raise. He cried constantly from the time he was thirteen months till he was three and a half. He's very intelligent and needs to be challenged and stimulated to be active. Everything else is boring to him, and when he is bored, he gets into mischief. We would appreciate any suggestions you might have that would help us lead our son. Also how to discipline. Removing privileges seems to help.*

This parent needs to be aware that every strong-willed child has at least one strong-willed parent, which inevitably causes power struggles. In power struggles too often we lose sight of *what* is right in this situation, in the interest of proving *who* is right. That is almost always a losing situation.

Major problems also arise when a parent feels sorry for a child after too rough a hassle, and in making up, unwittingly may rescue the child from the very consequences he needs. Also, when a child develops a growing guilt complex about the misunderstandings that go on, that child doesn't know what to do about it. And he may act out those unpleasant feelings in still more naughty behaviors.

There is certainly a need to teach or to discipline that rebellious youngster. What do you do, then, in teaching a willful child? First of all, parents, develop a plan. Sit down together (yes, and even with the child included), make a brief list of the expectations for responsibilities and behaviors that you hold for that little one. Decide with that child what will happen when he measures up to his very best—and when he doesn't. Natural consequences in my opinion are best (even better sometimes) than a spanking. Don't try to do all of this at once, however. Take one issue at a time and settle it, then go on to the next. Choose the time wisely when you are going to work on an issue. Give yourselves plenty of time and energy, such as during a weekend or the summertime, when the child's schedule and yours may be a little easier.

Prepare to levy those consequences through the loss of a privilege, the loss of television time, or playtime. Whatever is important to your child can motivate him to want to work with you on correcting the problems. Be persistent. Do not give in. Whether the child acts indifferent, angry, or sad, hold out, be firm and consistent. When he learns that you're in control, your child will give in and the next issue will be easier. Give him as much positive feedback as you can and remember how much you love him.

68.   EXPLAIN REQUESTS?   *We have a three-year-old son. When his mother or I tell him he can't do something, how much should we reason with him or explain? Is it all right to make him behave in a certain way, just because we say so, or is this a cop-out?*

I think what this father is really asking is, how much authority should he use in dealing with his child? Authority is a very important concept to understand. It seems to me that it is possible ultimately only if it is reasonable, fair, and in the good interest of everyone involved. Otherwise, authority becomes tyranny, and then rebellion takes place. Good discipline is certainly based on the strength and wisdom of the parents. If that wisdom is not conveyed through some explanations, I think the child will fail to understand what it's all about. He is much more likely to resent and resist the good disciplinary tactics of the best of parents.

Good discipline then outlines and teaches right policies or principles for living. These basic policies are applied in many little events. In our family, for example, we had a rule that we do not hurt each other physically or verbally—so we didn't need a number of rules that said, "Don't hit, don't pull hair, don't kick, don't pinch," and then discover that we forgot to say, "Don't bite," and so the child is all too quick to pick up that one little omission. So I hope you will understand this concept of getting some very basic policies, and then a lot of little things will fit in order fairly simply.

69.   TEACHING CAUTION   *What are some of the cautions that you think every child should be taught?*

There are a number of warnings, but I'd like to remind you that children fortunately are born with a *sense* of caution. Children are born with a fear of loud noises and a fear of falling, so that inborn, God-given sense of fear is the element that parents can build on in teaching good judgment and healthy cautiousness in all of life. Perhaps going chronologically through a child's life, *the first caution that should be taught is that a tiny child must be protected from physical dangers.* Little children need to be taught to stay out of household supplies that could be life-threatening. They need to be taught *bicycle safety,* as they grow older, and *water safety,* if parents live in an area where children can play in the water. All of those personal behaviors and situations can be taught with care and persistence on the part of the parent.

I would strongly recommend, parents, by the way, that you teach the child to observe those cautions *whether or not you are in the child's presence.* Many children will behave when parents are there to oversee them, but get a bit out of control when parents are gone.

The second area of caution that children must learn is *how to handle natural disasters or threats.* In my part of the country, we have tornadoes and thunderstorms. Lightning can actually strike and kill people, and that has happened many times, so children need to be taught where to seek shelter if they are caught out in a thunderstorm. In other parts of the country, earthquakes, avalanches, and hurricanes are natural disasters that can threaten or actually strike an area. Children must learn where to go to provide safety for themselves.

In homes there is another area of safety that must be taught and that is *fire protection.* Recently I met with a family whose home had been destroyed by fire. They were very fortunate in that they knew how to take precautions to get out of the house, so no one was hurt. Keep items put away in the home, so people don't trip and fall; watch the wiring and heating systems; provide safe locks—all of those are precautions that every family should take to protect themselves, their homes, and their children.

Sadly, in today's world we must also teach our children to avoid strangers, bullies at school, or even invasive, molesting neighbors and relatives, because people are sometimes tragically harmful. Teach your child to judge wisely, to behave cautiously, and you may well prevent some needless tragedies in their lives.

70. CONSEQUENCES *What discipline and consequences would you suggest for deliberate lying and bad language?*

First, discover why your child is lying or swearing. The most common reasons are these: the gaining of attention from peers; getting out of certain duties or disciplines; making themselves feel important.

The child who lies or swears is nearly always insecure and lacks a healthy self-confidence. As you step back and evaluate your parenting, you may discover that you have been too harsh, perhaps a bit inconsistent (letting the lies work now and then), and that you have not balanced your punishments with love and congeniality.

Start the discipline, then, by changing your parenting patterns according to the need. Be firm and consistent, but keep a caring and kindly attitude. Your child will learn even more effectively from kindness if you follow through.

Do make it clear that lying will not be tolerated and that there will be consequences. For example, if your child tells you she has cleaned her room when she really hasn't, go with her to clean it once and allow her to miss play or TV time or delay dinner until it is done.

For swearing, I suggest a child pay a fine for each unacceptable word. This fine may be taken out of his allowance, or he may be assigned a job to earn the money.

Be sure to explain clearly why these habits are harmful and that it is out of love you are punishing the child. If you really mean that, your child will recognize your concern and sooner or later, he will comply.

71. REWARDS *I would like to know how you can motivate children to work on their own at home and in school without always*

having to reward them. Our son is very bright, but he would rather talk or watch others work, instead of going ahead and getting his own work done. It gets frustrating for us as parents. We would appreciate your opinion on this subject.

This is a common problem. I would recommend that the parents talk through this issue. When you have determined a plan that sounds practical and possible for you to put into effect, then discuss it with your child. Let that child know there is going to be a new routine around there. The question is not going to be *whether* he will do the assigned job but *when*—now or at midnight—and let him know that every pleasure stops until responsbility is taken care of. Start with a household task that is reasonably time-limited—one that perhaps the entire family could work on together. Certainly at least one parent needs to work with the child in order to teach him how to organize his work, and actually to finish it.

The best reward for any child is your pride and pleasure in his achievements and eventually his own self-respect. It takes effort and time from you as parents to make that happen, but that time is perhaps one of the best investments in your child's future that you can make.

72. SUNDAY-SCHOOL DISCIPLINE *I work in the primary department in our Sunday school, and the problem I have is with a little boy in the third grade. Every Sunday he completely disrupts his class through his rowdiness. He may be what you call hyperactive. We hate to keep going to his parents every Sunday and don't want to tell them not to bring him. Very little is accomplished while he is there. He can seldom stay in his seat and he is never quiet.*

That is an extremely sensitive issue, and one that deserves a great deal of consideration. A Sunday-school teacher needs to have a take-charge attitude. A child somehow senses when the adult is *really* in charge. Now that's not enough for a child of this severe a behaviorial disorder—this is recommended for that particularly difficult child:

I suggest that the teacher visit in the parents' home or invite them into the class for a sit-down conference. Many times Sunday-school teachers try to catch parents in the hallway during or after church to discuss the issue, and they never really set up a definitive plan of action. So if you can, sit down together, ask what they would recommend, and what they have found that works to help gain this child's cooperation. If they have no such recommendations, maybe you could be ready with a plan that you would check out with them. Gain their permission and their backup for such a plan. Here is my suggestion for that plan: Make very clear to this problem child what you most want from him. Perhaps you simply want him to sit still in his seat, or you want him not to talk for ten minutes at a time. Make it a possible requirement, and one that is extremely clear to the child, to you as the teacher, and any helpers you may have, as well as to the parents. If he does sit still for a period of time, give him special praise and notice for that good behavior.

If he is unable to do this, I recommend having an assistant handy who can escort the child to the hallway and stand outside with him for a moment. Allow him then to come back in and try again. If the parents will cooperate, if you as a teacher and an assistant work together, I think that most children can be helped to cooperate, enter into the activities, and learn to worship in an appropriate fashion. (I often feel that there will be a special place in heaven for those who serve week after week as our children's Sunday-school teachers!)

73. HATES SCHOOL
Our fourteen-year-old son absolutely cannot stand school. He "hates it" in his words. Most of the time he refuses to keep his assignments current. He even goes so far as to refuse to do tests during school. We have tried just about everything. The problem seems to be that he is immature for his age, and he seems to live in a world of fun and games. We also have difficulty getting him to take responsibility with jobs here at home. He seems to get along in the classroom (usually), but his greatest problem is that since he is bored, he distracts others. He tells us and the school authorities that he doesn't have to do the work. Go ahead and suspend him, he says, or he can stay where he is until he's sixteen and can be legally out of school. He is mostly a sunshiny kind of boy, and most people warm to him. It's just that he puts up a wall and plants his feet like a mule.

The problem basically is simple to understand. It's the solution that's difficult. The issue, frankly, is one of learning basic responsibility. This boy is not responsible at home or in school. The causes of irresponsibility are also fairly easy to understand but hard to correct. First of all, most parents want their children to be happy, and to them, happy means *carefree*. So they allow children to grow through those early years without a great deal of responsibility, and then when they do give some tasks to the child, it's hard for him to carry them out.

Many times parents need the child's love and want it so much that they are afraid to risk adequate discipline.

When I hear of a child who is bored, I know that very likely he is depressed, and often he feels angry, helpless, and sad. Yet many such children will cover those feelings with a rebellious attitude.

These parents indicate that they have "tried everything." Oftentimes that means that there has been some inconsistency. Oftentimes there may be a difference in expectations between the parents themselves, and between the parents and the school.

The solution, then, demands that the parents must become unified in their expectations and the consequences. They must become tougher. Tough love does not pity or rescue a child. You need not be angry, tyrannical, or rude, but neither do you need to give in to a child who must learn responsibility. Parents must agree upon one or two issues and enforce those consistently, until the child learns that he has to comply. There must be absolute follow-through if the child is ever to learn to be responsible. If you will not give in, and keep the consequences fair but absolutely to the point, you will find, parents, that your child, even as a teenager, can learn to be responsible as well as productive.

74. FORGETFULNESS   *Other than constant nagging, what can parents do to help children remember things?*

It is a dawdling, daydreaming child who tends to develop the habit of forgetting. And such forgetfulness prompts parental nagging. What happens, then, when you stop nagging? The child still continues to dawdle and daydream. In order to avoid nagging, simply rely upon natural consequences. That is, if the child is late to meals, the family goes right ahead and eats, and whatever part of the meal that child misses, he simply misses, until the next meal comes along. You do not rewarm the food, you do not extend the mealtime, you do not rescue the child from that lateness. That reality is much more likely to teach a daydreaming, resistive, or dawdling child than a parental system of nagging or dragging the child to those activities.

The next step that parents need to take is to discover each child's basic strengths, finding the qualities about that child that are good and positive, and reflecting upon those. Commenting about them will help them grow and develop. As your child feels better about himself, the forgetting, which is a passsive resistance against the things that you most want him to do, will slowly disappear.

You need to give children *limited choices* in order to help them grow in responsibility. Stop their resistance by being wise and helping make the right choice. This is something you can teach them to do. Work out a plan that involves assigning responsibilities, setting rewards which may be only your praise and pride in that child. Planning consequences that your child agrees will help him remember, help him learn the lesson, and then follow through *consistently*. You and your child will both grow by practicing this kind of plan.

75. LYING SIX-YEAR-OLD   *How do you deal with a six-year-old who lies to stay out of trouble?*

Certainly six-year-olds are not above lying, and there are several important causes of lying. They range from the sublime to the serious, and I would like to list those. The least serious is that of tall-tale telling just for fun, but the child should not become confused between the imaginary stories and the real.

More serious causes, however, are that some children lie *to get attention.* Those who particularly do not get enough positive attention may do a great many negative things to get *some* attention at least, and such lying is a common behavior. Trying to *avoid work or discipline,* however, is the commonest cause of lying. Children are by nature perhaps just a bit lazy (and sometimes frankly a lot lazy!). So they often learn to lie to get out of work, or sometimes out of the consequences of not doing their jobs.

Well, what are parents to do then if they have a child who lies as this mother's six-year-old does? First of all, *tell your child to stop lying.* Then you need to evaluate what you are doing that might unwittingly encourage his lying habit. Are you, for example, too severe in the way that you punish your child? Are you too angry when you discipline your child? The frightened child is often one who lies in order to try to avoid the harshness of the punishment. Evaluate your overall relationship. Does your child need a little more affection? Do you all need more happy fun times as parents and children? A different approach in teaching and training perhaps? Make the necessary change and show your child that he can no longer get out of work or discipline by lying. He will then give up that obnoxious habit.

76.   ALLOWANCES   *Do you think children should receive a certain amount of money each week to spend as they wish?*

Yes, if that is possible—and in today's economy many families really cannot afford to give children an allowance. I would not want any of you to sacrifice unduly in order to provide that for your children. There are, however, some wonderful lessons that can be taught to young children by giving them an allowance. I truly do not believe the money should be given to each child to spend exactly as he or she wishes. It should be given to children to help them to understand how money is to be used, and what its value actually is.

Teaching children to budget is very possible by the age of six or seven, and certainly by the age of eight. If you can afford to give your child even a dime, give it to him in pennies, so he can save one penny, give one penny to Sunday school, spend a couple of pennies now for a stick of sugarless gum, or whatever he might be able to buy for a few pennies. Help the child to know that will be all of the money that he or she can spend that week for frivolous or unnecessary kinds of items.

Be consistent about the uses and needs of the money. Increase the child's allowance as his or her responsibility increases, and you will have taught a valuable financial lesson to your young child.

77.   PAY FOR HOUSEHOLD CHORES?   *My young teenage daughter always wants to earn money for chores she does in the house. She's forever asking me if there is something she can do, and how much will I pay her for doing it. I'm going broke. Help!*

That certainly is a problem and it does have a lot of ramifications. Some children feel that they must be paid literally for every job. Now I can understand children wanting money, but the amazing fact is that many parents fall into that trap. My philosophy about family living is that everyone should help one another within the family group. Everyone needs to learn to give as well as to get, and the family is certainly the arena for learning that. This daughter, however, is saying something really very fine. She is not asking for a donation. She is at least willing to earn the money, so while this mother is upset, I hope she will look at that one good point in this whole issue.

Here are my suggestions about this idea of paying children for helping: First of all, parents, remember that the final decision is up to you. I do recommend, however, that there be a family council, and that together you sit down and decide on some of these very important issues. First of all, budgetary matters must be determined for each child, and in this family council, you can determine what amount of money each child needs for that person's style of living. Household tasks must be done by each family member without pay. Those basic jobs should be assigned and rotated fairly among all of the family members. (A family council is a wonderful place in which to do that.)

Over and above these basic jobs, however, there may be some special jobs that are up for bid for extra pay. Whatever pay those jobs merit can be settled together, and that is then written down on paper and is clear to everyone. Encourage your children, as soon as they are able to seek jobs outside of the home, to find out about those possibilities as well as jobs within the house. Lawn care for neighbors, child care, helping someone else clean house—all of those are time-honored jobs that children, too young to get full-time jobs in a commercial establishment, can do to earn money. Then teach money management to your children. They need to know that there are limits as to how much money is available, and that they must budget the way they spend it.

Education

78. EARLY LEARNING   *Could you suggest what things I should be teaching my eleven-month-old child? I'm referring to such things as colors, numbers, shapes, and words. I'm wondering how and when to teach them and where to start.*

This mother's question is a bit startling, because I am involved in pre-school and early childhood education. I am a little concerned that a mother should feel that she needs to begin teaching academics to an eleven-month-old child. Early learning ideally is involved with the child's learning to feel safe; to feel warm and close; to laugh and love; and find the joy in life. The physical development of early childhood demands plenty of physical activity, sensory stimulation of the sight, hearing, taste, and feeling parts of the body. There should be a balance of that activity with cuddling, resting, and privacy. Children early on need the freedom to just *be*, to grow as God meant them to grow—and to be unconditionally accepted. Too many times, when parents become anxious about teaching children numbers and shapes and words, the unconditional acceptance becomes lost in the parents' concern about teaching the child. The child may feel stressed or pushed too much.

Early learning *is* possible. We know that little babies can learn a great many numerical concepts, but frankly I don't think that's too desirable. We have learned from studying children for a period of years now that those who learn how to read before school are no more advanced in their reading abilities by, say, the third grade, than those who do not learn until the first grade. So I recommend that parents not try too hard to teach children academic skills before they start school.

Preschoolers' tasks are basically to find and accept their physical abilities and their limits, to develop their creativity, to find and build sure foundations. As you and your child learn to relate lovingly, you will have taught that child the most important lessons of all.

79. PRESCHOOL HEADSTART   *My daughter hasn't been to nursery school, and I'm wondering if she'll be able to compete in* *kindergarten on an equal level with the kids who have already had some school experience. Do boys and girls who have been to nursery school have a head start over those who have not?*

Actually, I doubt it, but let me discuss that. So many children are going to preschool that I understand kindergartners are advanced, as compared to what they were some years ago.

I suppose the greatest advantage that preschool offers to a child is that of learning social skills. Many children live in neighborhoods where there are not many other children, and the chance to learn to share and cooperate, to take turns, and consider the needs of other children, may be a problem when that lonely child enters kindergarten. I think, however, that can be corrected fairly readily, so if your child has not been able to go to preschool, don't worry a great deal. Do follow some of these suggestions:

Teach your child to interact with others socially by inviting a child into your own home or taking your child to someone else's house to play now and then. Take your child to Sunday school or to some church event that will give her the opportunity to interact, and learn some of the social skills that school-age children must have.

Academically, you as a mother can teach your preschooler many of the basic facts that she could learn in a preschool situation. Basic colors such as red, yellow, blue, and green, can certainly be taught by you, as you teach your child to color and share in that coloring activity with her. Recognizing some letters and numbers can be taught by using an alphabet book or finding a very simple preschool-level book in your local library. Being able to follow directions, to be respectful, and obedient are among the greatest essentials for your child to learn, and who can teach your child that better than you as the mother or the father?

Teach your preschooler to learn to wait for and how to use the bathroom, because that is one big milestone that preschoolers and kindergarteners must learn. Be able to use the usual play equipment. Take your child to a park or a local play area where she can learn to swing, throw balls, skip, and do those kinds of physically coordinated activities that school-age children must master. Your child needs to be able to pay attention for fifteen or twenty minutes at a time. If you have enjoyed your child, offered normal social interactions with similar-aged friends; if you've trained and disciplined her consistently, fairly, and lovingly; if you're proud of her and her potential for good; *you need have no fear of any disadvantage for your preschool child when she enters kindergarten.*

80.   SCHOOL READINESS   *Most parents probably have mixed emotions about waving good-bye on that first day of school. They're glad for the new freedom they'll have, but a little afraid that Johnny or Susie isn't quite ready to face that big, cold world out there. Do you have any help for them?*

Yes, and I certainly can identify with those mixed emotions. On the one hand, when children are fretful and irritable, it's tempting to want to be rid of them and give them over to the teacher. When they are pleasant and happy, there is a joy in being with them. Then parents are reluctant to let go of them! So parents do have a hard time knowing which of their emotions is accurate, and in fact, if the child is ready for that big world.

When you're not sure, parents, don't be afraid to ask other people. If you have a trusted relative who can be reasonably objective, ask that relative. Sunday-school teachers are a great source of information that can help you to know if your child is ready socially, intellectually, and emotionally for that new experience. Many school districts now have a preschool screening test that can help you to know scientifically whether your child is actually ready for kindergarten. Boys tend to mature more slowly than girls, though we don't know why. But if there is any question, I strongly recommend that you allow your children to wait a year, and *particularly do I recommend that for boys.*

Physical Signs. Now there are some specific signs that you can look for to help you know if your child is, in fact, ready for school. The physical signs that you need to observe are these: Can your child hold crayons and pencils and use them reasonably successfully on paper or in a coloring book such as those you may purchase at your local dime store? Can your child dress himself and tie his shoelaces? Can the child use the toilet alone satisfactorily? These physical signs, if they are not up to par, will help you to understand that your child should wait a while and practice those physical skills.

Social Signs. Your child should be able to cooperate in play and in work with other children. Can she share and take turns? Is he able to show respect and compassion for other children's feelings and needs; on the other hand, can he protect himself when that is necessary? Emotionally, can your child verbalize most feelings? Is your child aware of her needs, and can she ask for the satisfying of those needs in a reasonably clear and acceptable fashion? Academically, is your child's attention span at least fifteen to twenty minutes? If not, there are several steps you can take.

What You Can Do. Read to your child over a period of time. Deprive him of some television watching to spend time developing his motor skills and academic interests. Then send him off to school with joy and confidence.

81. READING GROUPS   *Do you think it is a good idea to divide a class up by reading skills?*

If you can remember back as far as first grade, you may recall being placed in a reading group known as the "zebras" who could read fluently, or the "giraffes" who could hardly make out any of the words at all. Now your teacher may have used different animals but no doubt the groups were there. I have worked with school districts for a number of years now, and I have debated in my own mind the pros and cons of this issue. I do not frankly have an authoritative answer, but I do have some thoughts that I would like to share.

First of all, we need to think about what happens to a classroom of students when the slower readers are placed directly with the very gifted readers. The less-gifted child is very quickly going to run into the risk of feeling that there is no hope for him. *This very bright child is doing so well, and I must be very dumb.* That's really how children react, so the origin of children's reading groups came from teachers' concern to help children not to become discouraged by comparing themselves with one another.

On the other hand, putting children into different groups still does give them that opportunity to feel that they are stupid while others are more gifted. Children can quickly attach a value to success and failure that becomes personal, rather than just intellectual.

Perhaps it is more helpful to discuss the following concepts, rather than just arguing about whether or not to put a child into a labeled reading group. What I find to be so important to a child's success in school, as well as at home, is the acceptance of that child for who he or she is. Every child has some area of gifts and special abilities that are unique to him or her, and whether we call that child a *zebra* or a *giraffe,* the assets and the strengths are the important points for teachers and parents to understand and remember.

82. READING TO CHILDREN   *At what ages do children really enjoy having their parents read to them and benefit from it?*

One of the most pleasant ways for a parent and child to spend quality time together is in the sharing of a good book—no matter what the age of your son or daughter.

Perhaps the child who most enjoys his parents' reading is the pre-school child. I have a suspicion, however, that that's because parents fail even to think about reading to older children. Since the advent of television, children have become so entertained by that medium that reading to one another (or sometimes even conversing with one another) has become almost a lost art. The benefits of reading are so many that I would really like to list them:

It is, perhaps, more the sense of *intimacy* and *warmth* that reading together creates that is valuable, more so than the content of the story itself. However, I believe that reading together *teaches and models the value of reading and learning to children.* As you parents show joy and excitement in reading a good book together, you will inform your children that this is something they will enjoy, too. Furthermore, it exemplifies that reading and learning can be fun, not just that it's valuable and important, but delightful as well.

Taking off from the story in an informal conversation with children can help them to learn to read with comprehension. I'm finding a great many children in today's world may read very well, but truly do not understand what they have read. Furthermore, talking about reading matter can help children to apply the information in the book to real-life situations, *and that is teaching wisdom!* Use care in selecting the materials that you read so that they are not too serious and create a sense of resentment or heaviness; they are not so giddy or silly that it insults the child's intelligence. I wish for you real joy and warmth as you and your child share books.

83. TALENT SCOUTS *How can parents go about uncovering their child's talents?*

One of the important keys to building your child's self-confidence is to discover and cultivate those special talents and abilities that can make that boy or girl stand out from the crowd. Actually, parents need to be talent scouts, and that means that they must explore as many areas of their children's lives as possible. Let's discuss what these areas of life are all about.

First of all, I think of *cultural aspects of life.* Parents, help your child to explore the areas of art and music, literature, and photography. Share with your child your own interest in these various areas of life. Try to find a range of types of music, art, and literature to teach and guide your young child in those exploring expeditions.

Another area is that of *personal physical interests.* Expose your child to gymnastics, swimming, running, skating, skiing, tennis, soccer, football, baseball, basketball, and any of the other sports that you can think of. Not only does this develop your child's physical skills, but you may discover for and with your child some special area of skill that could become a lifelong joy, and perhaps even a professional ability for your child.

Nature hikes are certainly a favorite pastime of mine. Children need to learn about nature. Sitting and listening, or walking, can give you the opportunity to teach your child the joy of all of the sensations that nature can provide. Commenting about these to your child and helping that child want to explore and learn, could be the avenue through which that child may become a physician, a nurse, or a scientist.

Exploring, however, does not mean that you try to make your child become a master at every one of the areas that we have just discussed. Let these times of exploring be superficial at first. Take a look, dip into the various expressions of interest which we have discussed, and let your child have fun with them. It is out of this simple exploration that the final commitments to a life career will eventually be made. Get excited with your child over his efforts and interests and share your own. Praise the results of his projects and his skills and he will be likely to explore more deeply on his own.

84.   DETECTING LEARNING DISABILITIES   *What are some of the symptoms a child might develop if he had a learning disability?*

Those are fairly easy to define in some cases. First of all (and most commonly) is dyslexia, the reversal of letters and simple words. A *b* for example to a child with learning disabilities looks like a *d*, a *q* may look like a *g*. A simple word such as *dab* becomes *bad* to a child with a learning disability. Now that sort of learning disability can be helped simply by requiring the child to memorize by practicing again and again the right shape and the right name for that letter.

In many children the process and the problem of a learning disability is much more complex than that. In some children there is a difficulty in translating what the eyes see into a concept that the cortex or the outer layer of the brain can interpret. The same is true of the hearing: what a child hears simply may not get from all of those complex nerve tracts in the brain to be interpreted into something that is meaningful to a child. Such children have difficulty in what we call short-term memory. They have trouble seeing or hearing something, and remembering, even for a few minutes, what is going on. They may remember what happened last week or last year, but not what happened a few seconds ago.

Still another kind of school difficulty or learning disability has to do with emotional problems. Depression or anxiety about school with its failures, or about problems at home, can cause impairment in that child's learning.

The causes of learning problems are numerous. Of course, neurological weaknesses might be due to birth defects or some problem even before birth. It may be an inherited or genetic problem. I often see children who are preoccupied with anxieties that are too heavy to imagine. A child who is worried about his mother's health, or his father's accident, or an impending divorce, is bound to have difficulty learning about math and history. Children become discouraged through their own failures, or through seeing other children get ever more rapidly ahead of them, while they tend to stay the same or fall behind. Sometimes I find children feel guilty about misbehaviors at school or at home, and that guilt makes them feel inadequate.

Special classes and special learning techniques can help many children overcome learning disabilities. Have your little child build letters out of blocks or string, or something that he can feel and touch while he is creating the letter. Repeat the sound of the letter as he builds it, and so help your child to create the image within his mind, as well as in his hand while he is learning. Keep the child's mind free from worry by explaining the events of his life and assuming adult responsibility for the child so that he does not need to carry them. Praise your child's successes, and discipline him so he can become responsible. He will learn to succeed if you are patient and loving.

85. CAN'T READ?   *My son can't read. He has been through four years of learning-disability programs and has been to five different schools. I've had him in a Christian school this year, but I don't see any improvement at all. We had to put him in third grade because he couldn't begin to handle fifth grade. We are confused and very concerned. He's been living with his dad until this year, and now he's living with me and my new husband. In a few weeks I'm going to start working half-days, so I can work with him more and build a* *closer bond between us. I would like to help him learn to read, but I'm not sure how to begin. Can you suggest books or other resources for me?*

From the information given, I believe this child may suffer from dyslexia, or difficulty with learning to read. I would recommend that this mother go to her local library and seek out some books on dyslexia. You will find such books listed in the card catalog file in your local library. As well as going to your library, consult your telephone directory and see if in your neighborhood there is a group called the Orton Society. These are wonderful people who have banded together to support one another, and the dyslexic children that are involved in the group. They may be helpful in diagnosing and recommending help for a child with reading problems.

Minimum brain damage can cause this problem in children, and if that is true, fortunately children tend to outgrow it. In such cases children tend to reverse their letters so that a *b* looks like a *d* and vice versa. We really know fairly little about this complex sort of brain damage. *It is not retardation,* and there is a great deal of hope for help as the child matures.

Perhaps more commonly than brain damage, however, children have difficulty in learning through anxiety or depression, and that may be the case in this child's life. Because he has been through a divorce, he has shifted from one parent to the other, has had to adapt to a variety of adults, and has changed schools many times. These are my recommendations: This mother has already begun to follow them by rearranging her priorities and taking some time off to be with her child. I would strongly urge her, however, to spend more time playing with her son and developing a happy relationship, rather than working with him too much. Limit his study time to one or two thirty-minute intervals. Reward his efforts with praise and congratulations. Read to him at times about topics that he enjoys. Let him choose books that are easy for him, until he learns to develop some confidence in his skills. Do anything that you can to help him feel secure and settled. Love him and respect him. Help him to love and respect all of his parents, and I think in due time you will discover that he will overcome the problem with learning.

86. REPEATING GRADE   *What questions should parents ask if their child's school recommends that he repeat a grade?*

I have a list of questions that should be considered in deciding such an important issue. Whether or not to hold a child back is a difficult decision, and parents need to give it careful consideration.

The first question I would ask is: *How does his age and physical size fit with the other children in his present grade and in the grade that he would be in if he were held back?* If he is a great deal bigger or feels older than the class he would be in, he may resent it so much that he will rebel, and holding him back will not be effective in improving him.

The second question: *How badly are his academic skills lacking?* Is this true of all areas of learning or only one or two special areas? (If he is lacking in only one or two special areas, tutoring could help him to improve.)

The third question is this: *What are his social skills?* If he is quite mature, he may feel very out of place with younger children. If he is less mature on the other hand, he may feel even better with the younger ones, and that would help his adjustment if he is retained.

My fourth question is this: *What are the other choices?* Special classes for possible reading difficulties? A selected teacher who may be good with children like him? Those choices can help you decide wisely what is best for your child.

"He Must Repeat." If all of the answers that you have just considered converge and say, "This child is not mature enough, he simply is not facing the responsibility that he must learn. He needs strengthening in all of his learning," then, parents, as much as I know you may not like it, accept the fact he may need to stay in that grade and repeat it.

How to Handle the Decision to Repeat. Here's how you may deal with that: First of all, I'd recommend, parents, that you face your sadness. All parents have dreams and ideals for their children, and repeating a grade rarely fits that dream. When your dream is lost you have to grieve, so do your grieving and then accept the fact. When you have grieved through the loss of your dream, and you have accepted it, then I think you are ready to help your child go through the same process. Most children are sad if they have to repeat a grade, and lose the social contacts that they have built in the years they have just finished. You and your child together can explore the advantages of repeating this grade. Help him to see how he can improve his study skills and his learning foundations and how that will help him for the rest of his school life. Keep your attitude positive, and it will help your child to stay positive as well. Work closely with the school, and make next year the best year your child will have. Facing disappointments, overcoming them, and moving on—that's what you and your child can learn even if he must repeat a grade.

87. MIDDLE SCHOOL *Next year my son is assigned to attend a new middle school. I don't really like the idea of his leaving the* *grade school which is nearer to our home. Also I'm concerned about the older children and possible bad influences he'll have to deal with. What do you think of middle schools? (We have considered sending him to a private school.)*

Explanation. Unless you went to an old-fashioned one-room country school, you probably attended an elementary school, followed by junior high, and then high school. A middle school is a fairly new concept, and many communities are considering it. The "classical" middle school includes grades five, six, seven, and eight (the upper two grades of elementary school and the first two years of junior high school). Actually I find that there are some advantages to this idea and I'd like to discuss those first.

Advantages. First, it gives the child a longer time under somewhat closer supervision. For some time we have found that seventh- and eighth-grade children seem to get into a great deal of trouble. Problems that adolescents eventually have may often begin at that time. This may have to do with the major transition from a very protective elementary school environment to a much more independent junior high. This may come before the child is quite ready for it. The transition is more gradual through a middle school, with some added responsibility, but with continued supervision of a more careful type. Thus the young person has a chance to finish the early adolescent period as more of a child and not quite so much an adult as the junior high school would promote.

Disadvantages. There are some risks and this depends on how the school is organized. If it is set up to really be a larger but younger junior high school, then it could push children to grow up just as much as junior high, and even earlier. Be sure you check that out with your school staff and administrators. If that is the case, then I would suggest you avoid sending your child there. How well supervised are the children in the middle school? Do they have a home base, one teacher they especially can relate to? What freedoms do they have? You might give this school a try for a semester. See how positive you feel about it. A private school certainly may have some advantages for your child but all schools have problems. Above all, be in close touch with your child's teachers, counselor, and principal. Work with them to provide the best school experience you can for your child.

88. CREATIVITY   *Are some people born with more creativity?*
Or is it something that's developed?

Your son or daughter may not grow up to be another Beethoven or Michelangelo, but no matter what occupation they choose, they will benefit a great deal from a well-developed ability to think creatively. I am convinced that everyone created in the likeness of God is creative. God is the infinite Creator, and since we are made in His image we must be creative. Each person, however, is born with different potential and a different area for the expression of that creativity. We can trace through several generations many times and find special gifts for art, music, or other areas of creativity. Perhaps it's not so much, however, that they are born with this gift or have a genetic factor that makes them follow a certain path, but that they are taught this by the excitement of their creative parents.

Much creativity depends on the parents' encouragement and the providing of opportunity for that interest in the child to be developed. Whatever the child makes demands recognition and praise. (Be sure the child's classroom experiences do not spoil his individuality and creativity.)

89. MUSIC LESSONS   *Could you discuss some of the factors*
parents should think about if they are considering music lessons for
their child?

Parents naturally want their children to have the best and fullest life possible, and to some moms and dads that includes special lessons in music and other subjects. I think the very first thing that parents need to consider is whether or not they are willing to commit themselves to suffer through what can become an agony in the learning experiences of their child. There are about three phases that children go through in learning any special skill.

Excitement. Usually the first stage is that of excitement at the new opportunity. The opportunity to touch those keys and learn what those funny little black notes mean is usually very intriguing to children.

Boredom. This can be fairly short-lived and the second phase is one of boredom and resistance to the monotony of scales and practices.

Thrill of Mastery. Once a child gets through that difficult stage, however, she can then know the thrill of mastery. Somewhere in the process, children may hit a time of severe discouragement, if they find that this really is not a skill at which they are gifted. That may or may not happen to your child.

Let's talk about how it is that you can determine what to do for your child in the area of music lessons. First of all, *evaluate your child's natural giftedness.* I think all children need to learn and appreciate music, because music has been called at times the universal language. I believe every child should at least learn the basics of music. The notes, scales, and rhythm will enrich that child's life in even the enjoyment of hearing music played by other people (if not his own performance). Be careful to avoid rigidity. Most of all, avoid allowing your child to quit during that hard or difficult phase. Set up a plan (with your child's cooperation and perhaps with advice from the teacher) in these ways:

1. Keep practice time short enough to be bearable.
2. Keep the practice time frequent enough to learn the lesson.
3. Encourage a time to play that instrument just for fun, without the hard work of practicing.
4. Try playing that instrument yourself. Having your child teach you something about it can captivate his interest and promote his real work and effort in finding the mastery that can be such a thrill—such an advantage in his life.

90.   CHRISTIAN SCHOOL?   *Do you think a child should be put in a Christian school if at all possible, or should he be allowed to remain in the public school?*

That is a very important question today because there are many concerns parents feel about the public school system in general. There are, however, some disadvantages in Christian schools as well, unless the parents are very careful in their selection. I have known, for example, that Christian schools can become in a sense a reformatory, and a great many parents who are concerned about rebellious children send them there to get them straightened out. On the other hand, sometimes Christian schools may be so rigid and legalistic that they cause rebellion in the minds of the children who go there. I worry about Christian schools overprotecting children, or failing to prepare them for life in a secular, real world. There is sometimes a lack of balance in the various learning opportunities. Many Christian schools emphasize the spiritual growth but perhaps neglect the physical growth or the cultural opportunities that children need.

The advantages of a good Christian school, however, are worth considering, and if you have a very fine, balanced Christian school in your community, parents, I hope you will consider it for your child. The warmth and love of a truly Christian environment is one that would be ideal for a child's intellectual, physical, and spiritual development. The definite teachings of Christian principles and the reinforcement of family values can hardly be emphasized enough. You do, however, as parents, need to check out each school and decide whether the things that they teach are, in fact, congruent with what you teach, and if they are reinforcing the values that are special to you. A Christian school will many times help a child to answer the doubts of a secular society, and if the Christian school you select does not offer that sort of thoughtful environment for your questioning child, then I would seriously doubt if it will meet that child's needs.

There are several requirements that I suggest you look for if you are seeking a Christian school for your child: First, you need to find out if there is a *balance in the academic, physical, social, and cutural teachings of that school, as well as the spiritual teachings.* I hope that you will find in it a real sense of *genuine warmth and openness, that unconditional acceptance of each child as he is, balanced with structure and discipline,* and the kind of guidance that helps him to achieve and grow. I suggest that you look for a *general flavor of excellence* in the school, that the *environment be clean and neat,* as well as the *academics being well polished and geared to the child's growth.* Look for a *friendliness* among the staff, and especially between the faculty and students. The lives of your children will be influenced by the teachers who are in the school that you select. I hope you will find a great team for all of you.

91. HOME SCHOOL   *What are the advantages and the disadvantages of teaching your child at home rather than sending him off to school?*

These home schools are an actual substitute for public schools, and they recommend that parents totally teach their children, following a curriculum that this group has prepared. There are many concerns that the advocates of this plan share with a lot of people. They are worried about the bad influence of peers, the bad language, disrespect and dishonesty (that even very young children practice), and certainly those habits can become contagious. Home school advocates are concerned about the influence of agnostic teachers and secular humanism that can be taught in many schools. They are concerned about overcrowded classrooms, and they advocate the need of parent-child intimacy. They believe that parents' knowing what their child is learning is a vital concern. They claim successful achievement and all-around better education than even public schools.

Now I certainly can share the concerns that these folks express (and that I have just shared with you), but there are some disadvantages in this plan as well. I would like to present some thoughts for your consideration on this side of that issue:

First of all, in my experience, few parents can handle the constant interaction with children that such a plan would demand. They are required in this case to fulfill a dual role. Shifting gears from parent to teacher and back can be fatiguing and draining on both parents and children. Providing such constant supervision, and yet finding the energy to enjoy the child and relax and play together, is difficult at best if not downright impossible. In spite of claims to the contrary, I know frankly of less than 5 percent of my own friends who could adequately teach much of the educational material that children must master. Modern math is only one example of that.

In the elementary years of life children generally respect parents' opinions and ideas. Hence, it is the ideal time to expose children to the existing social and cultural forces about them. It gives the parents an opportunity to teach children how to understand what is wrong about these negative influences, how to stand against them and to establish their own healthy individuality in a problemed world. Most home teaching ends at the beginning of junior high school, and putting children at that vulnerable time into an outside world that they have not been accustomed to, can create problems for them. In the end, you must choose whether or not you will have home teaching for your child.

92. SUMMER CAMP?   *Many of us have wonderful memories of attending summer camp, but watching your child wave good-bye from the window of a moving bus can be a terrible experience for us parents of first-time campers. Will my child be homesick? Will he be sent home with poison ivy or broken bones? Will he be able to get to sleep without that bedtime story? These fears are real concerns, and while we know that summer camp can be hard on the parents, is it a good experience for the children?*

I think summer camp is a wonderful experience for children, but it certainly does need some good judgment and planning. Usually camp is good, but there are children who suffer severe attacks of homesickness and have difficulty adjusting to the numbers of children, the scheduled activities, and the new adults that supervise them. In order to find out if your child is really ready for summer camp, here are some questions that may help you: Is your special child *ready to go?* Because all of the other kids of a similar age are going off with excitement does not necessarily mean that your child is ready. Be careful to ask that question honestly, without overprotecting, and yet without pushing your child to go simply because his friends are going. By the age of nine or ten, almost all children can go to camp for a week, and they will really enjoy it. That doesn't mean of course that *every* child is ready even by that age.

Has the child had a previous unpleasant experience in being away from you overnight? Sometimes an overnight visit with a friend has been an unpleasant or frightening experience, and the child may still have some unhealed fear that could make going away for an extended time a very difficult problem.

Does the child fear that you want to get rid of him, or that you will give extra attention to a brother or sister while he or she is away from you? What is the camp's policy regarding phone calls home, or parent visits if the child does become a little homesick? Some camps are very understanding, and others are very strict about not allowing the child to start calling home. What is the camp program? Does it offer some activities that your child really likes and is good at doing? Or does it emphasize areas of life that your child doesn't particularly care about? If you have a lurking fear that this year may not be good for your child, do not hesitate to wait. There's always another year and perhaps next year will be a far better time.

Emotional Development

93. HUGGING YOUR CHILD   *Do children ever outgrow the need for hugging and cuddling from their parents?*

All of us, adults too, need a great deal of hugging and touching, so I really think children never grow out of that. However, they certainly do go through stages of time in which they would make parents believe they do not need that hugging and cuddling. Even in those difficult stages of the establishment of their own identity, children still need a great deal of touching. They simply need it in private, and they need it in different ways. Find the time of day at which children are the most accessible to that kind of stroking and touching. It is usually at bedtime. Make the rounds very privately and personally with each child. Try a variety of brief touches, a back rub, scratching the head; stroking the forehead or a little tickling may be acceptable at different times. Sit by the bedside, talk awhile, try some sort of touch, give them a kiss as you leave.

We need to understand that this seeming rejection is normal, so do not take it as a personal rejection by the child. As you stay patient and understanding, and remain available to your child emotionally, the warmth and the hugs may come and go. But the security remains.

94. PRIVACY   *What guidelines would you offer parents on the subject of children's privacy?*

There are three major factors that I think can help parents understand that need. One is the *age of the child.* The second is *the child's personality,* and the third is the *mood or the circumstance of the moment.*

Prior to the age of six or seven, children rarely need privacy, while parents need a great deal more privacy. So, parents, if you are struggling with this whole issue, try to remember how you felt, and how you needed some time alone when your children were younger.

Up to three or four years of age, a child needs to be always within sight or hearing of an adult. But after six or seven, a child begins to need some time alone—some secrets in order to become an independent individual.

By the age of ten or eleven a child's needs for privacy increase greatly, and during those teenage years, they need a lot of time alone. The personality category is one that really is subdivided into two groups. Some children are extrovertive and need and want very little privacy. The introvertive child enjoys and needs much more time alone, and that should be understood and permitted.

The big problems come not from these two categories but from the moody child who has special problems. They can create anger and hurt and worry on the part of both child and parent. That situation demands a great deal of parental ingenuity and sensitivity. Recognizing and respecting the child's need for time to think through and work through the anger or the hurt of a situation is very important. All children in my experience want to go slamming off to their rooms when they are upset and angry, and literally often bang their doors. I would not intrude on such a child for a little while. Give him time alone. Then go to the room and knock on the door and invite yourself into that child's room. I never knew a child who did not want the parent to come to him when his anger had begun to subside. Gently, courteously, and respectfully, talk with the child about the issue that upset him. Ask him how he feels about it, and help him put into words the problems that have troubled him. Help that child to think about what it is that he or she can do about it. Then ask your child what it is that you might be able to do to help. Don't lecture or scold so much as invite and offer, and you will resolve this question of privacy with your child.

95. SEPARATE BEDROOMS   *When our daughter was very small, my husband and I began letting her sleep with us all through the night. I'm embarrassed to tell you this but our daughter, who is our only child, is now ten years old, and she still insists on sleeping with us. When we refuse, she cries, and says that she is afraid to be alone in her own room. It's hard to say no to her. What can we do?*

That's not an uncommon problem. In fact all children love to share their parents' intimacy. It's understandable that this child wanted to share her parents' bed, but frankly I believe that three in any bed is one too many. No one really sleeps well, and I strongly recommend that it's time for this girl to sleep in her own bedroom. Mother and father need their privacy too, so these are my recommendations: First, parents, decide together that you deserve a happy marriage and that includes the privacy of your own bedroom.

Explain to your child, younger or older, that she will need to do some catching up on her independence, and you on your time with one another. Therefore, she will be sleeping in her own room from now on. Let her help rearrange that room and redecorate it, if possible, making it very much her own. Have her take a doll or a stuffed toy to bed with her, so she will not feel quite so alone, and she will have something to cuddle. One of you may sit with her a few moments after she retires, *but do not give in and go to bed with her*—she will tempt you to do this. If she awakens at night and is a little afraid and comes into your room, simply get up, tuck her back in her own bed, and kindly—but absolutely firmly—let her know that she is now a big girl, and that she must sleep in her own bed. You must outlast her tears and fears, and if you do, I predict that in a few nights she will be sleeping just fine, and so will you.

96.   QUARRELING NEIGHBORS   *We live in an apartment, and a number of times we've been awakened at night by our neighbors who are quarreling loudly. This has really been frightening and disturbing to our small children. How can we explain to them what's happening in a way they'll understand and that will calm their fears?*

Someone has wisely said that we choose our friends, and even our in-laws, but only God can choose our neighbors. And unfortunately God gives us neighbors sometimes who do seem to be an annoyance rather than a blessing. First of all, I would suggest that these parents explain to their children what is going on. Children all have little fights and quarrels of their own, so they can understand that even adults sometimes act like children, and that they too will get into fights and arguments. This could take some of the mystique out of those fights and the noises. It will help the children to identify a little bit more with the situation that is going on.

I do recommend that children get uninterrupted sleep. Perhaps those noises from the neighbors could be muffled by keeping low, soft music going. If that's possible in your apartment or in your home, then I do recommend that. Sometimes disturbances do get out of hand, and you may need to report those to the apartment manager or a neighborhood counsel (if that is available for such referrals). Try making friends with those neighbors, and see what God may want to do for them through your relationship. Perhaps they need the kind of friendship that you could offer them. This could, indeed, be a fine example for your children of how to reach out to those who are having difficulties in a loving, constructive way.

Help your children to learn from the mistakes of your neighbors.

They can see the difference between the angry fighting and yelling of those people and the healthy disagreements that you have established in working out the difficulties and differences in your own family. Knowing how to choose the manner of behaving in times of disagreement is a major lesson for a little child.

Your physical nearness and comfort for your little children at night can reassure them enough to restore their sleep. Take some time, get up from your own bed, and spend a little while talking, comforting, and cuddling your children. I think you will find that they will go back to sleep. By demonstrating the understanding, outreaching love that I have just described, you can not only teach your children to feel secure and confident in their own home, but you can teach them God's love as well.

97. OVERPROTECTION   *How can parents keep themselves from becoming overprotective of their children?*

That's a very good question. Recently I worked with a little girl in a public school. She was in the third grade. She took little, tiny baby steps when she walked. She talked in a babyish tone of voice and used a little child's vocabulary. Though she was very bright, she was unable to fit in with the other children, and was afraid to play in their active games. She was an insecure, unhappy child who cried a great deal. As we explored the reasons for this child's difficulty at school, we found that the mother had really enjoyed her daughter as a baby, and had unwittingly kept her child small, overprotected, and babyish, giving herself a little baby for a long time, but creating in her daughter a serious problem as she grew.

Reasons for overprotectiveness are important in understanding this whole problem. I find that oftentimes overprotective parents are those who either had overprotective parents of their own, or perhaps on the other extreme, they were neglected. In parenting their children too much, they essentially reparent themselves a little bit. It doesn't work too well, but I can understand their trying to do so.

Sometimes serious illness or accidents have hit a family, so that parents overprotect the child in an attempt to prevent such a problem from recurring, or perhaps to relieve some guilt for a past difficulty.

Parents often fear that they are being bad parents, and therefore they overreact to the usual vicissitudes of their child's life. There is a natural desire by a parent to be needed, just as the mother that I've mentioned, and that parent is tempted to keep the child little or dependent too long and too much.

The treatment, once we understand the cause, is not quite so hard as it might seem. The main difficulty of course comes from the parents' desire to keep the child dependent and close. It's so painful to let go of the child that that may be the hardest part of it all. Parents, you need to look at your own habits of growing up. How did you feel with your parents? Did they overprotect you, or neglect you, and how does their attitude toward you now influence your handling of your own child? Set that right, and you will help your child as well as yourself.

98.   CHILDREN'S MEMORY BANK   *My friend, who is studying psychology, says she learned that children store all they see and hear, even if they don't readily understand or use the information. This bothers me mostly because my husband and I have gotten angry and yelled at our daughters. What effect does this have and how can we reconcile these times with them?*

Children do indeed store up all experiences, good and bad. But children especially tend to remember the things that are emotionally charged, and that can be a very happy emotion or, unfortunately, it can be painful. However, being angry and yelling is one of the common characteristics of almost all parents, so I would not want any of you parents to go off on a heavy guilt trip. When your anger is aimed at correcting your children's problems and love really prompts that anger, then it is a healthy thing, and you need not be concerned. When in doubt about how your children feel about their experiences from the past, ask them. Children are very quick to tell you.

Let me give you another bit of reassurance. A picture that is a masterpiece always has contrasts in it. It takes the dark and the light, the bright and the faded colors, to make a picture really beautiful. And in molding the lives of your children, you are creating a masterpiece. It takes sadness, anger, joy, and peace to make those lives balanced and to teach your children the concept of reality. So do not be unduly afraid of what you have done to your children. In talking with your children from time to time, it is very helpful for you to review the past with them. Remind them of some events from their early childhood—times that perhaps they have consciously forgotten. In telling those stories from their past, you will have a wonderful opportunity to interpret to them the reasons for the things that happened. They will know then that it was love that prompted the discipline with all of its pain. They will forgive the pain because of the appreciation for the results.

99.   TEACHING LOVE   *Other than through the parent's basic care and feeding, how does a tiny baby learn about love?*

From the very moment of a child's birth on, that little baby is equipped with the emotions of anger and fear. You can see these feelings displayed whenever hunger or a wet, uncomfortable diaper makes him angry, or when a loud noise frightens him. But as far as I and others have been able to detect, a newborn infant has no concept or feelings of love.

Love is taught from loving parents—parents who love each other, who love themselves, and who love God. The warm exuberance over the presence of a baby is the presence of love. Love is not only caught, however, it is also taught, and the teaching of love is something that is essential for parents to understand. The tender care for the needs of a tiny baby or an ornery older child are equally important in keeping love alive in the life of that child. Love is taught by using a gentle, loving tone of voice rather than a harsh, angry, yelling voice. Love is also taught by saying loving and positive words to a child, encouraging that child, rather than scolding, lecturing, or putting down, even in the best-meant intentions of teaching the child. By the gentle touch and the close holding of a child, a tiny baby can learn to feel physically loved.

100.   CAUSE OF NIGHTMARES   *My grandson, age four and a half, has nightmares, and I'm concerned about him. He also cries often but not as much as he once did.*

Children's nightmares certainly are annoying, not only to the child, but to the parents as well. I find that when parents do not get their sleep and the children don't either, the fatigue factor causes a great deal of stress within the family. Actually, nightmares themselves are caused by too much stress in most cases. Sometimes that's because expectations are too high. I find that many times children in school, who are struggling for grades that are truly beyond their potential, have nightmares. Punishment that is too severe, or consequences that are administered with too much anger, can cause problems in a child's life that may come out through bad dreams.

We need not overlook illness, and certain physical causes as well, for the disturbances that are manifested in nightmares. I find that children who have difficulty breathing because of nasal allergies or asthma many times have sleep disturbances. Inconsistencies in the parents' (or teacher's, for that matter) handling of the child can create anxiety and nervousness, and the child dreams those out in nightmares.

At the other end of the spectrum of a child's life, sometimes too much freedom can cause anxiety. Many preschoolers have a great deal of freedom to roam geographically about the neighborhood, as well as too much emotional freedom, and too little closeness within the family constellation. We need to learn a little, I think, from baby animals. They like to cuddle and cluster together at times for security, and they rarely roam very freely or very far from their parents until they are nearly mature. Balancing your child's freedom and supervision is important.

Children need to have a great deal of cuddling and physical closeness, as well as emotional intimacy and warmth, if they are to be secure enough so that they won't have nightmares. Frightening experiences that children see or hear about often cause nightmares. Television programs or news articles, which are discussed around the table at dinner, can register in a little child's mind in a very frightening fashion.

Now dreams do help children to get rid of some of their fears, but they can become a vicious cycle in which the dreams begin terrifying the child. I have seen children dreading going to bed at night for fear of their recurrent nightmares.

The cure for nightmares really is fairly simple, once you understand the causes. Simply decrease the stress in your child's life. Give him that fine balance between freedom and expectations, and less severity in the discipline that you must provide. Spend more time with the child, particularly in the evening, reading stories, cuddling, playing happy games, and thus allow your child to go to bed, feeling confident, warm, and secure. I recommend leaving a night-light on; eliminate any frightening things from the room, such as pictures or shadows that might look scary at night. Surrounding your child with this kind of protection will not spoil him. It will offer him the security he needs to grow up happily.

101.   CHILDHOOD GRIEF   *My husband and I have two sons, three and a half years and eighteen months. We recently had a baby who was stillborn. Our oldest son was truly excited about the new baby. He had felt the baby's movements and heard the heartbeat while in the womb. The loss of the baby had many bad effects on him. He has begun wetting his pants, not sleeping or eating well, and his behavior is unpredictable and rebellious. We have explained to our son that the baby is in heaven, and will not be coming to our house to live. Our sons didn't ever see the baby or attend the memorial services. We believe many people would benefit from a discussion of*

whether children should be allowed to view a deceased loved one's body or attend the funeral services. These were hard decisions for us to make.

They certainly are hard decisions, and death is the ultimate loss with all of the helplessness and sadness it causes in the survivors. It's very difficult for adults to deal with death and certainly even more difficult for children. The stages of grief are important to review briefly: First, there is denial that it has actually happened, then a sense of loss, anger over that loss, and finally, preoccupation with the sadness, pain, fear, and guilt, that go along with all grief. Eventually, however, healing does come!

This child probably has experienced fear as well—fear of the adults' grief and his own pain; fear that possibly this death is a punishment for some of his naughtiness; fear that he himself might die if another little child could die. A child certainly is going to feel angry, and this anger covers and acts as a protection for his pain and fear. His rebellious behavior is simply acting out the anger he feels. These steps are those recommended in helping a little child deal with grief:

First of all, *use a great deal of verbal interpretation and explanation about the death.* Help the child understand that it is not his fault. You don't have to defend God, and try to make the death look okay, either, because at this time the child is not going to believe that or feel it. Later on, of course, he can, but not in the acute stages of grief. Be honest about not having all of the answers to the child's feelings, or even your own at this time. Reassure your child of your love and acceptance, even of his regressive and unpleasant behaviors. Baby him a great deal, and give him the comfort of your physical presence frequently. Encourage him to talk or cry out his fear and anger and guilt in words, if possible, or on a pounding board or in tears. Cry with him, if you feel like it, and comfort him. Usually I recommend that children attend the funeral home and view the casket or even the body. The ceremony of a funeral is one way of expressing the grief. Being there to see the person who has died, and knowing where the body is, somehow helps us all to complete that grief process in a more concrete and tangible way. Grief and loss are a fact of life. You and your child can and must learn to cope with and transcend it together.

102. LEAVING CHILD IN NURSERY *How do you leave a child in a church nursery? We've tried and unfortunately we've already done everything wrong. First of all, we kept our daughter out*

of the nursery until she was about a year and a half because she al-
ways cried there. Then when we did decide to leave her, we made the
mistake of getting her interested in some toys and sneaking out. She
really threw a fit, when she realized we were gone. Now it's really a
problem. My husband and I wish we could sit together through a
church service and not feel guilty about our daughter, screaming for
us in the nursery. She is now two years old.

That's a common problem, and I spent a number of months working in my own church's nursery, so I understand the other side of that difficulty as well. I do have a plan that I have found works a great many times, and would like to suggest it to this couple and any other parents. You will need to plan to miss the church service for a couple of weeks. You may alternate that between you, as mother and father, but this is what I suggest that you do. (With variations, this works in a nursery or any other child-care facility.)

First of all, explain to your two-year-old, who will understand a good deal more than you might think, that you are not going to feel sorry for her when she stays in the nursery; that you know it will be good for her to learn to play with other children, and to give you the freedom to attend the church service without her being there, being bored and nervous, sitting still for so long in church. Whatever your explanation, make it very clear and be sure that she understands what you are saying.

On the other hand, let her know that you certainly understand her fear of the strangeness, the fact that she will miss you, and that she wants to be with you. Now, when you go to church with her the next time (after you have given this ceremonious explanation to your child), take her with you to the sanctuary. Let her see where you will be sitting, and then walk with her from the sanctuary to the nursery. Knowing the exact route will give her a little more security.

When you place her in the nursery, leave her for as short a time as two minutes. Leave her, telling her that you will be back in a very short time, perhaps only a minute. Do return to her, so that she knows you will follow through, and that you will be back. The next time you leave, make it five minutes, and gradually increase the time that you are away. Always consistently returning to her will help her to know that she is not abandoned, that you *will* be back, and that you are reliable parents.

You will, of course, need to have the nursery supervisors aware of your plan so they can cooperate with you. I suspect they will be more than glad to have such a plan working, rather than to have a screaming child for an hour every Sunday. The following week, I recommend that again you go through this leaving and returning process. Within three or four Sundays, I can almost guarantee you will find that your child will be staying in the nursery happily playing away, and you may attend church with absolute peace of mind.

103. PARENT-CHILD DIFFERENCES *What kinds of family problems grow out of personality differences between a parent and child?*

A great many problems can develop. A pediatrician in New York City, a number of decades ago, began studying children and parents from birth. She followed as many as possible for a number of years, and her discoveries are worth thinking about. She found, for example, that a mother who was placid and loved peace and quiet, when she had a child who was energetic and into everything, developed a problem with that child from birth. Resentments began to grow between them that became lifelong and serious in their impact. On the contrary, a mother who was energetic and active might have a child who was very peaceful, quiet, and introverted. She could become very impatient and troubled about such a child, and again, set the stage for discrepancies and resentments that created disharmony in those families.

I find many a time that a mother loves to cuddle babies, and yet some babies simply don't like to be cuddled. They squirm or stiffen and simply will not relax and settle into the mother's arms. That again can cause resentment, and a mother's fear that somehow there is something wrong with her as the mother; or that the baby doesn't love her and unconsciously, from birth, there can come to be animosity and power struggles that set up serious problems later on. Family troubles oftentimes come from the fact that a little baby resembles some relative that has not been exactly desirable.

Here are some simple rules for living in harmony as a family: *Define your unpleasant feelings toward your child.* Who does he look like, or what is it that he does that creates problems for you? Make peace with that person, and reconcile those traits as a gift of God to your special child. Then learn to accept and love him *as he is.* Unconditionally, give that child the attention and the love that he needs. As you affirm your child, praise him, build up some hope for his worth and success. You will see that child bloom, and you and your child will grow together.

104.   ACCEPTING V. EXPECTING   *Isn't it a good thing for parents to have dreams and ambitions for their children?*

Whether consciously or unconsciously, most of us as parents have dreams for our children. Some of these hopes and dreams are for opportunities we ourselves missed when we were growing up. Or sometimes we want our children to relive exciting and happy times we did experience in the past. But whatever the source of those dreams, we need to be careful that they do not become an unbearable burden for our children, because serious problems can result. But to answer your question, yes, indeed, it's great—*if* those dreams are general enough to fit any and all children and reachable enough to prevent disappointments and failures. There are problems, however, with many parents' dreams.

I have known fathers who wanted a boy who'd become a great, muscular football player, and they had a little boy who would have been crushed on any football field. Parents want a girl who will be a cheerleader or the Homecoming Queen. Unfortunately, the daughter they are given will never quite measure up. The degree of the parents' adaptability to a different and possible dream can eliminate the disappointment of the impossible one.

There are good dreams, however, which parents can devise, and which any child can fit. The first one of these is the dream that a child have certain gifts. *Every child has those,* and the parents' dream of helping the child discover those unique, individual abilities and talents, and then valuing the ones the child is given. That is a dream that every parent should have.

105.   SECURITY BLANKET   *I have a question about my seven-month-old son. When he was three months old, someone gave me a very soft blanket, made out of a silky-type material, and he really likes it. In fact, he likes it so much that he absolutely will not go to sleep without it, and it has to be over his head. Is this normal, or should I try to get him to not be so attached to this blanket? It scares me to think of losing that blanket or having something happen to it, because he just would not sleep until I got another one. Should I do something to discourage his attachment to this one certain blanket?*

Actually this baby is in a large group of children, because most children become attached to some form of security blanket. Children need object constancy, and that means that they need something that is going to be consistently and absolutely the same, day after day after day. It is the sameness that seems to offer such children the security or sense of safety that they need. In fact, that's how the name came about: *security blanket.* Children are strange little bundles of receptor nerves. They pick up all kinds of impulses from the environment about them. They are highly sensitive to anything that acts upon those nerve endings, and touch is especially important in tiny babies. Smell, sight, and hearing, of course, are important as well. As children grow and become interested in their external world, they lose interest in the attachments that they have formed with objects and their own bodies, such as thumbs, security blankets, or teddy bears. Tucking those things away too soon, worrying about them excessively, simply creates insecurity that is often expressed through whining, crying, or nervous habits.

I strongly recommend that this child be allowed to have that blanket. I would even recommend that you take good care of it, so that it will last long enough to go through the stage in which he does need it! Eventually, of course, you will wean him from it. You will need to take it away from him to wash it now and then, because with the hard wear they get, security blankets do become very soiled. I would suggest that you substitute other soft or silky items for the particular blanket that the child likes. Have him take something else along to bed, so that he won't have just one item to become attached to. Since this child is only seven months old, he will have quite a period of time to use that particular item. I wonder if this mother might not want to purchase another blanket very similar, because he will become troubled (and needlessly so) if he doesn't have something that meets that need.

Someday, shred by shred, that blanket will wear away. If your child is twelve to eighteen months or older, I would let that happen. Substitute your presence for the blanket. Your cuddling and stroking of the child will get him through that loss with a minimum of grief. Both he and you will survive the loss of that security blanket when that must happen.

106. DIVORCE NIGHTMARES   *In a family where I baby-sit there was recently a divorce. There are two children, a two-year-old and a four-year-old, but I'm writing mostly about the older boy. He has constant nightmares about his mother. She was abusive and beat him when he was younger. Now she has visiting rights for an hour a month, but the four-year-old does not want to see her. He even has kicking and screaming fits when he goes. Their father wants them to* *know and love their mother, but for a week after the visits, they are hard to control. The father is open to suggestions about how to handle this, especially the nightmares. I'd like to know what advice, if any, I could pass on to him or what I can do when I'm caring for the boys.*

That is a very difficult question, and with the prevalence of child abuse today certainly a great many families must cope with this kind of situation. Children must have protection and reassurance, and this child particularly needs to know that his mother will never hurt him again. It might help this child if he were shown on a watch or a clock just how long an hour is. If he knows when the time is up and that he'll get to leave at that time, he is likely to feel a little more secure and less frightened.

I would recommend that this child's father teach him about his mother. If he knows, he could tell that son stories about the mom's childhood and how she grew up. Now I don't recommend giving any tragic details if she was an abused child, but enough stories to help your child see her as a person who also could feel as he does. It might be a wise thing to give the child a wild flower or a small gift to take when he has a visit with her, and help him feel good that he can give something to the mother. Now she may not act excited over it, but giving her something can help him feel a little happier, perhaps a little more powerful, and less frightened of her. The father and the baby-sitter need to allow and invite the child to talk out his fears, past, present and future. Verbalizing his anger, as well as his fears, can help to relieve the pressure and the tension within him, and enable him to get over the tragedy of his past.

This child is perhaps fortunate to be having nightmares, because we believe that through dreams and nightmares some of our fears are released. I would certainly recommend that the father or the baby-sitter take this child into their arms when he awakens at night. Comfort him, awaken him if possible, and get him to talk about what he has been dreaming of. Reassure him before putting him back to bed, and then at a later time again talk about the contents of the dream, reassuring him that he will not have to worry about those fears anymore. Comfort and reassurance, encouragement and love—these are the qualities that will heal the hurts of this child's life.

107. STOP WORRYING

My kids have been on their own for quite a while, and I know they can take care of themselves, but I can't seem to stop worrying about them. Is there something wrong with me?

Once a parent, always a parent. That's the way it is, isn't it? There's nothing seriously wrong with you. But perhaps you do have a lack of trust. Most worry is based on a failure to have a very solid trust in several special areas. In this case, those areas are these: You *must* trust your own good parenting. You do that somewhat because you say that your children have been on their own for a while, and you know they can take care of themselves. That indicates that you have been a good mother. You also need to trust in the children's basic good sense and responsibility; that they can take care of themselves is certainly evident. And perhaps most important of all is your need to trust in God's power and His individual care for those children.

Now stopping worry is not so easy, because it means that you must break a habit of a lifetime. These are some steps I would like to recommend that I think can help you break this habit. First of all, become aware of your worry, and that it is based on the failure to trust. Work hard to develop that trust in yourself, in your children, and in God. Separate the healthy concern that all parents feel at times for their children from the vicious cycle of destructive worry. *Be available to your children for help and advice but don't feel compelled to take charge of their lives or to tell them what to do.* Break the worry habit by these further simple steps:

1. Define the cause of your concern in its very simplest terms.
2. Determine what you can and should do about those concerns, if any.
3. Avoid doing anything for anyone else that will be healthy and maturing for that person to do for himself.
4. Do only what you decide wisely to do, and then only when your child asks. It's all right to offer help and advice, but certainly do not push that help upon the child, but rather wait for him to come and ask you for advice or help.

Give your child and all of his affairs over to the Heavenly Father. Visualize this giving over to Him and then leave that bundle with Him. Fill the void in your life that your children have created by their leaving home with volunteering and helping someone else, going back to school, or getting into some creative hobbies. You can *love* your children without worrying about them!

Entertainment

108. BABY-SITTERS   *Do you see any problem with hiring the high school girl next door to take over, when Mom or Dad take a night off?*

Unfortunately I have to answer that I do see a problem there, because recently newspapers have had large headlines about a young woman who is suspected of actually killing some children for whom she baby-sat. There are some actions that baby-sitters take short of killing a child that can also be damaging, and you, as parents, would not want that to happen to your children.

Many times the attitude of the sitter is so careless and indifferent that your children feel afraid and unattended to. The sitter may use her time to entertain her friends, either by telephone or in person. I have known sitters to have their friends come by and spend the evening, ignoring the children for whom they are responsible during that time. They may tease or abuse children, and it is not uncommon that little children have been sexually molested by baby-sitters in their own homes. Sometimes baby-sitters become hysterical, and do not handle a crisis very responsibly should it arise.

Be sure to screen your baby-sitters carefully before hiring them. Here are some criteria by which you might judge a good, reliable sitter, and you are blessed, indeed, if you can find such a person. They need to be *mature enough to have good judgment and self-control in times of crisis. They should never slap or yell at a child, or hurt him,* even when the child may need some controlling and discipline. (By the way, you must give your baby-sitter clear guidelines about the kinds of discipline that you use, and that you would want them to use in case that it is needed). The baby-sitter needs *to have judgment enough to know when to call you, as parents, and what she can handle in case she cannot reach you. The basic love of children, the ability to be kind and firm and protective* are qualities that I would look for in a baby-sitter. I'd like to have a baby-sitter who is energetic and strong enough not only to provide care, but to play with my child and to enjoy some fun together during the time they spend.

How can you know what baby-sitters are like? I recommend that you request references, and that you call those references and talk with them personally. I suggest you have a sitter spend some time with your child while you are there, and observe carefully the interactions that go on between them. When your child is old enough, ask him how the evening went after the sitter is gone. Observe carefully the condition of the house, the sitter, and the child when you return. If you have serious questions, come back unexpectedly, and pop in on that sitter during the course of an evening out. It may well be an inconvenience, but it may serve a good purpose in helping you to know whether you can entrust your special child to this person.

109. EVENING OUT *We have a four-year-old and a new baby. When we go out to a friend's house, or to a restaurant in the evening, is it better for them to stay at home with a baby-sitter or go with us? We don't mind taking them along, but wonder if it's too hard on them to go places where they can't talk or play as freely as at home.*

That is a good question and frankly I deplore the practice of always leaving children at home while the parents are away from them. On the other hand, I know the need of young parents to be free of the responsibilities of young children for bits of time through the week. So here are some practical suggestions:

It seems to me that one of the most important things I can tell young parents is to train your children, so they will behave nicely, and then you can take them along with you and enjoy them as well as having your friends enjoy them. Parents might plan some social life at home with their friends, in order to train those children. Sometimes this is a real strain on mothers who must prepare a company meal, but when fathers help, it can become a very delightful family evening.

Parents also need to take children out to family-style restaurants or quick-food places now and then, in order to teach children how to behave properly in a social setting. Many family restaurants provide entertainment and special menus for children. If you will select your restaurant carefully, you will find this an asset in teaching social skills to your children.

I question, however, if brand-new babies should be taken out very much. If they sleep well in an infant seat and are very calm babies, perhaps you can get by with taking them out for short periods of time. If you take a child to a friend's home, where it can be put to bed, then I see no harm in taking even a new baby out for an evening with those friends.

The question I think you as parents must answer in considering taking your children out is whether or not they are controllable so that you can *enjoy* your evening out with your friends; the children are not bored or exhausted; and other people in a restaurant are not irritated.

One of the suggestions that I would like to make for you parents is that you might trade off baby-sitting now and then, so the cost doesn't become prohibitive. Several couples who are friends can relieve one another and give some special time out. Of course, as a grandmother, I know that I love to keep my grandchild when my daughter goes out!

110.   TELEVISION   *Watching television is the kind of entertainment that many good parents believe ought to be eliminated from their homes. And yet nearly every family has one, if not two or three, TV sets that are on for a good portion of the day and night. Since television has become such an established part of our homes, do you think it's even possible for parents to turn it to an advantage?*

Yes, and studies have indicated how we might go about doing that. We know, for example, that with children who are a little bit slow to talk, parents can spend time in watching a child's program, and use the words and the objects in that program to teach language to the infants. They can teach children colors and many other facts by sitting and talking with them about the content of a given program. As children grow older, it is possible for parents to teach children from television the contrasting values of the world in which we live. While television may influence our society, yet it also does teach the values of the society in which we spend our time growing up!

What is wrong with violence, cheating, promiscuous living, and all of the many varied values that television teaches, both good and bad? By watching programs with your older children then, you can help them to understand what is good and bad about the program itself, but even more important, about the world that it depicts. You can use television to teach empathy and compassion to your children. For example, in a given program you might ask your child, "How would you feel if you were that person?" or, "What would you have done if you were in a situation like that person in the play?" Drawing the family together and offering a forum for discussions of all sorts is offered by television itself.

Television brings another opportunity to parents that I think is often overlooked. You can use TV to teach sharing to your children. I recommend that families not have more than one television set for this very purpose. Your children can learn to take turns choosing the programs they want to watch. All kinds of creative devices have been used by parents in teaching this concept of sharing and taking turns. Guidance regarding how to choose a program, and what makes it really worth watching, is another opportunity that you have with TV.

I find many families do not realize the need to teach respect for parents. Fathers sometimes come home from work, wanting very much to sit and relax and watch the news, but the children are greedily grabbing the television for their own interests. Parents, don't be afraid to teach your children to give you a turn at watching the news for a bit of time. You need not do that gruffly or rudely. You may model the very respect you want them to learn in the way that you do that. Do be creative as you evaluate your television set, and decide how you can turn it into a positive influence in your home.

111. CARTOON VIOLENCE   *Do you know the effects of violence in cartoons on young children? My husband and I have four children ranging in age from two to nine. If you could give me some insight into this subject, I would appreciate it very much.*

We in the mental health profession certainly are concerned about the effect of television violence on children. For many years, studies have indicated that violence *does* influence young children. One group of school-agers in California were studied a number of years ago after watching violent scenes, and then they were observed as they played afterward. The children who had watched the violence had a great deal more intensely violent situations between themselves than children who had not watched such scenes. Recently we have learned that even cartoons can have this sort of effect on children.

Furthermore, I am concerned about the effect on children who see the cartoon rabbit being squashed, and apparently dead, and then suddenly being revived and running about quite as usual. I worry that this may teach children that death is not final and injury is not real. That is a very bad concept, because it simply is not true.

Prior to the age of seven or eight, I think parents must monitor television programs. At this early age, children do not have the capacity to determine right from wrong very adequately, and they simply do not understand what is good or bad about the cartoons they watch. As you watch television with your child, forbid those violent, destructive programs. Now your children will survive without a great deal of television, and there almost always are a few good programs that you can permit. Even with those, I suggest that you watch with your children, reinforcing the positive ideas and views, and helping them to understand any questionable views or ideals that are contrary to your own.

If you are appalled (as I often am) at the kinds of programs that go on the air, write to your local stations expressing your views and clearly defining what you see as harmful in that program. Perhaps even more effective is a letter to the advertiser who sponsors that program. Tell them that you and your friends simply will not purchase their products, until they begin promoting more healthful and less violent programs for children to see.

112.   VIDEO GAMES   *Do you think it's possible that playing video games is harmful to children?*

I do think it can be harmful to some children, and recently the Surgeon General of our country, Dr. C. Everett Koop, has come out with some very interesting and very definite statements against video games. I do generally discourage video games, but on the other hand there are some assets that need to be discussed as well.

First of all, if you have your own video games, they can draw your family together around a fun occupation or activity. They can attract children to your home, so that you will know who your child's friends are, and how they interact.

In discussing this issue, however, let's review the arcades, where children go in droves to play these games. Such arcades are very often undesirable places. A great many drugs are exchanged in public game rooms. There is certainly a dubious atmosphere at best. Alcohol is common, and tobacco smoke is so heavy that one's eyes burn.

I feel concerned about the money that children spend in such occupations in the public arcades. There seems to be a compulsive need to play just one more game, with an almost excessive sense of excitement or tension that accompanies such activity. There is an undue competitiveness that is a part of many of these games. Some people argue that this is good, as it allows children to play out their aggression so they do not take it out on their brothers, sisters, or playmates. Perhaps there is some truth in that, but in many children, such activity may stimulate more aggression on the outside of the arcade.

Now let's discuss such games at home. When you parents are there to regulate your child's time and the type of game that is played, I wouldn't worry nearly as much as I would if your child were spending a lot of time in a community arcade. Even at home, however, a game can isolate family members, causing an unhealthy withdrawal. If you do get video games, select those that develop skill and coordination without violence. Limit the time spent on games, alternating them with more wholesome outdoor activities. Watch your children for any ill effects, and if you find them there, don't hesitate to weed out the video games that might be a part of the cause of those problems. Frankly, I trust the current fad will soon pass, so young people may do something more constructive!

113. ROCK CONCERTS   *You have a lot of contact with teenagers in your work. Could you say just a little about rock concerts and rock music in general?*

That's a very important issue today, and many parents are deeply concerned about rock music. In attending a seminar on the effects of drugs on young people, an important part of that seminar had to do with the music that our teenagers are listening to, because a great deal of the rock music does have to do with the drug culture. It promotes the highs of all sorts of drugs and many other kinds of misbehavior as well. So rock music certainly does have some points against it.

On the other hand, there is some very fine gospel music that is written to the rhythm of the rock beat, and that certainly does not have any bad words. In fact, this may be a bridge for many young people who have been into some very negative, destructive music into a much more wholesome approach, musically speaking.

There are some bases on which parents can help to make good decisions of all sorts, and certainly these decisions are important, when it comes to the kind of music your teenager should hear—even whether or not they should attend a rock concert.

First of all, you need to have complete information about the group that your young people want to hear. Some of them are definitely adverse. But there are some other groups that are not so bad, and at least do not promote drugs through their music. Be careful that you do have accurate information before you decide to be so rigid that you make your young people rebel.

Another helpful suggestion in decision making with your teenager is that you use the element of thoughtfulness, rather than emotions. Now young people are very emotional, and parents are too, but when those emotions clash, decision making does not come out very well. So be careful that you keep your feelings in control, and keep your decision thoughtful. It will be much wiser and more beneficial.

The third point is that any decision needs to be made on the basis of what is right for you and for your child. Not *who* is right, but *what* is right, is important.

The fourth suggestion is that as much as possible, you keep decision making with your teenager a democratic process, so that as little as possible you become the tyrant or the dictator. Now, if the teenager simply cannot come around in this democratic way to a healthy decision, then you will, of course, have to exercise your parental authority. Go with your teenager to a rock concert of the very best sort that you can find, and with the best wisdom that you have, help them analyze the effects. Then make a decision about the rock music that may be harmless, rather than destructive.

114. GRANDMA'S QUESTION *I am a grandmother and enjoy your books. I wish I had someone as sensible as you to talk to when my own children were growing up. I've been wanting to speak with my daughter about something, and if I handle it right, she won't consider it interfering. Each time her own teenage daughter, who is fourteen, wants to watch something on television that isn't too good or see a movie rated PG that has one or two bad words in it, they always get into a quarrel. I believe in taking a stand, but I wonder if she doesn't overdo it, as she sort of preaches at her angrily every time this comes up. How do you think she could handle this situation better?*

At this time in that child's life, she needs her mother to be much more a friend than the kind of authoritative parent she needed to be when the child was younger. By discussing issues in a less emotional and more intellectual fashion—really very much as one would talk together as mother and father or with adult friends—the mother will be able to help the girl express her ideas much more openly. This daughter at fourteen is approaching adulthood and needs to be taught how to think for herself, and how to determine what makes something right or wrong, good or bad.

Approval and disapproval of issues are really mental functions, and yet

I find that a great many parents confuse emotions with intellect. This is one area of life when you *must,* to be successful, separate those two parts of your personality. Think carefully and clearly with your children. Help them to understand the powerful influence of negative concepts, morals, and values in movies or television programs, so they will learn to make wise choices on their own.

Family

115. HOME ENVIRONMENT   *If you were to describe the perfect home environment for children to best grow and develop, what factors would be most important?*

There are many, many of these factors. One of the most secure things in my childhood was knowing *the extended family.* My grandmother lived with us until I was a senior in high school, when she quietly passed away. Her presence was a very influential factor in my life. The uncles, aunts, and cousins that surrounded us were very comforting in times of illness or distress. Help your child to know the extended family, and in today's mobile society, that is not easy. It demands special planning, the expense of telephone calls, and the time and trouble of writing letters. But give to your children that sense of the generations, and the extended family that will help him and her to feel the security of belonging to a clan.

The safety of two parents who respect and love each other securely is another major security-producing factor in children's lives. Parents, be sure that you communicate soundly and well, and that you keep the respect for one another obvious to your children, as well as to one another.

Giving unconditional, loving acceptance to each child for exactly who he or she is, is another essential to a secure family life.

Effective communication is equally important, because love is ever so wonderful, but it is not very helpful unless it is communicated clearly, consistently, and honestly.

Approval and disapproval must be communicated as well in a positive fashion, so *support, encouragement,* and *cooperation* become another essential in good family living.

Correction and *discipline* are essential for children to grow in their self-awareness, in interacting successfully with other people, and in learning a sense of compassion for others.

Providing a congenial atmosphere, where laughter of a wholesome sort is common, is very wonderful within families. Be careful, however, that that laughter does not become ridicule at someone's mistakes.

Show hospitality to the friends of your children, as well as friends for yourselves.

Make of that home that you provide for your children a springboard for their becoming healthy adults and a place for returning, when they need a shelter as they grow older.

116. COMPARISONS   *Our twelve-year-old has a problem with low self-esteem. I think it's due to his older brother and sister, who have achieved and do well in school. When this son was younger, he showed so much affection and an outgoing nature. But after observing his older brother and sister, and hearing about their good grades and achievements, he's developed an attitude that he can't measure up. His feelings of frustration are vented in a great deal of anger, and this has made me quite concerned.*

This mother has a beautifully perceptive attitude. Mother, I would recommend that you use your perceptiveness to interpret to your son, in a time of quietness and confidence, how you understand him, and that you can accept his frustrations. So many times children themselves do not know why they are frustrated and angry, and having someone explain it to them, reflect it to them in another way than they might even think about it themselves, can give them relief. A feeling of being understood and cared about is very comforting. Help your child to know that he can get over these painful feelings, even as he can get over his anger. And I would suggest that you teach your child that it is painful feelings that oftentimes prompt angry feelings. Remind your son of the qualities you so much liked earlier on in his life, and reassure him that by working together, you and he can get those back. Find the abilities and interests your son has that his seemingly more gifted older brother and sister do not have. Let him know when you are proud of him, even for small things, day by day. Help him see that in God's sight, his assets, whatever they are, are just as important as those of his brother and sister.

Now I would offer another practical insight, and that is that at twelve years of age, this boy is developing into a man. Some of his anger and frustration may have to do with those physical changes that are so important and so difficult for many young people to understand. Explain some of those changes and reassure him that these times will pass, and that his frustration and irritability will subside later on. Enjoy your son, and be careful to give him the praise that he needs. I believe that if you will follow these suggestions, slowly but surely he will come to feel better about himself, and you will have back that wonderful child that you enjoyed.

117. ONLY CHILD   *What effect does it have on a child (thinking particularly now of his personal growth and development), when he's an only child? And second, how can parents compensate for the fact that their child has no brothers or sisters?*

An only child can become rather selfish. He can expect, even more than the average child with several brothers and sisters, that the whole world is going to revolve about him and his needs and wishes. And yet there are many ways parents can compensate for that.

Some of the advantages of siblings can be described, and then parents can take these advantages and work them out through the use of friends. Certainly one of the wonderful things I enjoyed with my brothers and sisters was the fact that we had built-in playmates and friends. Working, arguing, and playing together were fine experiences of my childhood. Certainly friends can be imported to play that role with an only child.

There is a great deal of motivation through competition, and my family and I still love to compete in games and in arguments or discussions about ideas. This is a healthy sort of competition, and that, too, is a very important part of a brother and sister role in a family relationship. However, friends can fulfill some of that role with an only child. There is a security about family that's supportive and fun and intimate throughout the years. My brothers, sisters, and I still enjoy a great deal of mutual support and fun when we get together. You might perhaps seek cousins or near relatives to fulfill this particular role in the life of an only child. Learning to share, to take turns, to give and take, and be considerate, are qualities of life that brothers and sisters can teach one another.

Now there also are some disadvantages to having brothers and sisters, and these become the advantages of an only child. Sometimes brothers or sisters create a situation of partiality or unfair rivalry and competition in which one is too often the winner and the other too commonly a loser. Sometimes the division of the parents' time and attention becomes unfair or unequal, and an only child never has to worry about that particular problem. In a large family children sometimes have to share too much and may lose some of their own identity. The loss of opportunities for special lessons or advantages can be a major loss, when there are so many children that the family cannot afford many of those special privileges. How parents might compensate for the lack of brothers and sisters, then, depends upon the parents' creativity. They themselves can serve double roles, making the child share with them and taking turns with them. Teach your child a sense of duty, respect, and responsibility to others.

And whether you have an only child or several children, you can give to that child the advantages that are truly important to him.

118. GOOD GRANDMOTHER *How much time is too much for a child to spend visiting with a good grandmother? She would love to have her grandchild with her every day, if she could. In other words, how often should a child be around a grandparent?*

That's a difficult question to answer directly so I would like to answer indirectly. Let me give some thoughts to parents who are considering this very important question. First of all, oftentimes getting the grandparent and the child together may be inconvenient. Another important fact is the influence of the grandparent on the child. Is that grandmother, for example, going to support the parents' values and disciplines? Or is she likely to give in to the child and oppose what the parents are teaching? The child's attitude about visits, and the child's behavior afterward can give parents a clue as to whether or not the visits are really in his good interests. Does the issue of the time cause power struggles between parents and grandparents? Or parents and child? Such bad feelings and struggles may help you to decide very quickly what is right or not so good about those visits.

What are you to do then about relationships between your child and the grandparent? Think about the values in the relationship: the loving support that grandparents can give, the sharing of wisdom and the experience of years; fun times that parents don't always have time for. These are the benefits of grandparents. Consider also your own family values. You must have time for one another as parents and children, developing intimacy and bonding together as a family; forming your own traditions and customs. You must have time for that together. You may also want to ask your child his feelings about spending time with grandmother. While he can't have the final say about this yet, how he feels can be helpful in guiding you in your decision. Above all else, avoid bad feelings and power struggles. Those can catch your child in a vise that can damage him for life. There is never too much love. So find a way to enjoy and love one another, even among three generations.

119. FAMILY NUDITY *Do you think there is any harm in having my two-year-old daughter and her seven-year-old brother take*

their baths together? And what about letting them in the room, when their dad or I are dressing or bathing?

Parents need to keep an emphasis on the naturalness of young children's bathing together. If you, as a parent, have a morbid curiosity or an unwholesome attitude sexually, then I would recommend that you not allow this with your young children, because they will sense your discomfort. Above all else, children need to avoid that sense of shame or embarrassment about their sexuality, which is a wonderful gift of God to them.

As a parent, you do need to be present with children who bathe together, in order to prevent an unwholesome preoccupation with the sexual parts of their bodies. If they ask questions about the differences between their bodies, calmly explain those to them. Help them to keep their bath times short enough, playful enough, and also focused on toys, or just the splashing of water, so they do not become unwholesomely preoccupied. *Do be alert for your child's request for privacy.*

Now the question of whether or not parents should bathe with their children is a very common one. I find many fine parents who have bathed consistently and been around the house without many clothes on with their children. This has had no untoward effects whatsoever. On the other hand, many other parents have found the child standing back in awe, wonder, and confusion, and really somewhat disturbed by their nudity. Parents, I hope you will be aware of your own child's expressions. Watch the face and see if that child is a little bit in awe of the size of your body, particularly your genital areas. That can be very stimulating and frightening to a little child. If the child does not like that, then I suggest that you practice privacy.

120. PARENT'S FIRST NAME   *What should a parent do when their child calls the parent by the first name? My little boy is two and a half, and of course he has picked my name up from others. He calls me that, not continually though, and he laughs about it. I've been laughing about it too, and just replying, "Mommy." How do you think I should respond?*

I think this mother has responded wisely, but she reminds me that it is important what a child calls the parent.

There are some significant facts about the names with which children address parents, which I'd like to discuss briefly. What a name most conveys is the special relationship between you and your child. What name, to you as mother or father, especially says that *I love you* and *I am very, very close to you*? That unique bond between you and your child is the one that you need to think about, in deciding what your child should call you.

121. FAMILY LOOK-ALIKES   *What kind of problems can grow out of a child's resemblance to someone else in the family?*

It's a strange fact, but true, nevertheless, that there are many such problems. I am currently working with a family, in fact, in which that is the case. The mother in this family has found from the moment her little girl was born, that daughter reminded her of her mother. Unfortunately, she and her mother did not get along very well, and unconsciously she laid on this tiny little baby many of the negative qualities that she had experienced from her own mom.

You need to be careful then, parents, that in looking at your newborn baby, and seeing Grandfather's ears or Mother's nose, you remember that even though the child has some of the physical genes and chromosomes in common with those relatives, you can know the child is a separate individual.

Be careful that you love and accept your child individually for who he is, for what she looks like, and separate this child very consciously and consistently from those other people.

122. EFFECT OF DIVORCE ON CHILD   *My youngest son, age twelve, was only four when his dad and I divorced. I've never remarried, so I've had to be both mother and dad at certain times. He doesn't seem to want to do anything but watch TV or play sports. I have a time getting him to study, or even pick up his clothes. Sometimes I get so disgusted I could scream, and I usually just give up. It is so discouraging. Do you have any suggestions?*

Either directly or indirectly divorce now affects the majority of American homes, and I personally know of very few families in which some close relative has not suffered a divorce. This mother's question could be duplicated many, many times over. There are many feelings involved in every divorce. Grief over the loss, anger over the rejection, all kinds of very intense, negative, and destructive emotions are a part of divorce.

Children are especially vulnerable to those feelings. They rarely get those feelings worked out, because they don't know how to talk about them. They don't have the vocabulary with which to express them and the parents are so involved in their own distress that they are often not aware at the time of the divorce how urgently the child needs to deal with those problems.

Once the divorce is over, however (and the age of your child indicates that was some time in the past), you need to come up with some pretty specific decisions and plans as to what to do to straighten out this rather lazy, resistive, but unhappy child.

First of all, decide what you want him to do and choose only one item at a time. Select an area of his life about which you feel particularly strong, and then work out a plan for resolving that issue. At twelve, I strongly urge that you include your son in that discussion and in those choices, because his cooperation will be very necessary to make this work. Do you want him first, for example, to start by picking up his room and hanging up his clothes? Then what will happen when he does that? Perhaps he gets a little extra serving of dessert that evening. If he doesn't do it, what might happen? No television, no dessert at all. What will be meaningful to him and what will help him to be motivated to put in that extra effort to do the task both of you are working on his accomplishing?

How important it is for him to stop feeling guilty, helpless, angry, and for you to stop feeling helpless as well! Brag about him when he succeeds, simply and sincerely. Discipline him wisely when he fails. Together you can overcome the problems, and bring your child to a point of productivity and happiness in his life.

123. MOVING *I would like to know how we can prepare our nine-year-old daughter for moving to a new town. I know that moving can be upsetting to children but we have no choice in the matter. She's already concerned about a new school and leaving her friends behind.*

I recently came across a shocking statistic that said that the average American family moves fourteen times, and that concerns me because I know how disruptive those moves can be.

Such moves are certainly unsettling to children and parents alike. Unfortunately a great many families are moved without their having a vote in the matter. This involves a grief process. They're losing a great many things in such a move. So I recommend, parents, that you try to understand, practice, and teach the processes of grieving to your children. Exemplify those yourselves. As you teach your child, and as you practice getting through the stages of denial, anger, sadness, and then the healing, I think you will be ready for the next steps that are happier.

When you are through with that worst grief, begin to help your child see the adventure in the move. The excitement of a new and different area can be a part of any move as well as the grief. Keep (or make) your own attitude optimistic. Share the plans that you as parents must make with your child. Let them have a part in house hunting and selecting a neighborhood. Parents, I do want to urge you to choose your neighborhood very carefully. It's essential that you find a place where there are good schools, adequate libraries, safe shopping centers, and above all, a fine church, so that your child may have the spiritual nurture that he or she needs. In planning for your new home, give the child some votes in redecorating an older home, or planning a new home, if you are fortunate enough to build a new house. The color of paint for the walls, the kind of curtains that are chosen—all of these can help to make the new home belong to your child and can help her to feel a bit more comfortable in the new setting.

Above all let me recommend that you keep most of your child's old toys, old furniture, and belongings. Recently I met with a little girl who had had to move from one city to another, and she went through a very grievous time over that move. Tragically, one of the saddest events of all was the loss of her old teddy bear. It was decrepit and ugly, but it was hers, and losing that teddy bear produced a great deal of sadness and anger in her heart.

I recommend a ceremonious leave-taking when you must move. Have your child exchange some small gifts with friends—a photograph or an old book. A special book donated to the school library, farewell parties, a ceremonious time to say good-bye even with the tears those times will generate can make that leave-taking easier in the long run. Letters back, occasional phone calls and visits—all of these can help your child to finish the grief after moving and be free to anticipate the joy in the new home.

124. MIDDLE CHILD   *We have two boys, age nine and six, and a daughter who is two. My question concerns our second son, specifically, and sibling rivalry in general. In addition to his very low frustration threshold, he awakens almost daily irritable and complaining.*

It seems he can rarely find anything good about any situation. We have tried ignoring his complaining, and also being strict about his arguing with us about parental commands. This hasn't helped much, however. Both boys are good students and well behaved in school, but there seems to be more than normal competition between them. We have made an extra effort to make our second son feel special, and assuring him of our love for him, but our dislike of his attitude and behavior. Unfortunately, his sour outlook and continual testing often leaves me frustrated and exhausted, and precipitates a hasty remark that I might leave home because I can't stand him anymore. I guess I need help. Trying to manage our home and family, so he doesn't blow a fuse, is so wearing. He is not a tyrant, demanding his own way. He's just a frustrated, volatile, little boy expressing a need for help we can't seem to meet or identify. He does try to please when he's not a victim of his temper, and often gives me a hug following a confrontation. Any insight you might have would be helpful.

This child sounds like one who may actually need a little bit of professional help. Perhaps as much or more than the child, these parents need a little professional guidance. When a child reaches a state in which it sounds as if every transaction between child and family is a negative, unhappy one, then I feel that parents alone simply cannot correct that problem. But let me give some suggestions to this family so that they might begin to turn things around:

My first suggestion to this mother and father is that you *list all the resentments and anxieties* that you have about this child. Think through these areas of your resentment and concern, and pray about them, until you reach some understanding and honesty, some forgiveness about those traits or qualities that annoy you in this son. Then *list all the good qualities* that you may have overlooked in your concern about the problems. Be specific about these, and as you come across those good qualities in your son's life, comment simply but sincerely about them to him, so he can begin to see some hope for himself as being a good person, not just a problem child.

Together as parents and children, work hard to create a contract for change. Go by your son's bed at night, and tuck him in gently with caring and tenderness. In the morning, go and awaken him personally, rather than calling to him, so that perhaps he will awaken in a little better mood. Quietly and specifically react to those positive things as you come across them. *Then decide together what misbehaviors must go and how to-*

gether you will work out some better behaviors that will create loving and positive feelings within that family. As you develop some happy activities together, and build on the positive, even the very negative situation that has developed with such a child can be turned around to a loving situation within your family.

125. ROLE OF GRANDPARENTS *Several years ago my husband was transferred to Alaska, and that meant being separated from our families by thousands of miles. We felt sad that our children were so far from their grandparents, but we struck up a friendship with some older neighbors, and eventually our children began calling them Grandma and Grandpa. When the children's real grandparents learned about it, they were very hurt. I feel terrible about this and don't know how to correct the situation. Can you give me some advice?*

I would like to talk a little bit about grandparents in general. I really believe that grandparents' roles in a child's life are priceless. Perhaps that's even an understatement. These grandparents specifically are no doubt grieving because they can't be near their family, and understandably they resent other people taking their place and enjoying their roles in those children's lives. The best function of grandparents, in my opinion, is this: the simple acceptance and enjoyment of children without the need to train and discipline and do all of the heavy things that parents must do.

Grandparents usually have time to be more patient and understanding than parents do, and that's also very special in a child's life.

Let me say about these grandparents, that they should feel proud that they have played such an important part in their grandchildrens' lives that the family really needs a substitute for them. They may be grateful that others are willing to take over some of the functions they cannot perform. However, the parents of these little children should also be very careful to teach the children that their grandparents are really special. Perhaps they can best do that by using a different name for the foster grandparents. They might perhaps just call them Mr. So-and-So or Mrs. So-and-So, or Grandpa John and Grandma Mary—any name other than the one that they would use for their own grandparents would help those grandparents to feel better. Parents, be careful to have those children keep in touch with distant grandparents. Have them send to them the letters and the little pictures that they would give them if they lived nearby.

Parents, both you and your parents can love and understand the children, and "borrowed" grandparents need not threaten the real grandparents.

126. PARENTS' WILL   *We're in the process of drawing up a will, and along with the usual items, we want to put in a statement about who we want to have take care of our two children, in case something should happen to us before they are grown. We're wondering if it should be someone in the family, or possibly friends who share many of our interests and have similar life-styles. Also, would it be better to choose people who already have children themselves? This is really a difficult decision and any ideas you can offer us would be a big help.*

That certainly is a wise couple, and though this is a painful process (because no one would like to anticipate the death of both parents), yet it certainly is a necessary plan to make. There are several goals that parents need to consider in developing such a plan for the future of their children.

First of all, you want for your children the security and familiarity of their own environment. In imagining the loss of both parents, one would not like to imagine the children also losing their familiar surroundings and their own home, and so ideally one would think about selecting caretakers for them who could move into their own house, at least for a little while, and take care of them in that familiar environment. For some families that plan would necessitate the selection of relatives. For others, the neighborhood, the school, church, and so on could best be maintained by selecting friends who live in that neighborhood.

A second consideration is the values that you consider most important for your children. Whom do you know who will teach these the very best to your children? Again, for some of you parents, this may be relatives. For others who do not share the same values as your relatives, you may find friends could best reach that goal for your children. I believe that parents who have their own children can usually understand and adapt to other children more easily than people who have no children at all. That is not always the case but generally so.

Whomever you choose, I would recommend that you do this by formulating a plan. Cultivate those people as friends. Spend time together so that they and your children will get to know, love, understand, and trust each other. If there are major differences or lack of respect, it may help you decide to choose a different family. Offer a simple explanation of your plan to your children, so they understand who this special family may be in their lives, but avoid worrying your children or making them fearful of the loss of you, their parents. I hope that these plans will lie safely in your attorney's desk without his ever having to use them. But your peace of mind will be enhanced by knowing that they are there if needed.

127. CHRISTMAS PREPARATION   *What elements go together to make a family holiday special?*

These elements are so important, and unfortunately it's very easy to avoid them all unknowingly. I know at our house it's very easy at holiday times to become frazzled, and to find life's pace so hectic that the enjoyment is simply missing. I like to try to set the mood to be one of general congeniality. The goodwill that is so essential to Christmas is vital in the family as well. Smiles, laughter, and jokes are important all through the year, but Christmas is a natural time for such goodwill and happiness, as well as secrets and surprises.

Not only is Christmas a time of surprises and congeniality, but it needs also to be a time of quiet and peacefulness. Take time out personally, and as a family, to just be quiet and to look at the decorations and enjoy the packages in anticipation. Also meditate on the real meaning of God's loving gift of Christmas in our world. The inclusion of children in the decorating, baking, and preparations for Christmas is sometimes a bit of a trial to a busy mother, but it is also a part of the happiness and the building of traditions for children. *Building traditions is so essential!* Every Christmas we have a similar menu for the Christmas dinner and the Christmas breakfast. We have familiar tree ornaments, which we have saved from time immemorial, and each year I, as well as the children, love unpacking those and using them again and again on our special traditional tree.

The ultimate expression of Christmas love is in *giving*.

128. EXTENDING CHRISTMAS CHEER   *Can children learn to extend Christmas cheer to others outside the family?*

They certainly can. Children often are accused of being very selfish but they love to give, and can do so with great excitement and genuineness. I recommend that every family select another family who might not be as advantaged as they are. A group or a person with special needs can be a real stimulus to generosity for yourselves, as well as your children. Help your children, if you choose to do this, to avoid condescension or pity, and teach them their responsibility in giving to others, and in recognizing the needs of other people.

Furthermore, I think it's important that children learn how other people celebrate Christmas. In your community, there may be people from other ethnic backgrounds. You might read about the way other people celebrate Christmas across the country and around the world; there are many traditions that are fascinating. They might be ones that you would like to adopt into your own family.

In our community one of the major shopping centers has booths set up by many different foreign exchange students, and in each of those booths there are traditional Christmas celebrations that a particular country practices. Our family has enjoyed going to visit them year after year and sharing in the Christmas festivities of other nations.

Reviving old customs, which perhaps your grandparents enjoyed, might be very helpful to your children in valuing their backgrounds and learning to know from whence they came. If grandparents are not available to you, take your children to visit a retired person's home, and help them to bring joy to those people, as well as learning from them about Christmases in the past.

Some of the old customs, which we have shared with our children, are having them decorate a Christmas tree by stringing cranberries or popcorn. Christmas caroling is a tradition that seems to be lost. I recommend that you revive that. Even as a family, you might go to visit someone who is ill or elderly and bring them the joy of the Christmas season through singing those old Christmas carols.

Church traditions are very important in our families, and yet we like to visit other churches. Swedish groups, German groups, Polish groups, all of these have special religious festivities, and these need to be shared by all of us.

Special meals and recipes—all of these are traditions that you can build into those priceless memories for your family to give to their children in the future.

129.   CHRISTMAS GIFT SELECTION   *What suggestions do you have for parents who are shopping for children's presents?*

I'd like to make my comments really timely for the economy, because many parents may need to curtail their shopping considerably in more troubled economic times. I would recommend that you sit down with your children and prepare them ahead of time for the fact that Christmas may not be quite as generous as it has been in some years. As you sit together, mothers and fathers, set a budget for yourselves. The joy of Christmas can be totally spoiled by your worrying about paying those credit-card bills over the next six months!

Plan early, and by using your time wisely perhaps you might be able to make some of your child's Christmas gifts. Some of the most treasured gifts our children received at Christmas were doll clothes that I had designed and fashioned for them myself, or a hobbyhorse that a relative had made. There are many special gifts that convey the uniqueness of your love and your creativity without costing a great deal.

If you do have money to spend, I recommend that you look for gifts that include your child's creativity and development: a building set, paints, or music requires your child to put something into the enjoyment of the toy, and in turn get some development of abilities out of using that toy. Certainly that is a wise kind of gift to give.

Look at your child's life over the last six months, and think about things that he has truly longed for. Sometimes we give things that we see on the spur of the moment, or that the child happens to see on the commercials on television. As you look back over the weeks and months, you may remember something that your son or daughter has wanted for a long time. Giving that special gift may eliminate the need for a quantity of presents, because the quality of satisfaction that a longed-for item can produce is so wonderful. Be careful that you don't give so many things that your child cannot honestly appreciate them. On the other hand don't give so few things that your child may feel deprived. (This, of course, depends upon your child's age, personality, sense of values, and other facts of life upon which you can base your decision.)

Above all, be sure that Christmas is a time for the *giving of love*. The gifts you give must symbolize that—or no matter how much you spend, they will somehow miss the mark.

130. CHRISTMAS "ON YOUR OWN" *What help do you have for young parents who are still trying to decide where they'll spend Christmas?*

That certainly is not a question that can be answered with dogmatic facts. One of the memories that I treasure most of all are those big family gatherings involving several generations. Sometimes, in the hurry to establish a tradition within a young new family, there is the possibility that those transgenerational experiences and values can be lost. So whenever it's possible, I recommend that at least on alternate years, or on alternate holidays, young families try to spend some of those times with grandparents. The traditions of those grandparents can set the patterns for your own new family, and certainly can give wonderfully warm memories to your children. I think my children would agree with me that their memories of times together with cousins, aunts, uncles, and grandparents are very cherished ones.

Now sometimes the distances do make that impossible. The time and money that it takes to get to the home of a grandparent may, in fact, make that very difficult. Saving some time from vacations, saving some money if possible, is to me worth the sacrifice in order to be together with those special people on holidays. I respect, however, the young couples who feel pressed to separate from their families for their own reasons, and who need to begin building their own celebrations and traditions.

I suggest to those young couples that they invite the grandparents to spend some of those holidays with them. If that is at all possible, it can work in reverse that the traditions of the grandparents can be brought into the new home in some fashion. Distances and time may make the young couple unable to spend time with grandparents, but the grandparents in retirement may be able to travel to the homes of their children. When even that is not possible, I strongly recommend that you save enough money for a long-distance telephone call. That traditional reaching out to someone at holiday times is something I would reinforce. Shopping early and sending special memory gifts to those family members is something that can make the holiday time special for you and your children. When you cannot have grandparents with you, and you would very much like to, I suggest that you adopt foster grandparents—those who need a family and can come and spend some time with you. They can enrich the lives of your children.

131. NEW YEAR'S RESOLUTIONS   *What are some of the areas where parents may want to change course or make a fresh start as a new year begins?*

I think that's a valid question, and I hope every parent will think very carefully with us about this. The new year is a time to step back a few paces and take a look at one's own self, and the framework of the lives with whom we are associated. It's a sort of personal and family inventory—something that we all need to do at times, and certainly the new year is a logical time for that.

Parents, take a look at the general atmosphere of your family. Is it a happy, intimate relationship, which you all share, or have you unwittingly come to diverge and separate from one another more than you have realized? What do you think are the strengths within your family? As you define those, make a plan for how you will build upon them. Where are the weaknesses? Are you too busy, perhaps, and are your children getting involved in so many activities that they don't have time for you anymore? Whatever those weaknesses are, you need to strengthen them, and I predict your new year will be better than the last!

132. PHOTO ALBUMS   *Nearly every home has a box or drawer somewhere that holds a wealth of family snapshots. Please tell us what to do with all those pictures!*

I'm delighted to do that, because I find pictures are very important to people. One of the questions that I frequently ask in doing a psychiatric evaluation of a troubled person is this: If there were a fire in your home, what are the things that you would take out of that house? Almost everyone mentions the family photographs. So I gather that for troubled people, at least, memories and pictures are very important.

I strongly recommend that as mother and father, you set up for each child his or her own special photograph album. In that, organize your thoughts and the child's and the family's lives in such a way that you can create for the child from even before his birth those special things that you will want him to think about and remember later on. I strongly recommend that you start with the background of your child's life, and put in their photo albums the generations preceding them. Any pictures whatever that you may have of grandparents or great-grandparents, or the old family farm or homestead—whatever might be in your family— start with that, and give your child a sense of his past and belonging to some particular set of people.

Very important to children are the residences in which they have lived. The average family moves fourteen times, so that section may be quite sizable in some photograph albums! Pictures of the schools, the neighborhood, special spots in which the child may have had fun, would be wonderful ideas to include. Parks and picnics, vacations and toys, those are the things that someday your child can look back upon with pleasure. Another section should be reserved for friends—playmates and the activities that they shared—birthday parties and Christmas celebrations, very important memories.

Include significant people in the lives of the child: a teacher, a special friend, anyone who has been meaningful in the child's growing-up time. Symbols of the child's progress are also meaningful: sports events, school or church performances, science projects, special pets. All of these are memories that your child will treasure as he grows older and he himself starts a family. Your children will want to share this special set of memories with their children someday.

133.   SLEEPING ARRANGEMENTS   *What are the effects of children sharing a bedroom with their parents, or is this something that should be avoided? At what age is it appropriate for children to sleep in their parents' bedroom?*

Frankly, I prefer that children have their own bedrooms, almost from the time they come home from the hospital. A great many parents do not feel comfortable with that, and certainly I understand that they might want the child in the same room with them until he can adequately turn over and sleep through the night. In general, they want to know that their child is safe.

Having a child in one's bedroom usually interrupts sleep for both. Parents sometimes snore or make noises in their sleep that can awaken a baby, and maybe even frighten her. I used to be quite afraid when I would awaken at night and hear my father snoring. He was a *very loud snorer!* Concern for awakening the child can interfere with the parents' sleep. All in all, I think everyone gets much more satisfying rest when the child has his own room.

Still another reason for arranging for that when it is at all possible is that parents need some privacy. Their marital intimacy and their personal privacy are important values for a husband and wife, and having a child in the room can certainly interfere with that kind of healthy intimacy.

By the age of six weeks, if at all possible, I think children should have their own bedrooms. If they cannot have a bedroom, they could have a crib in another area of the house that is not quite so close to the parents. Sharing a room with a sibling is much more satisfactory, in my opinion, than sharing the room with the parents. A crib in the living room is certainly not a bad idea and can be something like a child's own private room.

Recently I talked with a woman who is a single parent. She has one child, and he is about seven years of age. She needed an arrangement for sleeping that would give them some privacy, and yet would take into account the limited space they had. Her creative idea was to find a bunk bed and to me that made very good sense. She took the top bunk so that she wouldn't have to worry about her son falling out, and he had the bottom bunk. They each had their own bed, and yet the rest of the house was kept separate for the entertainment of friends and guests.

However you arrange the sleeping for your family, I hope that privacy and consideration will be the important factors.

134. PREPARATION FOR A NEW PARENT   *I'm sure my three-year-old daughter is too young to understand the change that will be taking place in our home in a few months. Even though my fiancée and my daughter have a happy relationship, I don't know how to let my daughter know this woman will be her new mommy. I don't want to confuse her about her own mother or upset her unnecessarily. I'd appreciate any help you can offer.*

This is another very important question and one that a great many children are having to face. Many children lose a parent through divorce, and sometimes parents are lost through death. In either event, the child's problems are similar and the ideas that I have to offer, I think, will be helpful. *Sense of Loss.* The issues that are at stake are these: First of all, this little girl is going to suffer the loss of her father's time and energy to a new spouse. It will give her a feeling of displacement and rejection at first, and she's going to be very unhappy about losing his time to the new mommy. If the new mother is not aware of that, she may feel hurt and rejected in turn.
Sense of Disloyalty. Second, this child will suffer, perhaps, a sense of disloyalty to her biological mother. How can she love a new mommy, when she still loves her old mommy? She may think it's fine to have daddy's fiancée around as a friend, but not as a new mother.
Change in Life-Style. Finally, there will be many changes in the style of living, the family routines, and the expectations that a new parent will introduce.

How to handle these issues is not so simple. The first point I must emphasize again and again is to explain and explain and explain *again!* Do not take for granted that this little child will understand the new living arrangement and the advent of a new mommy. Help her to know that she doesn't have to choose between her "old" mother and the new one. She can love both of them and treat them each individually in her own way. Have the new spouse spend a great deal of time with the child alone (as well as with her father) before the marriage, so that the child will get used to her and she to the child. They need to know one another very well. Move slowly into the new parenting—both before and after the marriage, with simple explanations regarding the way it was with Daddy, and the way it will be with the new mommy. Expect some rivalry between these two parents. The divided loyalty and the manipulations that can come about through that are going to be there. If you expect them you will be ready to handle them by refusing to compete with the other parent, not tolerating the child's manipulations, staying together as adults, and working for the child. Tough as it is to create a new family together, both of you and your child can do it.

135. STEPPARENTS   *What guidelines do you recommend for getting a stepparent/stepchild relationship off to a good start?*

That's such a very important question because a great many families are sharing the problems of such a new relationship. Ever since the story of Cinderella was first told to a wide-eyed boy or girl, stepparents have had a bad reputation. Even though very few stepmoms or dads would come close to resembling Cinderella's wicked and cruel stepmother, there can still be difficult days in establishing this new family relationship. I do have some very specific guidelines that I think will help.

The first point I would make is that the stepparent *should not expect any specific behavior.* Keep an open mind, and explore the child and your own relationship with that child. Think about what you have to offer this individual and what the child has to give to you and can receive from you.

Second, *find a lot of good points about that child's biological parents.* It's very easy to subtly compete with that child's mother or father, and to find bad things about them, in order to make yourself appear better perhaps in your own eyes and certainly to the child.

The third recommendation is *that you specialize in understanding that stepchild's grief, confusion, and anger over the loss of his parent.* The child will often tend to cover his sad, tender feelings with aggression and acting out in a rude and unkind way. He won't want to choose between loyalty to the missing parent and the new parent that you are. If there was a divorce, particularly, he is likely to blame the stepparent for causing the divorce, or at least for destroying his dream of recreating his own biological family. By understanding the child's tender feelings, anxieties, and concerns, you will not blame the child or feel personally affronted or hurt by the child's misbehaviors or his reluctance, perhaps, to accept you as the new parent.

The fourth guideline is that you concentrate on kind, honest, and unconditional acceptance of the child as is. Now that doesn't mean that you must put up with rude or disrespectful behavior, but that at least you understand the child's honesty with you and accept that. Encourage the child to talk out the feelings that he has for you, as well as for his natural parent. Treat the child as you would a dear, young friend. Do not expect immediate parent/child relationships or rapport and work toward earning that while you are developing a friendly relationship. Don't crowd or push. Allow the child to approach you and offer your availability, but don't demand a sudden intimacy or response too soon, because that simply cannot happen. I wish the very best for you and your stepchild.

136. FALSE GUILT   *I am now working outside of our home after being able to be home with our children for six years. It was my husband's wish that I return to work, and I don't really mind. We do have a wonderful sitter, but some days the guilt is too much. I would really appreciate any help you can offer.*

First, let me define the difference between *real guilt* and *false guilt*. Real guilt comes when we *know* we have done something wrong. If you have been too harsh on your children, or if you have made mistakes in judgments and punished them for something that they never did, then certainly you will be guilty. That's fairly easy to correct by admitting the mistake, apologizing, and making it right. False guilt comes when we feel that we have done something wrong, but we honestly could not define what that wrong is. That false guilt is what it seems this mother is suffering.

Let me tell you how you can get rid of the false guilt and work through the conflicts that are a part of the needs of mothers who must be employed outside the home. First of all, explain how you feel to both your children and your husband. Let the children know that you're working simply because you must, and let your husband know that you are glad you can give him the support and help he needs. This husband is lucky that his wife is willing to be supportive of him.

If you will seek to build your entire family into a cooperative unit, everyone will have an easier go of it, and the children will indeed feel better about themselves, so I recommend having another of those famous family conferences. As the family sits together, explain to them the needs that all of you have, and let each one feel a vital part of meeting those needs. List all of the household and yard tasks, and assign them appropriately, and fairly, to each one in the family. This will give children a priceless sense of their value, and your appreciation for their input will help to build a great foundation for their self-esteem and your relationship together. Share the interesting parts of your job with your family. Try not to complain too much, but share the funny or even the not-so-funny parts of your job. Avoid competing with a baby-sitter. Work out a schedule that will allow time for all of you to play together as well as work together. Just keep in mind that working outside of the home need not be bad for you or your children.

137.   MINISTRY TO HANDICAPPED   *What can an ordinary person do to help the family of a handicapped child?*

The first thing I'd like to suggest (because I think it is so important) is to learn the difference between sympathy or pity and empathy. Families with handicapped children do not want to be pitied, but they certainly do need to be understood. You need to be sensitive to their feelings and problems. Being open to talking about the handicaps and all of the inconvenience and distress they may cause, without being intrusive, is a very important technique to learn. Avoid curiosity, but always be interested (and there can be a very fine line between curiosity and a genuine concerned interest).

Sometimes it's wise to wait for the parents of a handicapped child to discuss their problems with you, but be available to that discussion. Show the genuineness of your concern when they want to discuss those issues, and when they may need some help. Sometimes that help is simply to cry out about the stress and the worry of that situation. Learn to see the handicapped child as a person, a whole child, with only one area that is different or weak.

Here are some specific ways that you may offer to help: One of the most important for parents of handicapped children is that of offering to child-sit whenever possible to give the family a chance to get away without worrying because of the tender care that child will receive from loving friends. During times of stress, such as surgery or special treatments that handicapped children often need, offer your help. Take a hot dish by for the family's meal, or offer to do the laundry for a week or a little house-cleaning to help the mother especially. For the father, some time of free-dom from the demands of the household, as well as the needs of that special child, will be appreciated. During crisis times you might offer to take over phone duties.

An invitation to the entire family to come to your home for dinner or a party is something parents of handicapped children often lack. Many folks are uncomfortable with the handicapped child. If you are not un-comfortable, include that whole family in a very nice, warm interfamily social life.

Avoid platitudes such as, "It must be God's will," or, "You'll be better for all of this." While those are certainly true, parents who are in pain often resent such easy answers. Your loving, gentle presence in their lives, your quiet prayers, will be the greater help, the best answer for the handi-capped child and his parents that you can offer.

138. LEAVING THE NEST   *I'd like to know how you get your kids to move out after they are twenty-one. We love them, but we're worried because they seem quite satisfied to remain with us. Are we helping or hurting them by allowing them to stay?*

The Whys. A great many parents share this concern. Let us think for a minute about why it is that young people want to stay on at home. Some-times they need more warmth, nurturing, and attention—they simply haven't become saturated with their childhood dependency needs. Some-times there is fear and insecurity, maybe stated like this: *What if I can't make it on my own?* A great many young people are afraid in today's economy that they can't, and they don't want to face that fear of failure. Sometimes I have known young people to be selfish and greedy. For ex-ample, *I don't want to spend my own money on my needs, and it's easier to let Mom and Dad take care of me and foot the bill.* Sometimes it's just downright laziness. *Mom cooks, cleans, and launders for me. Why should I leave and do all of those things for myself?*

What to Do. So, parents, how are you handling your relationship with your grown children? Let me make some suggestions that will help you to decide whether or not they are going to grow up and leave home, or per-haps still stay on. First of all, I suggest that *you begin charging them a re-alistic amount of rent.* And as well, *charge for the services that you render to them.* Make this amount a fair one, not just symbolic. *Help your chil-*

dren find more personal resources for their own needs. They may, for example, find some of their emotional needs met by friends, activities, or hobbies. You may be able to withdraw your parenting and nurturing just a bit from them, so they won't have quite so much satisfaction from you as mom and dad. Then I suggest that you *discuss your feelings honestly with them.* Some children actually believe that their parents *want* them to stay on with them, and they need to know that *you're* ready for some independence and freedom; that you really would like them to move out and be on their own.

Stop serving them quite so adequately. Push them toward independence, even while they are at home, and ask that they help you some. Finally, set a fair and realistic deadline for those children to move out, and then help them pack. Invite them back now and then, brag about their moves toward independence; help them find a place to go. But do insist that they acquire their own independence *and that you get your freedom.* That is my wish for you and your adult children.

139. PROBLEM SOLVING RESOURCES *Many parents feel all alone when problems arise. But you don't think they need to feel that way, do you?*

As a matter of fact, they really do not. The range of problems that can occur, even in the most normal of families, is amazingly broad. However, the range of resources available to concerned moms and dads is equally extensive.

Recently a situation came to my attention that will exemplify what we are discussing. A school consulted me, regarding a young man who was a student there. He was having epileptic seizures. He was horribly embarrassed by that, and the school officials did not know how to handle it. When I talked with the boy and his father, I discovered that they had had no medical care for at least six years. They didn't have very much money and they were unfamiliar with the resources of their community. With only two telephone calls, we were able to put the boy and his father in touch with a very fine clinic, where the child had a wonderful neurological workup. He was put on medications that cost them nothing, until the father was able to find a job. The child came back to school and the seizures were put under excellent control. The resources were there; the family simply did not know how to touch base and find them.

Let me give a list of the resources that are present in almost any community in the United States:

First of all, I would recommend to you *your church.* Your pastor and the friends within that warm community oftentimes are very resourceful for many needs of your family. Then consider *your family's physician.* Your family doctor or pediatrician will know a great many technical resources and exactly which ones can help you in a variety of medical or psychological needs. Almost all *schools* have a school counselor or a school nurse who also can be extremely helpful in referring you to specialized areas for help.

If you're unfamiliar with the medical resources (or any other resources, for that matter) in your community, look for the listing of your *county medical society* in your telephone directory. Someone there will be able to put you in touch with reliable resources for a variety of needs. There often are area mental-health centers that are very low in cost, and extremely supportive for the emotional and psychological problems that your medical doctor may not be as skilled in helping as you need. *The specific foundations,* such as Myasthenia Gravis, Birth Defects, funded by the March of Dimes, and many other foundations, are available simply for the asking. Don't forget relatives and friends who care and are willing to help in many ways.

I find the problem with a great many families is that they are afraid to ask. They believe they should be able to go it alone, and then on the other hand they become rather hopeless and feel there is nothing anyone can do anyway. Don't despair, parents. If you have special needs, help is available.

Fathers

140. PRESSURED DAD *My wife and I want to do the best job possible of raising our daughters, and we try to spend as much time together as a family as possible. But one thing that really bothers us is that while people expect my wife to make changes in her life for the girls, a man isn't supposed to let children interfere so much—he's henpecked if he does. My friends at work don't seem to understand why I don't hang around the office any longer than necessary, or volunteer for extra projects anymore. A couple of guys even have said that I am hurting my future. But I feel like I'm doing a good job and not cutting corners on my work. Do you have any suggestions?*

My first suggestion is that you check with your supervisor or boss about whether or not you may have a risk of hurting your career. Certainly you will need your job to provide for that family that you love so much. I think you can get absolute peace of mind about that. Just explain to this person that you really value your children and want to spend time with them, but that you do not want to be unfair or neglect your job. Get that really clear so your mind can be at rest about it.

Then be quite certain in your own mind of your priorities. It sounds to me as if you are, but when you are absolutely sure, then you can take the jibes of your friends without so much trouble. I have recently heard of several men and women who have turned down major advancements in jobs in the interests of their children, and I respect that immensely. Such love and good judgment, such determination and courage, portray to me real strength of character, wisdom, and great love. It is not so necessary to advance in your job when your children are small as it is to advance the interests of your children themselves.

When you are absolutely certain and secure about your job, and know your position will be safe, then you can stand tall above the rank and file of all of your co-workers and anyone else who might challenge your values. You can be proud that you're building lives, strengthening a family, and certainly strengthening your own integrity. Fathers, I can't emphasize enough what a major influence in the lives of your children you are. You are the protector of your family. Enjoy that role.

141. TOO STRICT DAD   *The problem my husband and I are now facing is that I think he is too strict with our children, especially our two-year-old. When my husband was growing up, his own dad was extremely strict, to the point that my husband wished him dead a lot of times. He had a very troubled childhood. Do you have anything to say that might help us both come to a good and reasonable way of raising our children?*

I must say that the way parents are raised is so often the way they raise their children. In this family, I am concerned about the unbalanced parenting. The father seems very strict and extreme, where the mother is much more lenient and soft. In such unbalanced parenting, a vicious cycle can get going. The harsher and more strict one is, the more lenient and sympathetic the other becomes. There are two results that can evolve: First, parents get at odds with one another, and second, the child gets caught in the pinch.

Parents, above all, do not get in angry fights about your child or his discipline in front of him. That can create a geat deal of fear and guilt on the part of the child. In this specific case, I would recommend that the mother try to help the husband recall how he felt as a child. Now don't do that while he is upset with either you or the child. When he is relaxed and calm and perhaps feeling a little remorseful about being too harsh, help him remember his own sad feelings and identify with your child. Gently but clearly, help your husband see that his son could be developing feelings like his and that you, as the mother, want them to love, respect, and enjoy each other, and not feel angry or afraid. When your child can talk, have him or her go to the father and honestly tell Dad how they feel when he is too harsh or strict.

Do protect your children from abuse, but as much as possible, stay out of the middle. Having the children go directly to the father with Mother staying out of that middle position can help the dad to really hear the pain that he is unconsciously inflicting on that child. Comment to your husband on insights that you have gleaned from articles and books. Unfortunately, I find that many men are not very anxious to read, but if your husband will read, give him books and articles on child rearing that can help him understand, for example, the difficulties of the two-year-old stage and give him a bit more patience and sympathy with the child. Be careful not to overreact to a strict spouse.

Do not, above all else, set yourself up as the authority, the right one, making him wrong. That can create such a feeling of inferiority and inadequacy that he may give up and not even try to be involved in the parenting. When he does well, finds patience, and treats the children wisely, praise him and let him know how much you appreciate his efforts. Mothers and fathers, pull together.

142. FATHER'S APPROVAL   *I am especially anxious to ask you about children and self-esteem, because I have been aware of my seven-year-old son's problem in this area these past few months. It concerns me very much. He has a lot of God-given talents which we praise. He's a very good boy, and I tell him that I'm glad God gave him to me as my son. I'm wondering if his confidence would be better if his father praised him more.*

This mother has a very important question, and I can hardly emphasize enough how vital it is to build this healthy self-confidence in children. Let me explain clearly and concisely what parents need to do. First of all, *both parents* must work together. This mother is very wise when she recognizes that the child needs praise from his father as well as from herself. When both parents understand how vital self-esteem is, they can pull together in a successful fashion. Build success for the child, first of all, by assigning tasks and projects that he is realistically capable of doing. Second, help him by sticking with him lovingly but firmly and sternly (if need be) until he does those jobs the very best he can. Parents need to be fair about this, and firm, but never angry. And the third step in building successes for children is to praise them honestly and point out simply and clearly what was good about the job that they just did.

Give a lot of verbal approval. Tell your child what it is you like about the way he acts, how he looks, and what he does. Remember, you're not likely to be bothered about the things your child does well, so you may forget to compliment him on those routine, wonderful things that go on every day. Be careful that one parent does not try to balance out the other's sternness by sympathizing or overprotecting a child. Sometimes it's tempting to help a child a little too much. The affirmation of both parents will complete the child's needs for approval. Build together the self-esteem that will make your child's life a success, and that means both parents, working as a team!

Illnesses

143. HEADACHES   *What's the most common cause of a child's headache?*

The most common causes of headaches in children certainly must be due to physical conditions. There are several of those that I'd like to discuss. Emotional stress, however, is a close second as a cause of headaches in children.

Any child who has a *cold,* a *fever,* or an *illness* of almost any kind is likely to have a headache along with that illness. The stopping up of the nose, as you know, causes you to have a headache, and your child is no different from you. *Allergies* often cause headaches, too. Along with the nasal congestion and the watery eyes, there very frequently is a severe headache that accompanies that chronic problem.

Cutting of teeth or infected teeth sometimes can cause headaches. Even little babies can experience irritability from this. In older children eyestrain may be a problem and cause headaches because of the wrinkling of the brow and the furrowing of the forehead in trying to see a blackboard in school or a distant object.

There are *emotional* and *psychological* problems, of course, that can cause headaches, too. These I have to subdivide into two different groups, because there are true headaches from anxiety and worry or fear. These may be due to family burdens or problems that the child is carrying. (Sometimes you as parents do not even realize that your child is worried about your concerns.)

Sometimes your child's headaches may be due to a *personal overdrive.* Many children are so conscientious and responsible that they really try too hard to make good grades, or to get along well, or do the right thing. They have a certain sense of anxiety or tension that accompanies that effort and may result in headaches.

Sometimes there is *muscular tension* in the neck and the forehead that stretches and tightens the scalp, which actually is a large tendon. That kind of muscular stretching can cause a very definite pain, and yet that pain is due to emotional tension, rather than a physical illness.

I have seen children now and then who have pretended to have headaches in order to get out of particular jobs that they did not like. Headaches can sometimes be a means that a child has of needing to gain attention and love.

What are you to do in helping your child who has a headache? First, of course, *check the child physically.* If you're not sure, take the child to the doctor to be certain that there is no serious physical problem that is causing that pain. Of course you will want to take care of any such physical problems and get those out of the way. *Provide plenty of loving attention and happy times. Require the child to be responsible,* in spite of those headaches, and watch your own example to be sure that you are not creating a headache to solve your own problem.

144.   STOMACHACHE   *What are the most common causes of a child's stomachache?*

I'm sure all of us share in common those stomachaches that were very useful (when we were kids) in getting out of doing dishes, homework, or whatever the job might be. In my family, those excuses rarely worked and they shouldn't work in your home either. There are some important physical causes however, that parents must not overlook.

Physical Causes. Let me list these for you: One of the most common causes of real physical pain is that of either *hunger* or *overeating.* Severe hunger pains are something relatively few people in our country know well, but we do experience pangs when it's getting close to mealtime. Overeating and stretching the stomach can cause serious pain, and can be a problem that may even cause vomiting in some children. So be careful of how much food you allow your child to eat at a sitting.

The second cause of stomachache is *food intolerance* or *allergies.* Perhaps all of us have eaten certain foods that have caused a stomach pain or discomfort. Those foods need to be avoided, and that kind of stomachache can be easily cured. Having trouble with the bowels can also cause stomachaches. *Constipation* or an excess amount of intestinal gas can cause discomfort for many children. Give your child enough water and plenty of fruit in the diet, and the constipation should not become a serious problem.

Stomach flu is a very common cause of stomachaches and that can cause very intense pain. Usually that kind of stomach pain is accompanied by persistent vomiting or severe diarrhea and cramping. That usually passes within twelve to twenty-four hours, but if it is prolonged, you may need medical care to be sure that your little child does not become dehydrated.

The *aftermath of a course of antibiotics* for a strep throat or some other infection can result in stomachaches. This sort of stomachache is often associated with diarrhea or excessive intestinal gas. It can be treated very simply by giving your child yogurt or cultured buttermilk (if you can get the child to drink that), and reintroducing the normal healthy bacteria that are contained in those dairy products.

Many illnesses are associated with stomachaches. Strep throats, measles, which we rarely see anymore, and other illnesses may, as a part of their onset, be accompanied by a stomachache. Very rarely do we see *intestinal parasites* and *pinworms,* but those can cause some stomach discomfort.

The really serious stomachache, which you need to be aware of, is that of *appendicitis*. With that there is a fever of 100 degrees or more, and generalized abdominal pain that settles in the right lower fourth of the stomach and causes a very severe sort of pain when you press on the abdominal muscles or when such pressure is released (called "rebound pain").

Psychological Causes. Last of all, psychologically we can have stomachaches, either real pain due to the pressure and stress of a child's life, or actually made up for the manipulative advantage that I mentioned earlier.

Whether your child's stomachache is real or imagined, physical or functional, giving tender, loving care will be the proper cure.

145. SERIOUS ILLNESS *How much would you tell a child who might be sick for a long time, or have some permanent disability from their illness, or who might even die?*

That is a very sad thing to contemplate, and one that I do hope few of you will ever have to face. Unfortunately, such things do happen. There is a fine balance, in working with chronically ill or potentially fatally ill children, in keeping hope alive and allowing enjoyment of the life span that they may have, and yet being honest with the child regarding the ultimate end of that illness. There is always the possibility of some new scientific discovery that will cure cancer, or will save the life of a child who otherwise might die or be permanently disabled. So I always want to keep that hope alive, as slim as it may be in a given case.

Almost all seriously ill people, however, in my experience, have their own inner sense about the end result of that illness. Children are certainly no exception to this, and I do not recommend that you lie to your children, or that you pretend that something is true which is more optimistic than the actual facts define.

What can you do, then, if you have a child who is seriously ill and potentially facing death? First of all, *seek the physician's input.* Get as many consultations as you need to be sure of the facts that you must communicate. *Get help from your minister* to face the emotional and spiritual issues of that child's impending death or chronic illness. *Talk together as mother and father with each other, with relatives and friends,* until you find the inner strength to cope with communicating the facts to your child.

Then *tell the child frankly, honestly, all of what you know about that illness.* Give all the positives as well as the negatives and doubts. Offer the honest hope that is there, and teach the child to live each day to the fullest of which he is capable. Teach the importance of giving oneself to others in order to leave pleasant and happy memories with those who are left behind. Above all, teach that child the faith in a Heavenly Father who will give the strength to cope and the assurance of a life after this life. This can sustain and soothe that child as well as you through this difficult time.

146. HELP FOR EMOTIONALLY DISTURBED BOY *I have an eight-year-old son who is emotionally disturbed. Just recently, he was placed in a home for children with this kind of disorder. I'm hoping you can provide me with information that will enable me to cope with this situation when he finally does come home.*

That's a very important question and one that I work with almost daily. The most important guideline I can give to this mother of a troubled child is that she needs to avoid blaming herself or anyone else. Certainly she needs to avoid feeling guilty about the fact that her child has problems. I find that most parents do blame themselves or one another. That kind of blaming and guilt stops the solution to the problem, rather than helping. Work that through as quickly as you can, parents, if you have a child with emotional disturbances.

Then be sure to believe, *know,* that there is no shame in having such a problem. The attitudes of a great many people today still say that this is an embarrassment, and that somehow parents and children should be ashamed of themselves because they have such a problem! I do not agree with that point of view and would encourage you to give up such a belief (if you harbor it), and not tolerate it from other people. Many times such problems arise beyond anyone's control, and you need not be ashamed or embarrassed.

Work hard to understand the reasons for your child's problems. Many times those problems come from misunderstandings or troubled communication systems within a family. Those, of course, will need to be resolved and straightened out. Sometimes physical illnesses or other physical handicaps can contribute to emotional disturbances, so again there is the need to understand and not to blame yourselves.

A lack of correct information in child rearing can sometimes contribute to a child's emotional problem. Losses and grief that are beyond our control (or that of your child) are another part of the reason for emotional disturbances. Assess your input into your child's problems and make any changes you need to to prevent recurrences. Encourage the growth of your child back to health. Find good medical and psychological resources to help you to guide him when he returns. Look for the health and the strength in your child more than the disturbances, and learn to build on those strengths, in restoring healthy, loving communications and relationships. Find your own strengths. Develop and build on these. Develop your faith in God and ask for His guidance, as you restore the loving, healthy relationship beween you and your emotionally troubled child.

147. CAUSE OF COLDS *The current theory that exposure to dampness, wind, or chills has nothing to do with a youngster getting colds, has me wondering why these problems often occur after exposure. Your opinion, please.*

I think that the current theory that colds have nothing to do with dampness or chill is a little bit in error. Now true enough, if a person goes out in the cold and damp and has no contact with a cold-causing germ or virus, then indeed the temperature alone would not cause that infection. However, colds are caused by viruses, which often are harbored within our nostrils or the throat, and when we are chilled, fatigued, or our resistance is lowered, those viruses get into the tissues and cause an infection. The word for viruses that we call "cold viruses" comes from the fact that they multiply and grow in colder temperatures. So, getting chilled or being in a cold climate does have *something* to do with catching colds. Chilling also, in addition to encouraging the growth of viruses, alters the circulatory patterns of the body. Getting cold makes the capillaries and blood vessels on the surface constrict. That pushes the blood to the interior part of the body, where it pools in the deeper circulatory system. The superficial tissues, therefore, are less well supplied with the circulation, and the blood cells that fight off infection are not at the spot where they are most needed.

Colds (or any upper respiratory infection) are caused by three basic infectious agents. Most commonly they are caused by *various viruses,* and there are many of those. They can also be caused by *bacteria,* or they may be caused by a *mixture of viruses and bacteria.* Now viruses are numerous (so numerous, in fact, that we haven't even discovered all of them as yet). They are a little harder to identify than bacteria, and they cause a less serious infection as a rule, but unfortunately those infections are not healed by the antibiotics as bacterial infections are. So our own bodies have to fight off viral infections. Bacteria are easily identified under the microscope. They usually cause a more dramatic infection with fever, headaches, vomiting, and generally more severe symptoms. The nasal discharge or sputum from a bacterial infection is colored yellowish or greenish, rather than the clearer, whitish discharge of a viral infection.

We ought to talk for a minute about the treatment of infections or colds. Most viral colds, as we often jokingly say, last a week if they're treated vigorously. They last seven days if we do nothing at all. So for colds, just take good precautions, get plenty of rest, stay warm and in the house, and drink plenty of juices. Bacterial infections, however, often need to be treated with antibiotics. If you must be exposed to dampness, wind, or chill, be careful to wrap up warmly, and when you get back in the house, drink something warm. Take care of yourself, so you do not come down with that dreaded infection, a cold.

148. NO MEDICINE, PLEASE   *Some weeks back, my daughter told me she read that you advise a mild sedative for infants who fight sleep. She was really surprised. It would seem you could always be giving a baby some sedative—first for fussiness, then for teething, then for the first day of school! (Incidentally, this is not a letter of criticism, but of sharing, because I wanted you to know that at least one person who reads your books has chosen to avoid using drugs if that's possible.) I don't mean I wouldn't take a sick child to a pediatrician or an adult to a doctor, but I strongly prefer a nondrug* *route to a cure. I'm not some kind of nut, but I'm cautious because every so often a drug prescribed as safe is found to be somehow dangerous. Don't you think that if people would live right, and raise their children properly, there would be much less need for medicine?*

I certainly appreciate this query, and I respect the intent with which it was asked. In these days when medical science has made so many dramatic advances, it's easy to think that the answer to any ache or discomfort is to take a pill, and all will be well. This concern is certainly valid.

All of life is a matter of finding the right balances if we are to live it successfully. In medicine, that balance can be very delicate indeed. When I hear from parents who are exhausted and fatigued, because their children, night after night, keep them up, then I know that those parents and children are developing a vicious cycle of resentment that will cause serious problems later on. For such parents I would advise something that will help break that vicious cycle. Certainly I also agree with the avoidance of using pills for any and every whim that comes along. Knowing what and when to prescribe for a trouble child, a sick child, or family, is certainly a medical issue, and one that demands the good judgment of both parent and physician together. For the majority of healthy babies and resourceful parents, I wholeheartedly agree: Do not give pills or medications *unless you absolutely must.* The less reliance on medication, the better. God made our bodies so they tend toward recovery and health most of the time.

People can, however, become so opposed to medically supervised remedies that they may allow unnecessary pain to both themselves and their children. It is those extremes that I would like to help all of you avoid.

Nutrition

149. SERIOUS EATING PROBLEM *What is the solution to the eating problem of the child who just won't eat anything nutritious at all?*

Usually the eating problems parents encounter with their children are relatively unimportant, and many of them pass with time. Sometimes, however, an unwillingness to eat certain types of food can actually threaten a boy's or girl's health.

It does seem as if some little children simply will not eat that nutritious food. However, it is in the young child that the eating problems almost always begin. And more often than not, they have less to do with food than they do with a power struggle—a battleground that gets established between the child and parent. I will tell you parents—that is one battle you really will not win. I will never forget the time that I fed my youngest child those last few bites of egg, and later on (in fact, an hour later), when I took her by my office for her measles immunization shot, she opened her mouth to cry. I found those same eggs still in that child's mouth! I had made her eat them, but she had proved to me that she would not swallow them.

Now most little children have a well-built sense as to what they need to eat in order to stay healthy. For a period of time they may eat a great many fats; that must be what their little systems need. Later on, they'll eat more protein, and still later more vegetables that contain the starches and carbohydrates. As parents, give your children a little bit of freedom to know what they need. Of course feed them all of those items that they need, yet give them little bits of the other foods so that they will balance out their nutritional requirements and learn to eat various nutrients. Be sure you give them a daily vitamin, so that they do not become vitamin deficient. You will find that over a period of time they balance their diets quite well.

It is in older children that I have my major concern, however, and we're seeing a great many people today who suffer from what we call *anorexia nervosa.* These are teenagers, usually girls, who simply refuse to eat or, if they do eat, manage to get rid of the food by actually inducing vomiting or diarrhea. These young people always, in my experience, have some very deep-seated emotional problem, and that requries counseling and outside help.

What to do, then, with your own family? First of all, start with foods that your child really likes best, and that you as a family enjoy. Make the mealtime as pleasant as possible. Get both of the parents to cooperate so that you set the example of eating a little bit of all of the foods that are prepared. Clarify your rules for your child. Have a set time for meals. Do not allow snacks or desserts if some of the food that is offered is not finished. Start with small servings and add more as the child's appetite will accept that. Do not nag or punish or rescue the child. If he does not eat and clean up that plate, give him no more food until the next meal. Be kind and loving, but also be firm.

150. OVERWEIGHT CHILD *My five-year-old daughter is overweight. She is tall for her age, but is much overweight too. Should I put her on a diet, or should I just cut out all the goodies? I don't want her to feel deprived, but she will start school in September and I'm worried about her being teased. Also I am worried that this may be unhealthy.*

Yes, indeed, this mother's concern is wise, because it *is* unhealthy for a child to be seriously overweight. We know that a major problem for adults begins with the existence of excessive fat cells, even from infancy, in children who tend to be overweight. These fat cells are larger and more numerous than in other people, so the tendency to be fat is a lifelong problem, once it becomes established. Now there are certainly many reasons for a child's overeating. Understanding those reasons can help this mother to correct the problem much more readily.

One of the reasons children overeat that concerns me a great deal is that of *loneliness* or *boredom*. I find that children who are afraid of others, who don't have enough playmates, or enough other activities, tend to eat almost as a recreational activity. Often there is a family pattern of overeating. In our culture, eating has come to have many symbolic meanings. It can represent security, intimacy, comfort, celebration; all kinds of emotional needs can seem to be met through the habits of eating.

Overeating may become a contest of wills, almost a battleground or a means of getting even with a parent who is too bossy (as the child might see it), by a child who is too stubborn.

The solution, therefore, becomes dependent on understanding the reasons. First of all, of course, discover why your child does overeat and correct the underlying problem and reason. I suggest that you find playmates, so your child can be more active. Help her to join in a fun time with her friends, so she will not think about eating. Give your child plenty of warm, loving attention. Keep her mind off foods by your own presence in her life.

Start her on some sort of creative activity; getting her hands busy helps her mouth to be much less actively engaged. Help her to color, paint, model with clay; take her on long walks or nature hikes, to change her focus on life. Plan the menu for your family to be less caloric. Provide more raw vegetables, fruits, some eggs and meats, of course, for the proteins. Cut down on the starches, sugars, and desserts. Give a small vegetable and cheese snack between meals and at bedtime, so that the child will not be quite as hungry at mealtime. I recommend that you limit all seconds to low-calorie foods. Serve your child's plate and spread the food out thinly, so it looks like more but actually there is not such a quantity on her plate. Stay loving and understanding. If you can help your child now to win the battle of the calorie, you will have done her a lifelong favor.

151. UNDERWEIGHT *I have a three-year-old son who is underweight. I have been given some suggestions by his pediatrician on how to get him to eat what we eat, but I just can't seem to be firm enough to let him go hungry until he will eat with us. I allow him very little junk food. Do you think I should just wait until he outgrows this, or is it something that will affect him later on? He will not eat meat or vegetables, other than potatoes. At times I feel like such a failure. I would appreciate any advice you could give me.*

That is a problem, indeed, and I share this mother's concern. When my children were small, I worried excessively over how much they should eat. In fact, when we moved from our first home, when our oldest daughter was about five years of age, I cleaned out some unused cupboards by our dining-room table. There I found, to my horror, a row of dried-up little pieces of meat. My daughter had chewed on them for a bit of time, decided she didn't like them, and had very sneakily put them aside! She was perfectly healthy, and the lack of those very precious bits of meat had not hurt her one bit. So I began to learn from those experiences that children will eat what they need. This woman's doctor apparently does not feel that her son has a serious problem. Therefore, I would suggest that she remember that God the Creator has put into each child a tiny little biochemical computer. This computer tells that child over a period of weeks exactly how *much* food he needs and even what *kind* of food he needs. Frankly, many eating problems are *due* to mothers' and fathers' anxiety, and the power struggles and overprotectiveness that come out of that anxiety.

Here are some rules to follow: *Prepare simple, well-balanced meals that are attractive and tasty. Eat your own food with relish, Mother and Father, and set an example for the child.* Many children, in seeing the parents' enjoyment, will want to taste and also enjoy those foods. I suggest offering a child small amounts on his plate, allow him to eat all that he has, and then ask for seconds. Be sure at each meal to have at least one thing that the child likes, if that's possible. Most children love Jell-O, fruits, vegetable sticks, and puddings. These are all very healthy, nourishing foods for children. Be sure that the meats are tender enough to chew, so the child won't have to hide them as my daughter did. Be sure your child has only one small snack between meals (or even none at times), so that he will come to the table with a good appetite. Give him a simple vitamin, and be patient. In due time your child will get all the food he needs.

Physical Development

152. HANDEDNESS *Our two-and-a-half-year-old daughter sometimes seems to be right-handed but she uses her left hand with some things, like holding a fork or spoon. My question is, should she have a dominant hand by this age, or is it still developing? Is there anything we should do to help her?*

Yes, handedness is an important issue to parents, because ours is truly a right-handed world. Children who grow up to be adults with left-handed habits do have some difficult times in using equipment and in other areas of their adult life. Dominance is not truly established until perhaps five or even six years of age in many children. Now sometimes it happens earlier, when a child is strongly right-handed or left-handed, but much more commonly children start out life being ambidextrous. That means they can use one hand one time and the other another time, with equal skill. As they grow, however, it is important to encourage right-handedness when possible. It is equally important, however, not to force that to happen. The motor area of the brain is very close to the speech center of the brain. Many people believe that by forcing a child to change the motor activity from left to right hand, we may cause some problems in the speech area of the brain. There are ways to encourage the right-hand use as much as possible without making it a serious problem.

When the child is quite small and an item is handed to her, remember to place it in her right hand. When the child picks up something with the left hand that he or she may be using for a period of time, gently pry it loose from the left hand, and try placing it in the right hand—especially, as the child begins to use crayons or a pencil. Help the child to transfer that item from the left to the right hand while he is still young enough to use it with equal skill in either hand. If your child shows a strong inclination for the left hand, I strongly recommend that you allow it, because the attempt to transfer that skill when the child is strongly left-handed will not help.

Avoid turning a healthy sort of supervision as a parent into a destructive power struggle by forcing your child to change the handedness, which simply is not going to work anyway. It is equally important to look at your child's feet. A great many parents are not aware that their child may be right- or left-footed. So as your child is crawling, notice which foot or knee the child crawls on first. Watch on which foot he puts a sock or shoe first. Which foot does he start out with when he is running? It is helpful to try to get your child to correlate right-handedness with right-footedness, and vice versa, and not to have the mixed dominance of one foot and the opposite hand. Be careful to love your child, no matter which hand she uses. Don't worry excessively over things that nature itself will determine, and this need not become a serious problem.

153. HEALTH CHECKUPS   *Those visits to the doctor can really be expensive, and with that in mind, how often do you think a seemingly healthy boy or girl needs a checkup?*

For an older child, perhaps an annual checkup is often enough to see your physician. (It would be wonderful if the child stayed perfectly well in between those annual checkups!) Let us go back to the child's birth. Certainly a baby needs a very thorough examination at birth to be certain that there are no birth defects, or if there are, that they receive prompt, adequate attention. There are certain birth defects that may not show up until a little bit later, and so I strongly recommend that babies go in for a very thorough checkup again when they are about six to eight weeks old. Now if the child has any problem with eating or sleeping or functioning normally, even a three weeks' checkup may be advisable. But if everything is going quite smoothly, it's quite all right to wait until six to eight weeks of age.

At that time your doctor will be looking for any other problems that may have developed, or even then will be looking for some of the more obscure birth defects than can occur. An example of the kind of defect that may show up at a later time is a congenitally dislocated hip. In my pediatrics practice, I found several of those through the years, and they often did not show up until the child was several weeks of age.

After that six weeks' checkup, the child will need an examination about every two months until he is six months of age. A great part of those visits has to do with the giving of proper immunizations. Every child must be immunized against whooping cough, diphtheria, measles, and mumps. Those shots are so important that you dare not miss them. I must add to that list *polio,* because now that that has become almost extinct it is easy to forget the importance of giving those immunizations to your child.

Currently there is a great deal of concern regarding the rare but possibly serious reaction to whooping cough vaccine. Such a reaction is extremely rare in the first series of DPT shots. The likelihood of an infant's getting this severe disease is much greater than the outside chance of a reaction. Most young physicians and parents have never seen a case of whooping cough in an infant and do not realize how extremely dangerous it is to babies. Older children who get this disease are very sick with it for at least six weeks, but infants have a high mortality rate from it. Certainly you parents have the right to decide, but be sure you have all the facts.

Furthermore, your child's growth and development needs to be monitored carefully to be sure that some abnormality of the endocrine system has not developed, or perhaps a premature closing of the bones of the skull could take place. That could hamper the child's brain development. After six or seven months of age, probably an annual visit, or every three to six months, is adequate for the normal child.

When you know your doctor and he knows you, you may avoid an extra well-child checkup by telephoning in now and then to check with the doctor. If your child does become ill or has a problem, the doctor or his nurse may make an examination that will be adequate for the period of time. Most doctors will understand your financial concerns. Be frank with your doctor and discuss the facts of the financial problems. He will be glad to help you economize without sacrificing your child's physical well-being.

154. DENTAL CARE   *When do parents need to start their children on a dental-care program?*

I have a rather interesting answer from a dentist friend of mine. He indicated to me that as soon as a new baby's teeth begin to erupt, the dental care should begin. Now obviously the parent has to provide that care, but he recommends after feeding, that even a small child of several months of age have his teeth swabbed with a soft cotton swab, if not brushed with a very soft brush. I have not really seen a toothbrush for such a tiny baby that I would recommend using, but cleaning the teeth with a cotton swab is certainly a very logical process. My dentist friend states that the milk that new babies drink leaves a film on their teeth, and that film encourages the growth of bacteria that are part of the cause of tooth decay. Most parents don't think about that, and I have to admit I never did that with my children.

A child's diet is very important in providing good tooth development and preventing decay. I've already talked about the milk and the milk sugar that can feed bacteria. Too many starches and sugars of any kind also promote bacterial growth. Highly refined, soft diets leave tiny particles of food in the mouth and between the teeth that also promote bacterial growth. Providing at least some roughage foods that contain whole grains and crusts can help to rub off the film that collects, and may prevent some of the particle deposits that cause tooth decay. The old adage, "An apple a day keeps the doctor away," works for the dentist as well. If you don't believe it, try eating an apple sometime when you've not brushed your teeth for a little while. You will find to your surprise that after you eat that apple, your teeth feel very clean and fresh. There is an enzyme in the apple that actually cleans those teeth, so give your child plenty of fruit, particularly apples, to help promote good tooth care.

After every meal, children should learn to brush their teeth to remove food particles and to toughen their gums. Flossing a child's teeth is something that is very important, but I do not find very many young children providing that care. The in-between tooth surfaces certainly are cleaned best with that kind of attention. Don't neglect the child's baby teeth! It's easy to think that they'll soon be lost, and so we don't need to worry about them. A child needs to visit the dentist first somewhere between the second and third birthdays—first of all, to familiarize the child with the dentist's office, when there is no major work to be done, then to teach the child proper dental care. Use fluoride toothpastes, provide adequate soft brushes for plenty of brushing time without hurting the child's gums. These are all processes that will teach your child good oral hygiene, and will prevent the decay that can cause a great deal of trouble later on.

155. WATERBEDS   *My granddaughter is still sleeping in a crib, but her parents are getting ready to put her in a regular bed. They are planning on a waterbed. I'm wondering if this would be harmful to her growing bone structure. How old should a child be when he is given a waterbed? Also, how old when taken from a crib? I also have an eleven-year-old granddaughter with diabetes. Her parents just bought her a waterbed. What is your opinion of a child her age with her condition sleeping on a waterbed?*

Certainly the advent of waterbeds for children is new, but I understand from checking with authorities that these actually have some benefit for children. Recently a large hospital, which takes care of a great many tiny babies, has begun using waterbeds even in isolettes for their tiny, little, newborn babies. I understand the grandmother's concern because the traditional belief was that babies need a firm support for their wobbly little bodies. Indian babies in this country were wrapped on boards that were barely padded at all, and a firm mattress was certainly thought to be the very best for Caucasian babies.

Now, however, we know that this is not necessarily true, and the motion of the tiny baby on a water mattress can resemble the motion of the mother's body when he was still in her womb. The fluid movement that that child enjoyed before birth can be quite soothing and comforting to him after birth as well. It seems that the support of a well-constructed waterbed is quite adequate for almost all children. The only exceptions I can imagine are those that might have some special orthopedic problems that might require an unusually firm bed.

There certainly is no reason a person with diabetes would be hurt by sleeping in a waterbed, nor would it necessarily help that condition but it would be simply a matter of choice, so this grandmother need not worry about the waterbed for her grandchildren.

Now, when should a baby leave her crib and go into a bed for an older child? I would recommend that that be anywhere between two and five years of age. Some babies prefer the crib and the security of it for quite a period of time. Others, the more active ones, are climbing down and running around on the floor, when they still seem to be small enough that they should be in a crib. The important point is that the baby be in a bed that is safe and comfortable.

156. DELAYED PUBERTY   *What are the worries of a teen who may mature either earlier or later than his or her peers?*

The preadolescent and adolescent years can be difficult, even under the best of circumstances. That difficulty can be multiplied for the boy or girl whose biological clock is a little bit off from the majority of teenagers. Any differences certainly carry their own set of problems. Almost always early puberty happens to girls, or at least it is more obvious in girls because of their menstrual cycles. Girls who begin that cycle as early as the age of ten or eleven, very commonly feel as if they have been unfairly pushed into an adult world that they neither socially nor personally feel ready for. They somehow feel separate or different from their peers, and almost feel a sense of being abused. Especially in elementary school, I think little girls feel embarrassed or upset when they have their menstrual periods. If they ever have an accident that results in the staining of their clothes, they simply do not know how to handle it. They need help from parents and teachers to prevent such accidents and to take care of them.

Some people believe that beginning puberty early causes an early preoccupation with sexual interests, but I disagree with that idea. Sexual awareness is an issue that demands consideration on the part of parents and some protectiveness in order to prevent a child's precocious fascination with sexual interests.

The late bloomers in this field of puberty generally are young men. Those boys who develop late have as much of a problem as the girls who find the advent of their puberty early. Boys whose voices do not change as soon as their friends, who do not develop the hair growth and the other signs of their masculinity in reasonable timing with their friends, often feel left out, inadequate, different, and can develop a serious inferiority complex.

This is what you parents need to do about the situation: First of all, have your child examined physically, and let your doctor help to explain to the child whether or not there is any hormonal inbalance or need for concern, or to reassure the child that this is just a variation from normal. Be reassuring yourselves, and don't let your child feel different or inadequate because of the variation in his or her particular clockwork. Help your children to dress and groom in a way that will compensate for the difference in their development and enable them to fit more adequately into the social sphere of their peers.

157.   SHOES   *Do you think it's necessary to buy expensive shoes for children? Sometimes they outgrow them in a matter of months, and with three kids I hate to spend money we can't easily afford. On the other hand, I don't want to skimp if it's going to hurt their feet. One of the reasons I've avoided the discount places is because they are self-service, and I'm not really sure how to pick out shoes that fit. I've relied on shoe salesmen that seem to know what they are doing. Do you think the better shoes are really necessary?*

Sometimes better shoes (or more expensive ones) are necessary, and yet those times are fairly rare. There are children who have such normal feet that any shoes or no shoes are perfectly fine. But other children may have special problems of an orthopedic nature that demand special fitting. Watch your child's feet, therefore, parents, and see if they tend to toe out or turn their toes in. Notice the child's ankles as he or she walks. See if the ankles tend to turn inward or if the child walks on the outer edge of the foot. If you can't tell that for sure by watching the child walk, notice where the shoes tend to wear. If they wear on the inner sole, then it is possible that the child's ankles are a bit weak. If the outer part wears off in an uneven fashion, then the child's foot may be growing in a way that can create serious problems in later life. If that is the case, I recommend that you visit an orthopedic doctor who can tell you if the child's feet need special braces or special-fitting shoes. Certainly if it's questionable at all, go to a reliable shoe store, and have a very well-trained salesmen fit your child's feet.

For the normal, average child, the fitting of shoes is really very possible by an average parent. Here is a rule of thumb (literally) for fitting your child's shoe, if you go to a help-yourself shoe store. The child's new shoe should be a thumb's width too long. That is, if you press down where the child's great toe is and the end of the shoe, you should be able to fit your thumb in that space. It should be about half a finger's width, or the edge of your finger, too wide as you press the edge of your finger between the little toe and the edge of the shoe. You should have enough room to feel that finger settle in to the leather at that point. This gives room for your child's foot to spread a little, and be comfortable, and to grow enough to get reasonable wear out of the shoe without its being so large that it creates blisters or discomfort from friction. When you go to a regular shoe store with the shoe salesmen, watch how he fits your child, and you will learn some of the techniques for buying at least some of your child's shoes in a less-expensive store.

158. CONTACT LENSES   *At what age would you consider getting contacts for a child?*

That is a problem that I have certainly had to contend with personally, because all of our children wear glasses. My experience is, however, that very few eye doctors will consent to contacts prior to twelve to fourteen years of age. Twelve, in fact, is quite early. Soft contacts certainly are safer than the hard ones, which are still available, and formerly were the only ones that were given to children. But even soft contacts have some risks involved.

Contact Considerations. There are several issues that can help parents to know how to choose the time for contacts and when to avoid those. First of all, the *degree of visual impairment* is important, and children who are extremely nearsighted have to wear such very heavy glasses that the contacts almost become necessary. By placing contacts directly over the eye, the vision is much better, and the convenience is much greater. Still another issue that must be considered is the *degree of responsibility* of a child. Contacts take a great deal of care. They can be lost; they are very expensive; they must be kept extremely clean in order to avoid infections or injury to the eye. So if your child is not very responsible, you may find that neither you nor the child can afford the luxury of contact lenses.

Still another issue is that of the degree of activity of your child. Children who are in swimming or active sports are much more likely to have their contact lenses damaged, lost, or broken. Furthermore, broken contact lenses in the eye of a child can cause irreparable damage in some cases. I recommend that you evaluate your child's sense of responsibility, as well the degree of social damage that wearing heavy glasses can cause. *Ask* your *doctor.* You then should trust your eye doctor with a recommendation for the time and the way your child may move from glasses to contact lenses. I certainly suggest that you look into the possibility of an insurance policy during those active, growing-up years, when lenses can be lost very readily. Your child's vision is priceless. Take good care of it, for now and for his future years as well.

159. HOW MUCH SLEEP? *I am the mother of a growing three-and a-half-year-old, and I want to know how much sleep my little boy needs. Also, can he still be expected to take a nap?*

Certainly that is a question that a great many families struggle with. Believe it or not, little babies up to the age of almost six months need eighteen to twenty hours of sleep a day. There is a rather rapid decline in the amount of sleep that's needed after that time. Here are some factors that affect the amount of sleep that is needed by individual children. They can guide you in establishing bedtimes for your children:

Sleep Needs Guide. 1. The age and growth rate of a child certainly are important factors. I've already described the amount of sleep that little babies need. By the early grades, they need much less, and in adolescence they may revert to needing more for a period of time. As children grow rapidly, they do need more rest.

2. A child's health will affect the amount of sleep as well. Children who have allergies or upper respiratory infections, colds, or have fevers or any illness, will need more sleep than children who are in good health.

3. There is an inborn energy generator that also helps to determine how much sleep is needed. The amount of energy that's expended on a daily basis can influence the amount of required rest.

Telltale Signs. There are some signs that will help you to recognize when your child is beginning to get sleepy and needs to go to bed. Often children become irritable and fussy when they are sleepy. With my children, I learned that their eyes began to look sleepy. There was a little bit of a lag in their eyelids; they weren't quite drowsy, but their lids were just blinking. I do recommend that children have a regular bedtime, but that you establish that bedtime based upon the actual physical needs of your individual child.

Avoid the Power Struggle. There are some problems connected with sleep habits, however, and one of these is *power struggling.* Each child will want to determine his own bedtime, and that's a sign of his wanting some independence. If you're not careful, you will be hooked into trying to prove that you are the boss, rather than looking at the physical needs that are the real evidence of the bedtime to be established. Each child's brain and body will bring about drowsiness when he is tired, unless he has gotten into this sort of power struggle. Many babies give up their morning nap by a year of age. Children often stop their afternoon naps at the age of three or four, though some of them continue them even through kindergarten. A lot of children will have difficulty going to sleep at night, when they have had an afternoon nap. Eight to ten hours of sleep per night into early puberty is usually plenty, and even during puberty a matter of eight or nine hours is none too much. Keep bedtime a snuggly, warm, and intimate time—a time for the exchange of love and confidence, nurturing, and prayers, and don't let it become a power struggle in your family.

160. SPECIAL PROBLEMS   *How can parents decide if their boy or girl has a speech problem serious enough to merit attention?*

That's really not an easy question to answer because many speech problems of children are temporary, and they will outgrow them.

Delayed Speech. Here is an example of that: There was a little boy who simply would not talk. The parents came to the doctor repeatedly, asking for help. He checked the child's palate and tongue, and every area of the child's physical being, to find out why he was not talking. He certainly was not retarded. He was sent to various speech pathologists for a diagnosis and evaluation, and no one could find anything that was wrong. When that little boy became six years old and went to first grade, he suddenly began talking and has talked ever since. One of the concerns, then, is that of delayed speech. That is when a child has reached three or four years of age and is not talking. Frankly, we as medical people do not worry about speech delay until that time because some children do not talk much before then.

Abnormal Sounds. This is the second problem related to speech. The child who lisps and pronounces his *s*s as if they are *th*s, who confuses the *r*s and *l*s as well as other sounds that pose a problem for him—will certainly cause his parents to be concerned. Many abnormal sounds often are related to baby talk, and as parents talk in baby language to their child, the child continues that baby talk even when he is no longer small. Most children will outgrow this habit when adults routinely stop the baby talk.

Stuttering and Stammering. This is a very serious condition that worries a great many people. A friend of mine indicated that his little boy began stammering and simply could not get a sentence out. After a great deal of effort on their own part, he and his wife took the child to a speech pathologist. As she worked with them and the little boy, she discovered that the child, being the youngest of the family, simply was not able to get the attention of anyone when he wanted to talk. So he learned to stammer and stutter in order to keep the center stage once he did get it! Despite their doubtfulness that this was, in fact, the problem, the family followed her recommendation, which was to give the child plenty of time to talk, and plenty of attention. He overcame that difficulty very quickly. A refusal to speak because of anger or fear is not an uncommon thing. We call that *elective mutism.* If that is to be corrected, both the child and the parents must have the help of a professional counselor.

Almost all children learn to talk. They may talk too much or too little. They may talk with a little difficulty, but the important fact for you to remember is that communicating the love and concern you feel is what really counts.

161. PLASTIC SURGERY   *If you could afford to give your child either a better education or a better-looking face, which would you choose?*

That's a very interesting question, and one that many parents should think about carefully. There are a few basic questions that I'd like to suggest to parents who are considering this issue: First of all, who is it who judges whether a child's appearance is good or bad? Sometimes, because of certain familial traits or values, we think a child's nose may be too big or the jaw too small. Yet the ancient Romans considered a big nose a sign of intelligence! So you need to think about whether or not your child's problem is a real one, or an imagined one that's related to family or community values.

Just how abnormal is your child in comparison with his friends? What are the values of the child himself and herself? Is the child feeling really inferior or inadequate because of the appearance or the particular handicap that may be possibly corrected? It is rare in my experience to see children who are so abnormal that they really stand out as being ugly or different. Many of these children can have their problem corrected by simply learning how to style their hair, or, as they grow into the teenage years, to wear a little makeup. This can often solve that problem very easily. You need to know your child, and what it is that is bothering that child.

Let me discuss with you what you may do for your child: First, go to a physician and talk about the issue. How much will it cost? Is it possible that by having a psychiatric evaluation and determining how seriously the problem may affect your child's emotional health, that your insurance may cover the cost of plastic surgery? What can be done to correct the problem, short of going through the expense of the plastic surgery, if in fact that is possible? If corrective procedures are impossible, or you simply cannot afford to have that done, then you need to help your child to understand that this is a handicap. It is something that will cause some grief, but the child can get through that grief and go on to understanding that the whole of life is composed of many parts. As your child learns to compensate for the limits in one area, he or she will develop a greater degree of strength in many other areas of life. Developing academic skills, social skills, and activities that can be shared with other children, can more than compensate for the heartache of having an appearance that is not quite up to the standards that you and your child would like. Teach your child to use his own pain to learn compassion for others.

Sexual Considerations

162. SEXUAL PEER PRESSURE   *In your counseling, do you see teenagers who are feeling a real pressure to be sexually active?*

Yes, I do, and I really feel sorry for them, because many of them don't honestly want that experience themselves. They do feel left out, or somehow different from their peers. It's a sad fact that teenage pregnancies are extremely common and sexually transmitted diseases are epidemic. Whether we like to admit it or not, even teens from "good" families are not insulated from pressures to be sexually active. They can be made to feel amost abnormal if they are not as experienced as their classmates.

A very good friend of mine happens to be a teacher, and she came home from school one day to find her own eighth-grade daughter in a very risky position with a young man she was friends with. When she talked with her daughter about the situation and what could have happened, the child said, "But, Mother, I'm the only one of my friends who has never had sex." I think it was sad that a fourteen-year-old child should have to say that, but it was very true.

Peer pressure is so important to adolescent youngsters. Also, I find a great many children (and literally they are *old* children) feeling lonely. Out of their loneliness, they have a need for companionship that very quickly can become physical rather than just social. One little girl I worked with some years ago felt that because she was so lonely, she owed anyone who paid her any attention, even the purchase of a soft drink after school, a sexual favor in return.

The push of young people into a premature adulthood is a very common factor today. There's far too much information available to young people much too soon. There is too little comfortable openness with parents. The ability to talk about questions and feelings and find thoughtful answers within the family unfortunately is not very common. On the other hand, there is far too much exposure to sexually stimulating sights and ideas on television and in magazines. The local grocery store or drugstore far too often displays very explicitly pornographic materials, which are available to anyone—child or adult—for the looking.

The casual recreational attitude about sex—that it's simply something for fun—takes away from this very beautiful, significant part of life, its true meaning and value.

Parents, teach your children the real meaning of sex. Help them learn to be responsible in their social lives and for their sexual attitudes. Help them to learn the self-control that will establish the foundation for healthy sexuality and sexual relationships later.

163. DOLLS FOR BOYS   *I have a problem and can't seem to find a satisfactory answer. I have considered consulting a professional, but have been unable to find a suitable one in our area. My little boy is three and a half. At a very early age, he showed an interest in dolls, so I exposed him to dolls, thinking I was doing the right thing. Now I'm wondering if I didn't make a big mistake. I'm very concerned, and don't know how to handle this problem. I don't want to make him feel guilty or rejected because of this, but he senses his father and I being uptight about this. He likes to dress in feminine clothing, and always pretends he is the mommy or the girl when pretending. He is an intelligent boy, and seems well adjusted in other ways. Do you have any advice for me?*

Dolls a No-No? This is not an uncommon problem, and actually I would like to address it in two parts. The first issue is fairly simple. That is whether or not boys should be allowed to play with dolls. Frankly, I am very much in favor of little boys learning to play with dolls, because I find a great many men have difficulty in learning how to be daddies. A part of that difficulty lies in the fact that little boys historically have been discouraged from playing with dolls, and in not playing with dolls, have failed to learn some of those parenting techniques.

I would suggest, however, that Daddy show little boys how to play with dolls, and that he teach him how to do this as fathers do with little babies. This will give the child a masculine technique, rather than a feminine or motherly technique in playing with those "children."

Sexual Identity. The other issue is that of a child's preference for feminine clothes, and identifying in a feminine role. That is a serious concern, because that can become a very *major* problem when the child reaches puberty and is searching for a sexual identity. I strongly recommend that between the ages of two and a half or three and five or six, that little boys spend a great deal of time with their daddies. If little boys like to dress up, I see no harm in that. Help them to dress up in Daddy's big shoes, hats, jackets, or shirts. Dads, take time to teach your sons what it is that you do in your work lives. Have them with you when you work on the cars, mow the grass, go fishing, or whatever you do, even though that demands some extra attention and energy from you.

164.   EFFEMINATE SON   *I'm beginning to get very worried about my ten-year-old son. I've caught him dressing up in my clothes, and he seems to thoroughly enjoy it. Am I overreacting? Can you help me know what to do?*

That is a distressing question, but there is help for this mother. First of all, develop a loving, happy relationship with your son. Sometimes children want to dress in their parents' clothes in order to feel close to them. I would be a little concerned that your child's seeking after your garments may be a symbolic means of his seeking a close, loving relationship with you. He may, of course, just want to feel the softness of the texture of your clothes. He can have this in a soft, silky shirt of his father's, or in a soft toy.

Help your son develop a warm, positive relationship with his father, too. Include other male relatives and adult friends who can be models for him, as to what kind of a man he would like to be someday. Explain to your son that he needs to learn to be a man when he grows up, and so he needs to play dress-up in Daddy's clothes. He may enjoy that just as much as he does dressing up in Mother's clothes. Punishing or disapproving of you son's effeminacy will drive it into hiding and cause guilt and fear. He may be afraid that he is different from other people, and that something is wrong with him. As his mother, you need to understand his needs for your approval, for closeness, warmth, and softness.

Avoid undue worry or overreacting. I have seen a great many parents so worried that their child may become a homosexual that they actually drive them in that very direction. Simply encourage maleness in your son. Be proud of those masculine traits, and reflect them to him in compliments. Find ways to turn his effeminate tendencies into masculine gentleness. Your son can actually grow in his own unique way into manhood, and you will be very proud of him.

165.   BREAST-FEEDING CONFUSION   *I am the father of a three-year-old daughter. Her baby-sitter is nursing her baby, and naturally my girl is fascinated. Unfortunately, the mother uses rather misleading euphemisms for the process of breast-feeding, which I* *feel may confuse my daughter. How can I correct her impressions without causing problems with the sitter's family?*

That's an important question. Frankly, I would like to suggest to all parents that being simple and open are the hallmarks of wholesome education of children in any area. If you are going to provide for your child healthy sex education, obviously you need to know what the subject is about. So parents, it is important for you to have information. You may get this from any junior-high-school physiology book, or simply from your own practical knowledge as parents. This father may be the one who will have to explain to his child what is actually going on.

In teaching his daughter, the father must have a wholesome attitude about all kinds of matters—certainly about the mother's physiology, the facts of breast-feeding, as well as how to communicate the information to his child. This father can explain to his little girl, when he has her at home, that the baby-sitter's feeding of her baby is a part of God's wonderful plan for nurturing and protecting a little tiny infant. However, the mother's body and the process of breast-feeding deserves a proper name and explanation. It need not be embarrassing to tell this to a child, and I would hope that the baby-sitter, too, could feel less awkward and a little more open and frank in her discussion of feeding her child. Dad, teach your daughter several accurate facts under the correct names when she asks questions. Tell what she asks, but invite more questions if she has them.

If you need to have a baby-sitter, parents, please be careful that you tell them what you want them to explain to your child. There are many situations that arise in a baby-sitter's home that need explaining to a little child. It's important that the parents tell the baby-sitter what is okay and not okay to discuss with their child.

166.   BIRDS AND BEES   *My mother and father never talked to me about the birds and the bees. Now I am the father of a young son. Is this something I should do or that my wife should take care of?*

My answer to that is, "Yes." *Both* you and your wife should be involved in teaching your child about the birds and the bees—and the rest of his sex education as well. I recommend strongly, however, that you as a father and mother begin with yourselves. Talk about your child and what you want him to know about sex, but especially what you want him to know about his own personal sexuality. Unfortunately, this area creates a little nervousness or embarrassment to a great many parents. Begin by asking yourselves this question: What kind of spouse and parent do I want my son or daughter to become? Discuss this question broadly and deeply until you are comfortable with it. Neither be ashamed nor flaunt a false liberalness.

Be aware that each parent contributes to teaching a child about these concepts. Mothers can give to a son a very special slant on how it is that his future wife and his own daughter may feel toward him. And fathers certainly need to be a model to a son, and in turn an image to the daughter of the kind of husband she may choose someday. There is no way that one parent alone can give really adequate sex education to a child.

From talking and planning together about your values and what it is you want your child to learn, I recommend that you go on to the actual teaching of your child the simple, natural facts of life. Many people have made a joke for so long about the birds and the bees that they forget that it's a wonderful beginning. Teaching your child how it is that bees carry pollen from one flower to another, thereby fertilizing that flower and making it possible for it to become seed bearing in turn, is a wonderful way to begin your child's sex education.

How is it that birds lay and hatch eggs? How is it that birth takes place in the lives of pets within the family? These are simple, natural ways of teaching your child about sex. Keep the information that you give to your child simple, direct, to the point, and appropriate to his age. Be calm, natural, loving, and keep the door open for future communication. You can help your child to grow up with a wholesome attitude and identity as a sexual being.

167. SEX EDUCATION TIMING   *What help can you offer to parents who don't want to give their children more sexual information than they need, but do want to keep ahead of what's on television, and even what other kids are offering?*

Believe me, it hurries any parent today to stay ahead of television and their children's peers! A great many children have too much sexual information far too early. The most important guide I can give parents is that they must set a climate that promotes questioning in any area of the child's life, including sexual issues. Whenever the child is concerned or interested or hears a comment, that child will feel perfectly free to talk about such issues with the parents. You must be aware of your responsibility to teach sex as well as other subjects to your own children, and not give that over to other people quite as readily as I find many parents doing. You must look for avenues through which to teach. Start where it's easy. We have become so advanced in our sophistication sexually that the simple means of teaching children about sex has been forgotten. Those simple facts about biological procreation are a wonderful beginning in helping them to understand human sexuality.

168.   CHECKPOINTS FOR SEX EDUCATION   *What are the attitudes about sex children should have learned by the time they reach school age?*

There are five in all. Not only is it important for a child to develop those attitudes, but frankly they must begin with the parents. First of all, there is *a child's attitudes toward his body, so important in this whole concept of sexuality.* If the child feels that part of his body is shameful, and he is embarrassed about that area, then he will come to marriage later on with inhibitions and misconceptions that can make his marriage unhappy. Parents, you need to teach your child that his body is beautiful, that God made it, and that he needs to value it and give it dignity and pride. Obviously not being ashamed does not mean that a child flaunts his body or exposes himself to others either. The concept of privacy is just as important, along with the dignity that involves, as the recognition of the beauty of a child's physical being.

Emotionally, *children need to have open, accepting, and honest attitudes toward sex.* And that attitude, parents, comes from you. I have worked with families many times in which the parents were so ashamed or embarrassed to talk about any sexual area of life that the child could not have that open, unashamed attitude. So you need to talk with one another, read wholesome books, and share your ideas with trusted friends, until you become comfortable with your own feelings about sexuality.

Intellectually, I think *parents need a good deal of information to help them with their sexual ideas and attitudes.* I find many families not having a vocabulary with which to discuss sexual issues. So you need to learn the names for the various parts of the body, as well as their functions, and any junior-high-school textbook can provide those. You don't have to go through medical school to learn.

SEXUAL CONSIDERATIONS   189

Socially, it is extremely important that *you teach your child to respect the privacy of other people.* Many times I have seen parents who are shocked by children who investigate one another's bodies and evidence curiosity, which results in exploring that can be frightening to the child, as well as the parent. So you need to teach your child not only to respect and admire and appreciate his own body, but to respect others enough to give them the privacy and dignity they deserve.

Spiritually, I think it's so important that you *teach the child the awe of his body as being part of God's creation.* As you share all of your attitudes, let them be positive in the teaching of sexuality to your child.

169.   TOUCHING MOMMY   *Help. Over the past few months my four-year-old has become extremely preoccupied with my breasts—both when I am undressed, and also when I am fully clothed. I first tried ignoring her behavior, and dressing when she was in another room, but that isn't always possible. I then tried to explain that she should not touch my breasts around other people, because it is a private part of my body. Her question then was, "Can I touch them when we are alone?" I don't want her to think of this as ugly or forbidden and yet I don't want it to go on. Incidentally, she saw me breast-feeding over a year ago and was not at all interested then.*

Actually many three- and four-year-olds develop an interest in Mommy's breasts. In my experience, this almost always relates to a time that they have seen their mother or another mother nursing a baby. Even though this was a year ago, the child would not have forgotten that experience, and there may be some special reasons why now she is renewing her interest. Frankly, I see this as a natural curiosity, and it gives parents a wonderful chance to do some good sex education. Explain to this little girl (or your son, if he is curious), the purpose of a mother's breasts, and ask the child for any questions he or she may have about Mother's body. A little girl may be curious about why she is a little girl and yet she doesn't have breasts. Explain to her then that someday she will develop breasts, and even help her to know how and when that will happen. With either a boy or a girl, it is important to interpret to them that you know they like the feel of soft things and being a soft mommy is a part of the cuddling that all children and parents can enjoy. Explain frankly, however, that you simply do not feel good being touched or stroked on that part of your body—either alone or in front of other people.

170.   SQUEAL LAW   *My question concerns the so-called squeal law. Do you have any ideas on how we can legally help fight for the rescinding of this protective law? My daughter has been on medication since she was nine weeks old. It can cause a serious reaction with other medicines, and I can't believe that she could go to any federally funded clinic and receive pills or other birth-control devices without my knowledge or consent.*

I certainly share this mother's concern. There are several dangers that the ability to get birth control without parental knowledge creates. Some of these are very subtle and a lot of people, well meaning, simply do not think about them. First of all, this practice takes away the rightful status and position that parents hold with the child—the protective, authoritative role that is God-given, in my belief. The practice of giving birth control to young people without parental knowledge essentially says to that young person, "You and we here at the clinic know better than your parents what is right for you. We will become your ally, and we will give you permission, even though your parents might not." That, you see, causes a dividedness in a family, which is a very damaging and serious matter. The justification advocates of this practice offer is that giving birth control to young people will prevent the incidence of unwanted pregnancies. Statistics, however, prove that this simply is not true. During the years that such devices have been available to young people, the birth rate among single young women has risen from 10 percent to as high as 17 percent, by one study that I learned of recently. Now if you want to take action, here are some suggestions:

Learn the name of your congressman, the one who represents your district, as well as your state senator, and write them giving your reasons or these reasons that I listed. This mother's case is a particularly excellent one, and one that is not at all uncommon. Let me come back to the practical level, however. It is your opportunity as a mother and father to teach your child the risks of taking birth control when she is not ready to do that. The risks of becoming sexually active and the complications that all of that part of their lives involve, are those that you as parents can guide and control in some degree with your child. Keep your communications open. Keep your love clear and constant. It is that love and your guidance that will always be the best protection for your child.

Social Development

171. UNPOPULAR CHILD   *If you could see that your child was very unpopular, would you step in and do something?*

I think that I would. It's obvious that every child can't be the most popular in the class. But it can hurt when you see that your boy or girl is left out. *Advantages.* There are some positive values in a child's being popular that I'd like to list. One is that being popular reinforces a child's sense of significance and self-worth, and every child needs some of that. It opens a large opportunity for children to be a good influence on peers, when they have many friends among a group in their class. Simply, it's fun to be popular, and well liked, and to be part of a large group of friends. There's a sense of security in belonging to a group of people that is really universal. All of us need to belong to a group.

Disadvantages. Being popular, on the other hand, can become a goal in itself, and in this case a child can be driven by that need to have many friends and to be well liked. In doing so, she can lose the individuality and personal values that are so essential to a child's later real maturity and integrity. Being popular can, in its very risk, involve a sense of insecurity. While on the one hand, it makes the child feel secure to belong, the fear of losing one's position in a group can preoccupy a child's attention and cause insecurity.

The worst risk of all is the possibility that a child's sense of worth, instead of coming out of himself, becomes dependent on the values and the relationship within that group. I think that is something parents really need to watch for.

Solution. What, then, is a parent to do about a child who is not very well liked? First of all, I would suggest that you find out how your child treats and reacts with other children. Be sure that your child is kind, thoughtful, and empathetic with other children, not selfish and demanding. Evaluate your child's personality. Some children simply prefer being alone. They are not lonely. They like their own company, and are very satisfied to have only one or two friends.

If your child lacks social skills, teach him how to play with other children, how to talk with other children, and how to be a considerate and thoughtful friend himself.

172. HELP FOR A LONELY CHILD   *What can parents do to help a lonely boy or girl?*

They can start by beginning to understand why the child is lonely. The causes are almost always focused in some serious degree on a lack of self-esteem. The child simply does not feel as good as others, or he would be out there mixing with them and a part of them. Insecurity is certainly one of the problems that causes loneliness, and I find that comes from the child who has had to move too often, with repeated losses of friends. Or perhaps it's the child who has a brother or sister who is much more successful and popular. The overprotected child often is lonely as well. Parents who tend to do too much for a child unwittingly create in him a sense that he can't do anything. Hence the child feels afraid of or unequal to other children. The overcriticized child becomes lonely, because he is afraid or ashamed, or really unwilling to risk further mistakes and more criticisms by failing.

The cures of loneliness are something I would like to focus on in some depth. Parents, first of all check out your own feelings about your child. If you resent that child, or you feel very worried or tense about him, he will sense that as reflecting some defect or problem within himself. If you feel that he is incapable, take a look at his strengths. Begin to praise your child's efforts. 1. *Reflect to him* everything that he does at all successfully. Do this simply and sincerely, but do it regularly. 2. *Require your child to do something,* whatever it might be. Help him to do it the very best that he can, and then praise the effort he has made, as well as the results of the effort. That's one of the best ways that I know to begin building self-esteem in your child. 3. *Check out the possibility of unfavorable comparisons,* if not by you as parents, perhaps by other relatives, or even by your child himself.

Work at exploring new interests, abilities, and activities. As your child develops some skills that he or she can share with playmates, you will find that the friendliness automatically happens. Children will crowd around him to learn the exciting new skill that he has mastered. Help your child with his social adjustments. Find some new friends, maybe one or two at a time, and bring them into your home with you, where you can teach your child to play comfortably and successfully with someone else. There are times when the problem has become so severe that parents' efforts alone are not enough. Do not hesitate to seek a counselor to help you to know how to help your child to be loving and happy.

173. RESTAURANT MANNERS   *We thought it would be a good idea to occasionally take our children with us when we go out for dinner. But it can really be a hassle. Is it too much to expect children to sit quietly in restaurants?*

Frankly, I don't think that it is too much to expect, and yet I can understand why children have a hard time. In church, they understand that it's very quiet. In school, they have to behave a certain way, but a restaurant is kind of in between. Most people are quiet, but they are talking and moving about, and so I think it can be confusing to children. Up to the age of three, I frankly do not recommend taking children out to nice restaurants. True enough, many calm, adaptive babies may lie in their infant seats, or sit happily in a high chair through a fairly long meal and behave quite well. But from eighteen months to three years of age they simply are restless, have a hard time sitting still, naturally want to be active, and do not understand the restrictions of a restaurant. I would make these suggestions however, if parents would like to train their children to eat out with them:

First of all, plan a game at home pretending it's a restaurant. You can teach your child how to order, how to sit and wait for the meal, and how to eat properly in a restaurant. If a child can do it at home, and knows what to expect, then try the next step. Go to a fast-food place, and live out the game as you have at home, but following the routines that the restaurant would expect.

The next step is to go to a family restaurant, and try a little longer time with a little more formal atmosphere. When your children can handle these situations, then try a rather nice place. Now make the rules and expectations very clear. Tell the child that he must sit still until the meal is over. Take crayons and paper along, or some small toy that the child can play with during those tedious times of waiting. Tell your child that he may go to the rest room only once. (My children use to love to make trips to the rest room, and that can become quite annoying.) The child may want (and may in fact need) to sit in the parent's lap at times, if the age is appropriate, and if he gets tired of sitting in a high chair.

Make the consequences for any infraction of those rules quite clear. The first consequence, for example, would be that the child must leave his own chair, and come and sit in the parent's lap or be close to the parent, so his body can control those active little child bodies. The child may need to be taken out of the restaurant for a short time with a firm reminder that he must behave if he would return. Of course the child may need to be taken home. A spoiled meal once or twice is a small price to pay for teaching a child meaningful discipline and consistent training. Be clear and firm. Children will sense your uncertainty and vain threats and test you out. With time, firmness, consistency, and creativity, you and your child can learn to really enjoy the luxury of eating out.

174. THANK-YOU NOTES   *Do you think that children should send thank-you notes for every gift they receive?*

No, frankly I don't think so. I think that would be going back to the old rigidity and legalism that can be very stiff and not very truly gracious. A personal, verbal *thank you* does very well for many occasions. A birthday party for a younger child can provide the opportunity for a direct thank you at the time the gift is opened, and again when the friends depart. I think that's adequate for a younger child. We don't want to become so rigid about ceremonies that children even lose their sense of gratitude, and would rather not have a gift than have to write notes that are too numerous. A special telephone call can be just as effective in expressing appreciation as a written note.

I do believe in giving special thank-you notes on certain occasions, and here are some guidelines that I hope will help. First of all, be very careful that you teach your child an honest sense of gratitude. Do this by not giving too much, by your own expressions of sincere gratitude, and by the attitude that you teach your child. It's important, once your child really feels grateful, that you help him express that gratitude. It's important that you have thank-you notes available for children who are not able to write very much, and that you help them in composing those notes. In fact, it's fun for the parents of a five- or six-year-old to sit down with the child and print, with the child's help, a very simple expression of the gratitude the child feels for a Christmas gift or a birthday gift, which may have involved a good deal of effort for a grandparent to send from a distance. Helping them relive the fun of the gift, and putting that fun down in words, can give the child a good foundation for the pleasure of writing notes, rather than the burdensomeness of that task.

As the child grows older and more capable, the parents need to do less of the writing and composing, and give more and more of that over to the child. Set up a specific time for this to be done, making that time a very definite ritual and following through with your own responsibility—that of seeing the note was written. You, your child, and the gift giver will all be pleased that appreciation was shown in this way.

175. UNDESIRABLE FRIENDS *I'm very upset about our twin boys, eleven years old, copying their friends' actions and mannerisms. This has really been a problem. One boy's friend is very nice but very hyper, and picks his food apart like a monkey. My son gets very angry at me when I ask him not to act like his friend. My other boy's friend is not a bad boy, but is being raised by his grandparents, and is very spoiled and rebellious. I just don't understand why my sons can't be themselves. Do you think they have a bad self-image?*

Not at all. Friends are a very important part of a child's life. Interestingly, children need their parents' approval of their friends much more than their disapproval. Look at the positive aspects of your children's friends and comment on those. The children themselves will pick up the defects and the negative aspects of those kids.

Here are some suggestions for you and your children's friends: First of all, welcome them into your home, but be around and observe. Of course you need to make your rules very clear and make them stick. You can do this without embarrassing your child or estranging your child's friends. Help your children to see the wonderful qualities of those friends and learn to emulate those qualities, but also help them to understand their faults.

Having an imperfect friend allows great opportunities to compliment your own children for the areas of their lives in which they perhaps are better than those friends. Without putting down their friends, compliment them, and let them know that you appreciate some of their good habits and good mannerisms. Teach your own child to help his friends to become better people. In doing that he will learn to feel better about himself and you.

Spiritual Training

176. TEACHING INFANT ABOUT GOD   *What can a mother do in the first year of life to teach a child about God? Is prayer all we do at this age?*

Certainly prayer is not all we do, and yet prayer is very important. The most vital part of a little baby's life is the development of a sense of trust, and it is not hard to understand that sense of trust in mother and father is the quality that is later transferred to trusting the Heavenly Father. As the new mother comforts her little baby, provides for his safety, cuddles him with her strength and warmth, provides the brightness and joy and stimulation in life; as the mother feeds the baby, provides loving sounds, the consistency that a child needs, she is teaching that child the basic sense of trust that is so important.

Fathers are important in this process as well, and many times when mother's arms are tired and begin to tremble a little, the father's taking over the care of a fretful baby can provide exactly the strength that little one needs to respond in trust and confidence to the parents' presence and power.

God designed parents to teach a little child what He is like, and it is not necessary to say a single word to teach a little child how to be confident, trusting in his parents.

You need to be there for your children and for your little tiny baby; simply your availability and your loving attention will teach him that basic sense of loving trust in a Heavenly Father later on.

177. EXPLAINING GOD TO SMALL CHILDREN   *What words would you use to explain God to a small child?*

That's indeed a difficult question, because a great many adults do not have very good words to explain God. When I give psychiatric evaluations to people, one of the questions I routinely ask them is what they think about God, and what does He look like to them. I receive a variety

196

of answers. To many adults He is a harsh, punishing parent. To some He is a wise, loving, sense of power. How God enters into your lives as parents determines greatly how you will communicate Him to your child.

One of my best examples in understanding God was the time that my father had me watch a baby chick pecking its way out of the shell. He taught me that God was a wise Creator, who had a wonderful plan for how it was that things should happen in nature. My brother explained to me how lightning releases nitrates into the soil, and yet lightning and thunder had been very frightening experiences to me. Understanding that they had a purpose in nature made God's power magnificent to me. The cycles of water from the water in the lake to the vapor in the air to the rain that waters the soil was another example, as I studied science, of God's marvelous plan for the world. Walking through fields of wheat or a garden made me aware as a child of the teamwork that man and God put together that creates the providence for our material needs as human beings.

Some of the words that I like and have used in trying to teach about God to my children are these: I like to think of God as being loving and warm. When I taught my children in this fashion, and read them stories from the Bible, I would hold them on my lap and demonstrate to them, physically, the love and warmth of my human parenting. I taught them to compare that with God's heavenly parenting.

Describing God as wise in His plans is a part of the examples that I have just given. See God as protective. Despite the rigors and dangers of nature, there are a great many protective devices as well, such as the little animals that are so colored that they fit into their background to protect them from predators. See God as powerful, energetic, and always positive and creative. These are the adjectives with which I have tried to explain God to myself and to my children. I hope they help you in teaching your child about God.

178. TEACHING YOUR CHILD TO PRAY   *What special lifelong lessons about prayer can be taught only in the context of everyday family living?*

If your child attends Sunday school regularly, then no doubt he or she is learning certain Bible stories and other lessons there. But I hope you haven't relegated all of your boy's or girl's spiritual training to the church experts, especially in the area of praying, because no one is in the position that you the parent are to demonstrate to your child how prayer enters into everyday life situations. Your question is indeed a practical one. I think almost all of my lessons about prayer came from my particular family, and the way that they practiced prayer. I recently had an experience with my oldest daughter and my grandson that I'd like to share with you, because it's such a wonderful example of the practicality of prayer in a child's life. She and her son, our grandson, had watched a television program in which a mother was suffering from cancer and had to make decisions about giving away her several children. Andy was horrified by the program. (They had not anticipated that it would be so sad, or perhaps he should not have watched it.) He had bad dreams for a number of nights after watching that movie, and as he and his mother talked about the program, she realized that it was a part of those bad dreams.

They were talking about God one day, when Andy said to his mother, "Mommy, maybe if we asked God, He'd take away my bad dreams." So that night at bedtime they prayed a very special prayer about those bad dreams. And, as He always does, God the Heavenly Father answered that prayer, and Andy slept very peacefully from that night on. It was a wonderful lesson in faith for him, as well as for his mother, and a renewal of my own faith came out of that special story.

The answers to prayer promote growth in our own faith. It is an example for the lives of our children that they, too, may learn to trust the God who loves them, as He loves us the parents.

179. CULTS   *Is there a certain type of person who perhaps is more vulnerable to cults?*

Yes, there is a certain type of person, but perhaps it would be helpful to start with a description of the characteristics of a cult. There are so many new groups springing up around our country today that it is sometimes hard for parents and young people alike to know whether this is really a basically fine Christian group or a cult.

Several of the characteristics that are easily detected are these: There is a rigid structure and unbending rules with a very strong authority person. These characterize all cults. There is always a charismatic leader, someone who is easy to follow and very dynamic. Almost always in today's current cults, this is a male. Furthermore, there is a serious brainwashing that includes sleep deprivation, intensive behavior, and mind-control techniques; the structuring of the entire day of time, so that people involved have little opportunity to get away and think independently and to be individuals.

The people who are susceptible to the energy of the cults are these: First is the adventurous, exploring type of young person who has his mind open to anything and everything. He may have little judgment or experience and little training in how to make value judgments. This person, while he is very susceptible to cults, oftentimes is also wise enough to get out of them.

The second type is one that worries me more. This is the type of young person who is lonely, who has not been close to a father and, in fact, may not have a father at all. Through the cult such a person may seek friends, a sense of belonging, and actually a father figure. This person really concerns me, because what the cult seems to offer is that important sense of belonging or a family togetherness which he is craving.

Another group of young people who are very susceptible to cults are those who have low self-esteem, high dependency needs, and the willingness to submit to any authority, be it good or bad. People who adapt well to cults adapt well in all of society, and they are those who have a tendency to get along with almost anyone with whom they associate. The energy, the demands, and the structure of the exploitive cults in our society today is something that every parent and young person needs to recognize and be prepared to avoid.

180. FAMILY PRAYER TIME *How can we make family prayer time more exciting for our teenager? What kind of system can we develop to make this a real family time?*

That's a very important question, and it reminds me again of my growing-up years when prayer time was such a beautiful part of our entire family's schedule for the day. I would like to recommend a book written by Rosalind Rinker. It's called *Conversational Prayer*. Ros Rinker was the first person who taught me that prayer really is simply conversing with God. Doing this together as a family brings the very presence of God into the heart of the family. This can be a natural and warm part of every family's day.

For teenagers prayer must be reality centered. I don't believe they really go much for long prayers or very idealistic kinds of prayers. The traits of teenagers are important to think about in considering your prayer times. They're looking for their own personal identity, and their near independence becomes of great concern to them (and you). They explore, they disagree, they challenge and doubt. All of those characteristics are essential in their learning to pray. How they see God, of course, must involve seeing Him as real, understanding, powerful enough to be doubted and challenged, and loving enough to come back to a warm relationship, when they have finished their doubts and rebelliousness. Bible readings, I think, need to show actions and the feelings of God. The Gospel of Mark is an action book, and one that bring us the very living dynamic of Jesus Christ: Christ in the temple, stilling the storm, energetic, honest, compassionate, and wise. These are all qualities that I think would appeal to any teenager.

In prayers I recommend that there be some worship, because certainly we all need to worship and adore the Heavenly Father. But I would recommend for teenagers that there be more expressions of gratitude for God's past help in their lives, and the answers to the prayers they have prayed. Specific requests for today's needs are a normal, natural expression of a teenager's prayers. As you pray for Sally's test and John's date tonight, I think it will help them to know that God is really concerned in the little affairs of their lives, as well as the big ones. Moms and dads, don't forget to pray for patience and wisdom for yourselves. Real conversational prayer is just that.

181. SUNDAY-SCHOOL DROPOUT   *What can you do if your child doesn't want to go to Sunday school? My eleven-year-old son says that it's boring, and he doesn't enjoy it. His class seems to be fine, and the teacher is good, so I'm baffled about my son's resistance to Sunday school. Will I be helping him any if I insist on his attending?*

That's a very important question, and one that a great many parents are interested in. There are several reasons children should attend Sunday school. Obviously we want them to learn about God, His Word, and His world. We want them to see the importance of the church and its function in their lives, as well as in the world in general. And we want our children to make friends with those who share our spiritual values.

There are also several reasons children resist going to Sunday school. They oftentimes, unfortunately, have an unhappy relationship with one or both of their parents, and sometimes they resist going to Sunday school because they want in some strange way to reject their parents' values—to "get even" with them for some parental hurts. Also children are often influenced by their peers to think that Sunday school is kid stuff or for "sissies." Sunday school is, in fact, in some cases not geared to the specific age or needs of given children.

Today children are spoiled by having so many entertaining events in their lives. They come to believe that everything should be entertaining and exciting, and Sunday school just can't always be that. Children may have stayed up too late the night before and are simply too tired to get up and go to Sunday school.

Whatever the reasons, there are some answers to a child's resistance to attending church and Sunday school. First of all, as parents, be clear about the value of Sunday school for your child, and explain those reasons to your child in a logical and firm fashion. Also be clear about your expectations of his attendance. He doesn't have the choice about attending regular school, and frankly I think he doesn't need to have the choice about attending Sunday school and most youth activities, even through high school. Take a look, parents, at your relationship with your child, and find out if you have unknowingly been causing some hurt in his life that has resulted in resentment and a need to get even by rejecting your values. Don't be too critical of your church or Sunday school, but constructively take a look at your son's class. See if he is learning the values and having the kind of environment there that are conducive to his wanting to go and gaining some profitable experiences there. Help your church make your Sunday school a truly worthwhile experience. You always help your child when you teach spiritual values, self-discipline, obedience, and respect.

182. ROLE OF CHURCH   *As a church leader, I've been discouraged by the attitude of some parents. It seems to me that whenever things go wrong in their families, or with their kids, they blame the church. If only the church had a better youth leader; if only the youth program was stronger—things would be different. It seems to me that the basic spiritual leadership should belong to the parents. What do you think?*

Certainly, ideally, I emphatically agree with this person. Children's values are best taught, modeled, and reenforced by their parents. Today, unfortunately, many parents have dumped those responsibilities on the church, the school, almost anyone they can find. I would like to write for church leaders, however, and you parents read this also, if you wish.

A number of years ago I was doing some speaking at a ministerial seminar and was concerned about the permissive attitude of the church in those days. Leaders were taught, they told me, that they should "hook" young people by providing entertainment and keeping them happy and excited in the church. I think perhaps unwittingly such a philosophy has attracted young people and has taken away some of the responsibility from the parents, so the church needs to take a look at how it may work together with parents establishing a team for the young people. As children grow, they are bound to test out their own ideas and their families' values. If the church differs, or is not involved in that teamwork approach; if the church is more lenient or provides the excitement that I have just described, children will learn to take advantage of that. Parents may be left feeling a bit helpless and not knowing exactly what their role should be. Offering a really rugged study course for young people on practical issues, taking a stand for right against wrong, can really support the parents' values and help the young people as well.

I think young folks need opportunities for service, and many churches in my community have begun teaching young folks to give as well as to get, and I am excited about that change. Doing work for elderly or handicapped people; tutoring minority students, are activities young people can perform that will help them to share the love of God in a practical way.

I think sometimes churches are misled about this whole area of confidentiality. They may earn a teenager's loyalty at the risk of withholding information that should be shared with his parents. So, church leaders, I would strongly urge you to get together with the parents of the young people that you are concerned about. The church and the parents must unite to develop the guidance and protection young people need.

183. BIG PEOPLE'S CHURCH   *We want our preschooler to begin joining us in big people's church on Sunday nights, since she is really too old for the nursery and no junior church is available. So far every attempt has been embarrassing, with lots of whispering, crawling, and distractions. Other kids her age are joining their parents during the service. Should we persevere and hope for the best, or wait a while and try again?*

Certainly that is an important question and it takes me all the way back to my own childhood. I can recall vividly feeling so bored, and as if I absolutely could not sit still for one more minute. Fortunately, my parents were quite understanding. My mother had a way with a pencil and paper, and when she realized that I simply could not tolerate one more minute, she would take out that paper and with her pencil create the most marvelous pictures. Then my father would have his turn. In his suit pocket he kept a sack of wintergreen candies. When he knew that I simply could not sit still another minute, he would rustle that paper very softly, and I knew that there was help on the way. That piece of candy somehow helped me to get through those endless moments.

Church really is not geared to preschoolers and perhaps cannot be. Frankly, what they can learn from adult church is quite limited. I think it's ideal if a children's church or activity time is available geared to the comprehension of younger children and the shorter attention span that they have. These times can give to a child something very special. In fact, I worry about children developing lifelong resentment against the church because of being expected to sit too still, too rigidly, for too long a period of time.

Family togetherness, however, indicates that having a child sit with the parents may be a very warm and loving thing. Children need to accept the discipline and training of learning to sit still for a period of time, and doing something that the parents decide is good for them.

There needs to be a growing awareness on the part of the child of the importance of worship, the Christian fellowship, and the church. Start with what is possible for your child then. If it's necessary for him or her to be in church, give them a short period of time, and then take them outside for a time, and perhaps back in, so that they gradually become accustomed to the time and the structure of the service. Provide some of those quiet little distractions. Gradually increase the child's time to sit still. Use some firmness in requiring a little extra time and attention, so the child will grow in the controls that will be important, not just in church, but in other activities and in school later on. Be careful to keep God's house a place to which you and your child love to go.

184. SANTA CLAUS *If your children were small today, what would you tell them about Santa?*

What I would tell them is very easy for me to answer. Complications sometimes arise, however, from having two parents in a family, both of whom have different ideas about Santa Claus! I came from a family to whom Santa was a fantasy and a pretense and a very enjoyable one. Some parents come from families where they treasure their early childhood memories and beliefs that Santa was very real. So a compromise becomes necessary. In our family, a very interesting thing happened that I'd like to share with you.

Our son was our second child, and when he was about eight years of age, he decided that it was his duty to reveal to his three-and-a-half-year-old little sister that Santa really did not exist. A bit irritated at his premature revelation, I said to him, "All right, since you've told her that, now you go ahead and explain it to her." Well, to my amazement, he did a marvelous job! He told her very kindly and gently, as a very mature little boy of eight can do, about the beautiful symbolism of Santa Claus. He explained that Santa was not real, but was pretend, and that you could pretend and still have fun. His sister accepted it very calmly and without a single tear.

Actually I think that's the ideal situation, where we explain to children that Santa Claus is a symbol of congeniality and happiness, of secrets and excitement, of suspense and teasing, and of giving. And he can become to children a delightful experience. By letting them understand from the beginning that Santa is make-believe, we can separate for our children then the beautiful *reality* of the person of Jesus Christ—that He is and was very real—and in that reality, we can help them to understand the awe and the wonder, the sacredness, the infinity of God's love, the quietness of God's giving, the quality of His giving that is so unique. I think both aspects are important to children.

Teens

185. *Our eleven-year-old daughter is our oldest child, and I am concerned about the great amount of peer pressure she feels. There is a lot of pressure from her classmates to dress a certain way and also to achieve. This is very hard on her and also on her father and me. Do you have any suggestions about how we can help her?*

Yes, I do. That question is one that applies to many, many families today. In fact, I've had mothers of five- and six-year-olds concerned about their children's being taunted because they didn't wear jeans or shoes of a certain brand. In today's economy, few parents can afford those expensive items, and I do not think it is healthy for children to believe that they must have "name brands" in order to measure up to their friends.

Parents, get together and decide where you will allow your child to be similar to her peers, and where you will set the boundaries, and require her to be an individual. When a child is so different that he has no relationship with other friends and peers, he can be socially destroyed. (I knew such a child once. He was not allowed to watch television, go skating, or do any of the things his friends did, and he really felt very isolated and strange.) On the other extreme, I know parents who sacrifice so much that they almost become enslaved to the whims of society and their children's friends.

Once you as parents have gotten together on your values and what it is that you can and will allow, then I suggest you include your daughter in a discussion. Listen to and respect her points of view, and then share your ideas with her. Be frank about your reasons for setting some limits on her. This may be just financial stress, or it may go all the way to your awareness of her need to develop her individuality. Consider a clothing budget that she must live with, and then help her within that budget to decide what she wants to buy.

Begin a quiet campaign together, Mom and Dad, and let it reflect to your child consistently your value of her special individual gifts and abilities. In developing these qualities of her being and her character, I hope you will find that she gets such a healthy degree of self-esteem that she will not need those external items to feel good about herself. And you will have prepared her for the still-greater teen pressure to come!

186.   PREPARING FOR TEENS   *Since parents can't stop the teenage years from coming, what can they do to get ready?*

They really *do* need to get ready, and this is the time to strengthen the child's personality foundations and prepare him or her for the onslaught of those difficult teenage years.

First, I think it helps to remember your own preadolescent years. What difficulties were particularly troublesome to you, and what would have helped you (or what did help you), to get through those times? One of the main issues today is to explain to the child the physical changes that will be beginning in the preadolescent years. Preparation for puberty is something that can hardly be overdone. So learn what you must in order to teach your child about the sexual development that he or she will be experiencing; how to understand the opposite sex, as well as themselves.

Remember that even now the child is beginning to experience the contrasts between childhood and adulthood, and is beginning to make little explorations into the adult world from time to time. That involves that delicate balance between being dependent and childlike, and becoming more independent as adults must do.

Many preadolescents feel socially inadequate, and don't quite know where they fit with one another, or certainly, with adults. Work very hard with your preadolescent on developing and improving good communication skills. Be careful to listen to your child, as well as to talk with him or her, and learn to listen with your hearts as well as your ears. Balance carefully the parenting skills that you have developed up to now, and the need to become, more of the time, a friend to your child. Develop the intellectual skills, and the finely tuned ability to disagree without being disagreeable.

Not only must you prepare your preteens for puberty with its dramatic physical changes, but you must help them to learn how to prepare to go from being the top level in their elementary school to the bottom level of junior high school (unless, of course, you live in a community where there is a middle school that can help children through that difficult academic adjustment). Give them social opportunities and responsibilities to help them explore and test out how well they can cope in such situations. This will help you parents to know how much guidance they still need. Give them as much freedom as they can safely handle, but as much protection as they need!

187. TEENAGE DISCIPLINE   *How should parents approach the situation when a teenager has done something that's really wrong?*

Well, first of all, the parents need to verify the facts that would tell them that there has been a wrong done. I will never forget the time that we had a call from the police station about our adolescent son and his friend. We were told that they had been caught shoplifting from a local market. We could not believe that this was true. Nevertheless, I know that such things do happen in even the best of families, and so we went to the police station and checked out all of the facts. Gratefully we discovered that it was a case of a wrong identity. It had not been our son at all. You need to be sure that the facts are accurate before you make an accusation, or try to decide what kind of punishment to administer.

If you know that a serious wrong has been done by your child, my first recommendation is perhaps the hardest. That is that you "cool it," as the kids call it. Simply do nothing until you get in control of your emotions and can handle the situation with wisdom and caution. Then sit down together with your child. Both parents, the child, and any one or two other significant people (in private, however) can discuss the situation that has arisen. I recommend that you not question the young person if you are certain that he or she has done the act. Asking them questions can often allow them to add to the crime the problem of lying about it. Review with the child what was wrong with what was done. Be sure that the child understands what he or she did, and why it was wrong, and how it might hurt a number of people as well as themselves.

Help the child reach a decision regarding the act. It is one thing for you as parents to know that it's wrong, to be concerned about it, and to want to have changes. It will not help your child to grow in maturity and understanding unless *he* knows what was wrong about it. Until he wants to repent, or change that behavior, and decide to never repeat it, your concerns as parents will not really effect a change.

Once the child is willing to admit the wrong, be sorry for it, and be willing to make a commitment to change, then together you can set up a consequence that will be meaningful to your child. It should be one that will help him to see the seriousness of the act, and to make the commitment to prevent a recurrence of that problem.

Sometimes you need to see if there has been a reason for the misbehavior. Perhaps the child is seeking attention or acting out some worry or anxiety, or simply has been careless or used poor judgment. If serious wrongdoing is repeated, I urge you to seek counsel that will help diagnose and cure such actions.

188.   BIRTH CONTROL INFORMATION   *Would parents who feel very strongly about sexual morality be encouraging their teenagers toward promiscuity by telling them about contraceptives?*

That's a question that a great many parents have asked and they certainly deserve an answer. By the time their children become teenagers, parents should have taught them a sense of morality. By that I mean what makes a particular act right or wrong. They should have given their children a set of values to live by and have taught them how to understand their sexuality, and control their impulses; how to be sensitive toward each other (young men and young women); responsibility in their actions and reactions with one another in social and dating situations.

If that isn't true, however, they need to begin very quickly to develop that kind of an attitude on their own part as parents and teach that to their children. I think that parents intuitively know when their children are becoming interested in or actively involved in sexual practices. When that happens, or when you have that sense of imminence, parents, you need to think about these choices that you have and can use in helping your child.

Your first choice, of course, is to simply ignore it and hope it will go away. That's naive, so I hope you will not make that choice. You may angrily blame or accuse your child, or blame yourselves for being poor parents, and you may try to set up rigid consequences that are more likely to produce rebellion than improvement. One of the saddest situations I knew was a young woman who at nineteen was pregnant out of wedlook. When she explained to me how it was that she had allowed herself to become sexually active so early, she said to me that her mother had been so strict that she simply had to rebel in order to prove to her mother that she couldn't boss everything she did. (Those were her exact words.)

So parents, be careful that you not become so rigid that you push your child in the very direction that you want him to avoid. You may, at the other extreme, permissively give birth control information and thereby wordlessly permit or even encourage your child to go on in that sexual activity.

Best of all, you may thoughtfully and prayerfully sit down together as parents with your teenager and ask that person why he or she is becoming involved in sexual activity. What are the needs that drive her to that? Is there a peer pressure problem? Is there a fear that she might lose her boyfriend if she does not cooperate in those activities? Try to help your adolescent understand and meet her needs in wholesome ways.

189. UNDERSTANDING TEENAGE PREGNANCY *From your experience with pregnant teenagers, what would you say a girl in this situation needs the most from her parents?*

Interestingly, one of the most important aids that a pregnant girl seems to need is the help and support of her father. She needs her mother, but during this time, somehow dads are very important. In working with a great many teenage pregnancies, I found one of the common denominators of almost all of them was a remoteness from their fathers. They very much wanted to be close to their dads. They loved and respected them, but they felt very estranged. So, Dad, you need to spend some time with that daughter, even though it's a very sensitive situation in her life. This can give her a chance to understand herself and her relationship with her boyfriend, because many times that boyfriend is symbolic of you as the dad. Many children (and so often they are really children at heart) do not know why they become sexually involved, or how it was that they allowed themselves to become so irresponsible as to become pregnant. There are some points that you need to understand, parents, in this regard.

Many times young people's involvement in sexual activity comes from their need for someone to love them—someone to prove to them that they are desirable—someone to belong to and to hang on to. Many young women have a need to feel feminine, and lots of their boyfriends have a very big need to feel masculine. Some young people actually have a desire to have a child, and they want to become pregnant. The desire to gain attention from their parents and especially, as I have said, from you fathers, is a major subconscious (and perhaps even a conscious) part of the needs of these young people. Searching for a tangible evidence of love is a very common denominator in the young people who become sexually active.

So from these needs and inner feelings of teenagers, parents, I hope that you will see that what the children need most from you is acceptance, the security of your definite commitment to them, even in the midst of this serious problem, and the will to help them make some sense out of this tragic situation in their lives.

190. TEENAGE PREGNANCY AND PARENTS' FEELINGS
How can parents handle their feelings when they discover their teenager is pregnant?

My experience with both parents and young women who are pregnant out of wedlock has been tragically extensive. At first parents go through all the stages of grief. They want to deny that this has ever happened. Shock and denial are almost always followed by anger. "Why did you do this to me?" or "How could you?" are common verbal responses.

Then there comes a preoccupation, a sadness, a real depression. Often there is guilt. ("I have failed . . . been a bad parent.") Parents may blame one another, or the school, or the boy. There are all kinds of very strong negative reactions that parents experience in this crisis.

Let me reassure you, parents. You *will* recover from all of these painful feelings, and eventually you will be restored to a peace of mind and a joy in living again.

How can you cope with these strong feelings? Express them in words to one another, to your physician, perhaps your pastor, or a trusted friend. The more you can talk about the sadness, the pain, the worry, the anger, the more quickly you will recover from the intensity of those feelings. Above all, let your daughter know that despite the pain that this event causes, *you still love her.* Never allow her to think, even for a minute, that you will abandon her, or fail to help her through this time.

Get good counseling for yourself and her, and, of course, good medical attention for this mother-to-be. Listen to your child without condemning her or judging her. You will need to make some very important decisions in the days ahead, and you will need to work together to make these determinations wisely.

191. WHAT TO DO FOR A PREGNANT TEENAGER
What steps would you recommend that parents take when they find their unmarried daughter is pregnant?

Medical Examination. First of all, the parents need to get that young person to a medical doctor. A physician must make the diagnosis of the pregnancy, being sure that the mother's state of health and that of her unborn child is potentially the very best that it can be. One of the major questions that a young mother must have answered is when that baby is likely to be born, and the preparations that must be made prior to that time depend on knowing that with some accuracy.

Counseling. In addition to seeing a physician, I strongly recommend that the family go together, certainly the parents and the daughter, to a counselor who is skilled in such issues. Making choices about this child and its imminent birth is something that very few people can do very well alone, because of the high level of the emotional factors involved. Sometimes seeing a clergyman is helpful, because many times young women feel very guilty about their irresponsibility and the hurt they have caused their parents.

The choices that are available are those that we must list whether we like them or not. (Actually no choice at this point is likely to be a very optimistic one, but you must choose the one you think is the best.)

Possible Solutions. Marriage is possible in many cases, though not all. Usually this is not wise, since 70 to 80 percent of teen marriages end up in divorce within less than five years. The second choice the girl faces is to *keep the baby* and raise it herself, and usually that demands a great deal of help from her parents. You must be honest about whether or not you can conscientiously offer that choice to your daughter. The third choice is to place the child for *adoption,* and for many young women this is the best. Certainly it can be done through a qualified agency, which can provide a fine family to raise the child when the young woman is not able to do that herself. *Abortion* is one of the choices your child will be offered. I strongly recommend that you do not choose that avenue. Talk with your clergyman. Speak with a counselor. Take enough time to think carefully about this decision, because the aftermath of abortion is often fraught with serious guilt and depression.

Whatever the decision that must be made, be wise, take enough time to make that decision carefully, and consider the future of your child and yourself. Be prayerful, and I know that you will make the best decision that you can make.

192. COLLEGE? *How can parents and young people decide if college is the right move?*

A decade ago I would have had no difficulty answering that question very glibly. "Of course, all young people should go to college." That simply is no longer true, and there are many trades and occupations available to young people that do not require the formal years of college that I used to think were so essential. Some guidelines that can help parents know how to advise their children are these:

One is the *student's own motivation.* When that young person has studied conscientiously and has reasonably good grades, has an interest in going on to college and learning the kinds of material that colleges present, then I would love for that person to have an opportunity to explore more advanced educational adventures.

The second guideline is *the teachers' and counselors' recommendations.* Speak with your child's counselor or teacher and take their advice as to whether or not it is worth the expensive investment in sending your child to college.

Still a third guideline may be *the very practical consideration of your ability as parents to afford to send your child to college.* Loans and grants that were once so plentiful are not as easily obtained today. You must consider whether or not you can afford it. Helping to earn their own expenses is, of course, still an option for young people. Their willingness to do so is a fine test of their motivation.

Special vocational testing and guidance can give you additional help in knowing your child's best abilities lie in academic pursuits or in those of some other occupations, such as electrician's or mechanic's training, or many of the other vocational skills that now provide excellent opportunities for making a good living. Among the other options to consider are *trade schools.* Some young people need to take a job for a while (if they are lucky enough to find one). This is risky, and the child may become so addicted to the paycheck that he may not want to leave it. On the other hand, jobs can become so boring and monotonous that students will realize they want more education, and then can go off to college with great motivation.

Junior college is a wonderful opportunity that is not very costly, allows the young person to have a little more time at home to grow up, and this can help him to know what he really wants to do later on. *State colleges and universities* generally are less expensive than private schools; *church-related colleges offer some moral protection* for young people and should be a part of your options.

Do what is best for your child. Help to think that through carefully; get all of the help and counsel that you can; and I trust that you will make a wise decision with your child, one that will guide his future in positive directions.

193. REBELLION OR INDEPENDENCE? *How can parents tell if their teenager is rebelling or just trying out a new idea?*

There are some very specific guidelines that can help parents to make that differentiation. One is the young person's attitude. A truly rebellious teenager almost constantly has a hostile, sarcastic, or cynical attitude. He is secretive over prolonged periods of time and becomes manipulative and rather tricky. It's hard for the child or parent to really trust one another if he is a rebellious teenager.

Not only is the teenager's attitude important, but so is his behavior. The committed rebel is potentially destructive in the things that he does. If not destructive in the sense of suicide or some physical damage, the rebellious teenager is destructive of himself as a human being. He does things that disqualify him for trust or respect by other people. Rebelliousness also is generalized, and includes rebelling in school by not getting the schoolwork done. There is also rebelling socially by misbehaving, sometimes in serious ways; rebelling at home by not following the rules; refusing to attend church. Across the board there is a resistance to the rules or expectations of the family and society in general. As parents examine themselves, I find that many of them discover that they have been too rigid and controlling for too long a time. Resentment of that is another one of the characteristics and causes of the rebellious teenager.

On the other hand, the child who is going through a healthy search for independence argues at times over a specific idea or value, and needs to argue in order to stretch his own intellectual growing process. He needs to be listened to and argued with, in order to develop his self-respect and establish his real beliefs and values. Such a person soon returns to his basic goodwill and love for his family.

It's important to give your child room to grow, and preventing the rebellion that otherwise can occur is a great responsibility that you as parents share.

194. TEEN FINANCES   *Our high schooler needs to develop financial responsibility. He has his own bank account, but we buy all his clothes and give him money for school lunches and other expenses. He works part-time, and we're wondering what kind of bills he should be paying for. Also, how can we get him to keep financial records? Should we expect him to budget?*

Today's economy has been a very healthy motivator for all families to learn to appreciate what they have, as well as to help children learn to live within a budget for themselves.

Let's get back to the high schooler in our question. Both of the parents need to form some basic agreements regarding the lessons they want their child to learn. Then arrange a kind of formal business meeting with the son. Discuss the following issues very openly and frankly, but kindly and intellectually:

First of all, *what are this son's expenses and the family's? What is the cost of living? What are the son's future plans?* Is he going away to college, or does he plan on some special job training? Does he want to buy a car, eventually get his own apartment? What are the costs of all of these rather major things that children sometimes want a few years down the road? Discuss together how he can best prepare himself financially for those future plans, and what you parents can and cannot do to help.

As you talk together, help him outline a simple budget, and then help him to refine this in an account book, which he can purchase at any local dime store. If this son or daughter is not going to college or into some special training, then I think he should begin contributing to the family budget, saving some money, as well as planning for his own future. Keep this a positive and helpful issue and avoid disapproval or blame. I think you will find that your child will not have to rebel or be rude, but will benefit from your experience and your thoughtful guidance.

195. AMBITIOUS TEENAGER   *My high schooler loves to be a part of everything. Class officer, school play, athletics, and more. He does carry responsibility well, but I'm wondering when I should help him say no. How many extra activities are good for a teenager?*

Perhaps I can answer that by saying that only those activities that teach him to be a better person or allow him to serve or help other people are the ones he should pursue—assuming, of course, that he does some things just for good, wholesome fun!

Help him to formulate his own priorities and his own philosophy of life in general. I suspect that first of all, most thoughtful parents would like their teen to focus on the *growth* of his character, so activities that would encourage this may need to be at the very top of that young person's list. His or her own quiet time, being involved in youth groups in church or service organizations that serve the needs of the community, can be a wonderful means of helping your young person to grow spiritually and develop healthy character.

I certainly do think that young people need to be involved in activities that increase their *emotional awareness.* These are the activities that will teach your young person how to understand his or her own feelings, and how to communicate those sensitively and kindly to others.

Your child needs to develop this *sense of creativity,* so any task that can help your child discover his unique talents and abilities is important. Exploring and developing those, expressing them in creative and wonderful ways—certainly all are a part of good, extracurricular activities.

Intellectual development really matters too, and your child needs to be part of activities that will discipline and strengthen his mind, sharpen its use, and develop its breadth and depth.

Social interests are important, so your child needs to be in some activities that will help him to learn to befriend other people and to understand and associate with people of a broad variety. Many young people get into cliques and little organizations that can become a bit snobbish, even when they don't intend to be.

Physical development also is of great value, so give your child some activity that will promote that. Above all, give your child time to think, imagine, meditate, and just *exist,* and you will have done him and yourself a great favor.

196. CLOTHESHORSE   *My daughter has an insatiable appetite for clothes. We have an average income, and can provide a reasonable wardrobe for her, but I get tired of hearing her ask for more and more new things to wear. We argue a lot about this. How can I convince her that she doesn't need so many new clothes, even if we could afford it?*

One authority on children has stated that children really want only a small percentage of the things they request, and I suspect that's true of this girl as well. Why then does this girl (and literally millions like her) ask for so many *things?* One reason is that they are testing out the parent's ability to say no. Power struggles are very common between daughters and mothers (and sons and dads, for that matter). The inconsistency of the parent in being able to set limits causes children to have to test out the authority again and again. Also, the child may feel unsure of herself as a person—so insecure, in fact, that she uses clothes to bolster her ego. (That is, unfortunately, a poor way of building a good, healthy ego.) Peer pressure obviously is very important to teenagers, especially, and pushing one another to fit into their particular mold or be rejected or ridiculed is a common practice among young people.

What then can this mother and the millions of other mothers like her do? The first suggestion I have seems to have nothing at all to do with clothes. Actually it has *everything* to do with it, and that idea is to *develop a meaningful relationship with your child.* In such a relationship, based on respect and the sharing of fun together as well as love, you will find that your child will come to respect your values and accept your limits in a much more reasonable fashion. Help your child to learn some solid time-tested values for herself, so that clothes lose some of that high significance in her life. Help her develop such a firm, healthy self-esteem, that she really will not need that external reinforcement of fine name-brand expensive clothes. Together establish a fair and unbending clothes budget for your daughter—one that absolutely will not be compromised. When she has a certain amount of money to spend, she can choose how she wants to use that. In this fashion the budget becomes the authority, rather than you as the parent having to always set those limits. Yes, you and your child can even settle the issue of clothing!

197. PARENT-TEEN COMMUNICATION   *My fifteen-year-old son is going through what I call the "grunt" stage. It just seems so hard to get him to talk about school or girls or anything. How can I get him to communicate? He'll have periods when he's very open, but in between, silence. When I ask too many questions, he thinks I'm prying.*

That letter reminds me so much of my own daughter. When she was fourteen years of age, she and I were really at odds with one another. I changed my working schedule so that I could be at home when she got home from school. I had the juices and the potato chips (or cookies or whatever I thought might appeal to her) handy, and the stage was set for us to have a wonderful time of communicating. Except, unfortunately, that just did not happen. I would ask her how John was that day, and I would get, like this mother, a grunt. I would ask how the test was, and I got another monosyllabic answer, one that I couldn't really interpret one way or the other. Before very long, she was off to her room and all the communication was lost. I was hurt beyond measure, because I loved her very much, and I felt her slipping away from me.

Fortunately, I asked God's guidance, and that of a great many friends, and came to an understanding of what was going wrong. As a matter of fact, my daughter herself told me. She said one day, "Mother, you are absolutely yucky! You ought to know that I am not four years old, and you can't talk to me like you did when I was four. I'm fourteen." And to her, at fourteen, that was pretty old. Even though she sounded a bit rude, I understood what she was saying, and I quit trying to talk to her as if she were a child. I looked through my days desperately for any event or sight that I thought would be of interest to her. The next day after school, over a soft drink, I said, "Kathy, let me tell you what happened to me today." And I told her a story that was somewhat funny. It was a miracle, because I hadn't yet finished the story, when she said, "Oh, Mom, did that really happen to you? Let me tell you what happened to me." And we were off to a major change in our relationship.

Our wonderful Jewish friends have a marvelous ritual. They call it the Bar Mitzvah or Bas Mitzvah rites. At this time their young people experience the transition from childhood into the adult world in their worship ceremonies. They know rather clearly when the child leaves off being a child and becomes a young adult. In our own families, we can develop this transition, much as I tried to do with my daughter. It is largely a state of mind. My invitation of my daughter into my adult life was my sharing with her the events of the days through which I lived. Parents, share feelings, events, and thoughts with your child. I think you will find that he in turn will share with you. Express interest without prying. Understanding your adolescent is so important if you are to grow to become adult friends in the years that follow.

198. SHOPLIFTING *Just how serious or common is the problem of teenage shoplifting?*

The problem is very common, and unfortunately it is not limited to teenagers. There has been a great rise in shoplifting among even the elderly in our society. Many stores now have store detectives to pick up those shoplifters. If I were a parent who had a shoplifting teenager, I would be grateful if he or she got caught the very first time around, because getting caught can put a great deal of fear and honest respect in that young person's mind. Perhaps more important than what to do about it, is understanding why they shoplift.

One of the reasons I have experienced is that they are *craving excitement,* and somehow it becomes a bit of cat-and-mouse game. "Can I get this bit of makeup?" or "Can I take the flashlight without anyone picking me up or realizing that I have it?"

Testing the limits of authority is another reason for young people's stealing. Pitting their cleverness against the mentality of the shopowners is a challenge to many young people. Very rarely do the young people need the items that they are stealing, and the commonest shoplifters are those from more affluent families. They seem to need attention, to be noticed, and that prompts many misbehaviors, including the shoplifting. Almost always, in my experience, the habitual shoplifter feels unloved, unimportant, unattended to by their parents or other significant adults. They are unsuccessful people who somehow feel that they can achieve some sense of importance through this habit. A great many young people steal to support drug habits, and that's a very strong motivator.

If your child has been caught shoplifting, require that child to restore the item at once. If he or she has used the item or damaged it, so it cannot be returned, require them to earn the money to pay for it. Evaluate the total life pattern of that thief and your entire family, including yourselves. Correct the weak spots. Check out their friends. Correct the lack of time and attention that you may have been giving to that young person, and build loving and successful relationships for your child and you.

199. PARENT BURNOUT   *Right now I'm experiencing emotional burnout because I am the father of three teenagers, including twins in junior high. They are all strongly expressing their need for independence. Can you suggest something that will help me bear up under all the pressure?*

Being a parent is not only a twenty-four-hour job, it's a lifetime assignment with few, if any, vacations! I certainly can understand that this father needs some help. Here are some practical suggestions that I would like to leave with this dad and many others. Perhaps they will help them to find joy again in being parents.

Find ways to make friends with your teenagers! Share your experiences and feelings with them on a daily basis. Let them see you as a human being—a friend of theirs. Ask them sometimes for comfort and reassurance. Let them give you a back rub, or be a sounding board for you regarding some problem about which they may have some good ideas. Find some private times with each child, and do learn to laugh together. A great deal of tension can be relieved with a little bit of humor.

Invite your children to new privileges and new responsibilities, rather than letting them demand them. For example, suggest to your children, "Let's all do the basement and garage on Saturday, and then we'll go play baseball or go fishing." Or, "If you kids will do the yard really well, we'll all do something special this evening." This often makes work more a pleasure and less a drudgery. Show your interest in them, their friends, their activities, their likes, and dislikes. Avoid condemning them but invite their discussions. At this time, you will not be able to pound your values into them, but you can at least demonstrate those values through the joy of your own life and your own values.

INDEX